W9-CKY-442

NEW YORK STATE PARKS

A Complete Outdoor Recreation Guide for Campers, Boaters, Anglers Hikers, Beach and Outdoor Lovers

Bill Bailey

Glovebox Guidebooks of America

To our readers: Travel outdoors entails some unavoidable risks. Know your limitations, be prepared, be alert, use good judgement, think safety and enjoy New York's terrific outdoors. *Be bold!*

Special thanks to Commissioner Bernadett Castro, Beverly Wittner, John Barr and all the staff at all the parks. New York state parks are blessed with some of America's most skilled and dedicated staff.

Copyright © 2003 by Glovebox Guidebooks of America/Bill Bailey

Cover design by Dan Jacalone
Cover photo courtesy of the New York Parks, Recreation and Historic Preservation Department, State of New York
Editor, William P. Cornish
Managing Editor, Penny Weber-Bailey

Published by: **Glovebox Guidebooks of America**
3523 N. Gleaner Road
Freeland, MI 48623-8829
(800) 289-4843

Library of Congress CIP.

Bailey, William L., 1952-

New York State Parks Guidebook
(A Glovebox Guidebooks of America Publication)
ISBN 1-881139-18-2

Printed in the United States of America

10 9 8 7 6 5 4

Contents

Foreword

Welcome to the mighty roar of Niagara Falls, to the miles of white sand and surf at Jones Beach, to the majestic sights from historic Olana, the 19th-century Moorish villa overlooking the Hudson River, or to Ganondagan, where a 17th-century Seneca Nation town is celebrated. Join the 65 million visitors who enjoy the most dramatic number of state parks and historic sites in the nation.

New York State today carries on a proud tradition dating back to 1850 when Washington's Headquarters in Newburgh was acquired and preserved as the nation's first state historic park, Planting Fields Arboretum in Oyster Bay, Long Island, are for all New Yorkers and visitors from all parts of the nation and the world to enjoy for generations to come.

Besides the solitude and tranquility of pristine forests and sparkling lakes that complete the network of more than 200 state parks and historic sites, there is year-round recreation action. White water rafting and balloon trips, camping in winter and summer, hiking on thousands of miles of old and newly blazed trails, swimming, fishing, picnicking, nature trails, snowmobiling, biking and golf are but some of the activities to experience.

On behalf of New York State, the Office of Parks, Recreation and Historic Preservation welcomes all. We invite you to visit the parks and historic sites of the Empire State all year-round. Have a great time!

Bernadette Castro

Bernadette Castro, Commissioner
New York State Parks, Recreation
and Historic Preservation

f

Introduction

Welcome to New York state parks where 65 million visitors annually enjoy roaring waterfalls, white sand and surf, cool mountain hikes, woodland camping, fascinating historic sites, top quality fishing, boating and a proud tradition that dates back to 1850. New Yorkers and visitors from around the country come to enjoy dramatic scenery, solitude, pristine forests and sparkling lakes.

New York has one of the most diverse, interesting and spectacular state park systems in the country. In fact, the state was the first in the nation to protect and preserve parks and historic sites. The wonderful network of parks and historic places offers recreation and educational programming for people of all ages and abilities. For the adventurous, the parks offer whitewater rafting, kayaking and backpacking, or you can enjoy quiet bicycling, golf, swimming, jogging, tennis, sun bathing and plenty of winter activities.

Virtually anything you're looking for in the outdoors can be found in New York. Perhaps it is their diversity which explains why year in and year out New York state parks has one of the highest attendance rates in the country.

New York is a melting pot of industry and agriculture, mountains and streams, cultured cities and fertile rural life. It is a state of bounty and beauty; qualities reflected in each state park. Variety is no surprise in the state. Each region is unique and together they provide a total outdoor experience. While each park is unprecedented, they have many points in common. For more information about the state parks and historic places call (518) 474-0456.

Camping and cabin reservations

Reservations for all state-operated campsites and cabins, including those which remains open through the fall and winter season, are available by calling toll-free, 1-800-456-CAMP or by mail, on forms available from State Parks, Albany, NY 12238, (518) 474-0456, TDD (518) 486-1899; or the Department of Environmental Conservation, 50 Wolf Road, Albany, NY 12233-5253, (518) 457-2500.

Empire passport

The Empire Passport provides vehicle entry to nearly 200 state parks and recreation areas for a full year, April 1 to March 31. Purchase can be made in person at most participating facilities or by mail: Passport, State Parks, Albany, NY 12236.

Golden park program

The Golden Park Program provides New York State residents 62 or older free entry to state parks and recreation areas any weekday, excluding holidays, as well as reduced fees for some activities, i.e. swimming and golf. Simply present your current New York State Driver's License or Non-Driver's Identification Card to participate.

Access pass

The Access Pass provides New York state residents who have certain permanent disabilities free entry to most state parks and recreation areas and free use of the many facilities. Restrictions do apply. A Group Access Pass also is available to certain organizations. For an application or detailed information contact: Access, State Parks, Albany, NY 12238.

Group camping

Accommodations for groups vary among state parks and are available at Allegany, Darien Lake, Clarence Fahnestock, Harriman, Higley Flow, Letchworth, Moreau Lake, Watkins Glen, Wellesley, Southwick Beach and Chenango Valley state parks. Details and reservation procedures are available through the parks or the regional offices.

Inns and hotels

In addition to cabins and camping, you can also choose an historic inn or grand hotel for food and lodging at New York state parks.

Glen Iris Inn, Letchworth State Park, Castile, NY 14427; (716) 493-2622. Open from April through early November; guest rooms, fine food and gift shop.

Bear Mountain Inn, Bear Mountain State Park, Bear Mountain, NY 10911; (914) 786-2731. Open year-round; guest rooms, American menu restaurant and gift shop.

Gideon Putnam Hotel, Saratoga Spa State Park, Saratoga Springs, NY 12866; (518) 584-3000. Open year-round for elegant meals, lodging and fine gifts.

Alcoholic beverage regulations

No one under 21 can possess alcoholic beverages, except in the presence or a parent of guardian. Groups of 25 or more need a permit from the park manager; call in advance. Alcoholic beverages are generally permitted in camping, cabins, picnic areas and marinas. The are NOT allowed at bathing facilities, in public buildings, on walkways or in parking lots.

Exceptions:
• **Long Island Region:** All patrons must have a permit to bring alcoholic beverages into parks, except for the campgrounds at Wildwood, Hither Hills and Heckscher state parks.
• **New York City Region:** Alcoholic beverages may not be brought into the parks.
• **Niagara Frontier Region:** No alcoholic beverages permitted between May 1 and the last Friday of June, except in marinas and at campsites.
• **Taconic Region:** No alcoholic beverages permitted from April 1 through the last Friday in June, except marinas and campsites.

Pets

Pet restrictions vary, check with the park manager. Where pets are permitted, owners must insure that their pets are not a nuisance. Pet owners must take measures to insure sanitation and be able to produce proof of current rabies inoculations. Restrictions on areas where pets are allowed do not apply to hearing or seeing guides.

Golf

There are 15 state-operated golf courses in the state parks of New York.

Environmental education

Nature programs in the state parks include guided trail walks, special programs for schools, teacher training, specialized programs in subjects ranging from astronomy to zoology, or the simple pleasure of a self-guided walk with the aid of a map and trail markers. Throughout the state you will discover museums, a zoo, nature centers, arboretums, nature preserves and skilled outdoor educators ready to teach you about the natural history.

Nearby attractions

Many state parks are near other attractions. For tourism information write the Empire State Development, Division of Tourism, One Commerce Plaza, Albany, NY 12245 or call 1-800-CALL-NYS.

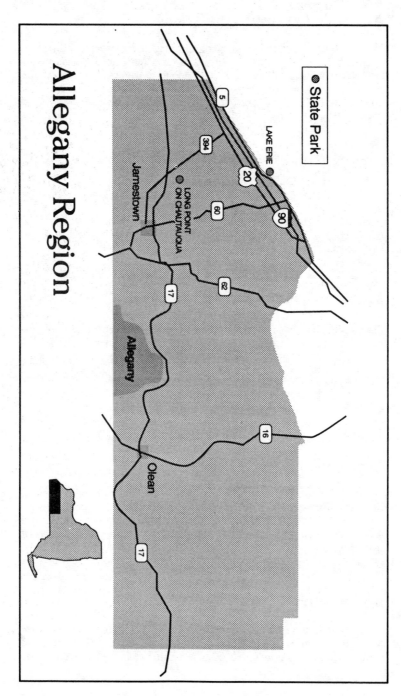

Allegany Region

● State Park

LAKE ERIE ●

LONG POINT
ON CHAUTAUQUA ●

Jamestown

Allegany

Olean

5
394
20
90
60
62
17
16
17

Allegany Region

This easternmost region spans three counties, containing rolling farmlands, crystal blue lakes and remote mountainous tracts. First occupied by the Seneca Nation of Indians, the area was also settled by farmers, lumber companies and the Quakers. Today, visitors will discover 100 miles of trails for hikers, bicycling, skiing and horseback riding.

There are three state parks in the region: Allegany, Lake Erie and Long Point on Lake Chautauqua. Each offers a variety of recreational opportunities.

Allegany has 65,000 acres that contains 300 tent sites, 380 cabins and three group campgrounds.

The sprawling park also has 55 miles of snowmobile trails, 30 miles of cross-country ski trails and nearly 70 miles of easy to moderately difficult hiking trails.

Long Point has been a favorite destination since the 1890s. The 40 acre peninsula has a huge marina and day-use areas.

Allegany State Park
Land: 65,000 acres

Allegany is the largest state park in New York, and it has been called "the wilderness playground of Western New York" since it opened in 1921. The park opened with only 7,100 acres, growing over the years to 65,000 acres that now contain rustic cabins, a beautiful lodge, restaurant, beaches, camping, fishing, 135 miles of hiking and a chance to see all kinds of wildlife.

Amasa Stone Jr. originally purchased the 7,100 acres for $40,000 from John Casement in 1873 with the intention of developing a private game preserve. Fortunately, I suppose, the game preserve never happened and many owners occupied the land until the state purchased it and appointed a park commission to operate the huge area. Since, Allegany has become one of the best examples of melding public recreation and active use with preservation and stewardship.

The huge park wonderfully blends gift shops and busy camp stores with wilderness trails, outdoor education and fun family special events.

Yet there's plenty of solitude to be found. From a rowboat you can enjoy fishing or bird watching, or nature photography along a woodland trail. The park also features two beaches, game fields, winter sports, fossil hunting, active beaver ponds, family movies in the campground amphitheater, guided tours and a natural history museum in a wonderful historic inn.

The huge park has a fascinating cultural history and is the only park in the state that has strata of Mississippian and Pennsylvanian rock, laid down more than 325 million years ago. The region was once homesteaded by Quakers and later gave up quantities of natural gas and oil. In the park visitors will also see wonderful rock formations and conglomerate rock beds. Some interesting formations are easily seen near Bear Cave on the Seneca Trail or at Thunder Rock in the southern part of the park. Plan on several visits just to get to know the park.

Allegany is an Indian word meaning *"beautiful waters."*

Information and Activities

Allegany State Park
2373 ASP Rt. 1, Suite 3
Salamanca, NY 14779
(716) 345-9101

Directions: The park is on the southern boundary of the state, west of Olean and east of Jamestown. Use Exit 18, 19 or 20 from State 17 or from U.S. 219 in Salamanca.

Emergency numbers: 911 system; park police, (716) 354-9111.

Campgrounds: The state park has campgrounds that contain 323 sites, half of which have electrical hook-ups. They are open from early April to mid-December. The large, well-stocked Red House General Store and adjacent laundry are at the entrance to the sprawling main Allegany campground where small sandy sites are located. The general store has camping equipment, lanterns, grills, charcoal, ice, propane, toys, firewood, paper towels, coloring books, toiletries, camping foods, cleaning supplies, fire starting sticks, small saws, snacks, ice cream and tons of soft drinks. The store also has a small video game area, three outdoor picnic tables and a bike rack.

Some of the back sites in the A loop are against a natural area. Sites in the B loop are on varying elevations with gravel pads and brick fire boxes. The loop is shady. Site 14 in the B loop is the most pleasant, surrounded by scattered boulders and jumbo rocks. Site B 18 is ideal

for a large RV rig. Loops in the C and D areas are up a gravel road and many of the heavily used sites have a woodland view. The shady sites are devoid of ground vegetation. Sites in the C loop are great for small RV units. Sites in the E loop can be uneven. Sites E 10-14 are open and large. E 16 is oversized, while E 19 and 21 are very shady and near the bike path. E 24 is gently notched out of the woods. E 35 is an attractive electrical site in a grove of pines. There are some pull-through sites in the E loop and this loop is near the general store. Many campers and anglers will enjoy the mountain stream that runs along the campground.

The Cain Hollow Campground near the lodge, on small Quaker Lake, is far from the developed areas, offering 164 sites along concentric loops. About one-third of the sites have electricity. This campground has a bathhouse and beach, and a terrific view of the surrounding tree-covered mountains that often have hazy tops. A modern, colorful play-ground and ball diamond are near the entrance to the lightly-used campground. There are five washhouses in the campground. This quiet part of the park has a wonderful view of the mountains and is away from the developed areas.

Sites 1-42 are up a hill along a hard-surfaced road. Most of these sites are wide open and sunny, and all of them have electrical hook-ups. Sites around the outside perimeter are against a natural buffer where you could get under limited shade. The view and access to hiking trails are excellent, but the quality of camping in this particular loop is only fair, unless you like open sites.

All other spurs and loops of Cain Hollow are shady and hilly, offering very good camping sites. Site 57 has excellent privacy. Most of the sites are separated by a wall of vegetation, making them private. The pads are of grass and thin gravel. Site 64 is notched into the woods and near the small washhouse. A woodchuck hole is at the end of this spur, near site 73.

Sites 75 to 164 are mostly grassy with good midday shade. Sites 84, 88 and 94 along a rise, not far from the multi-door washhouse. Site 95 is heavily shaded and carved out of the woods. If you like open sites, try 102 or 104. Both of these sites have firmly packed gravel and would be great for larger RV rigs. Look for sunny sites scattered throughout the loops. Sites 136 and 139, at the foot of a wooded hill, are good for RVs. Nearby, sites 141 and 143 are carved into a low hill, above the road. Site 164 is a prime site at the end of a narrow lane that ends in a heavily wooded spot. Next to it is a wonderful tent site, 163. Site 161 is kidney-shaped and wooded. There are many more good tent sites in the 150s. Sites 78 and 79 are private sites, elevated above the road.

The park operates a group camping area that is comprised of dormitory-style buildings in the Quaker Area. This group camp (the park has three group campgrounds: 2 in Red House and 1 in Quaker) is about one mile from the small camp store.

Cabins: Allegany State Park operates 380 cabins in 28 trails or colonies. Some of the cabins are winterized and most have electricity. There is a two-night minimum on all cabins; during the summer, cabins are rented for a seven-day minimum. The maximum occupancy is six people. Call the park or the reservation number (800-456-CAMP) for a detailed fact sheet that describes which cabins have wood heat, fireplaces, furnishing, number of rooms and so on.

Cabins 1-18, the Sugar Bush Trail, up a gravel road into a grove of tall pines. The simple, primitive cabins are rough-sawn and green on varying elevations and have a central bathroom, stone fire rings, refrigerator, wood floors, simple table and four cots. Cabins 16 and 18 are the nicest in the colony.

Cabins in the Quaker Area are rustic and some of them are streamside. Cabins 1-6 are called the Ward Trail Cabins and all are scattered along a stream. They are under a canopy of mature trees and separated by about 30 yards of lawn area. Each of the remote cabins has a small

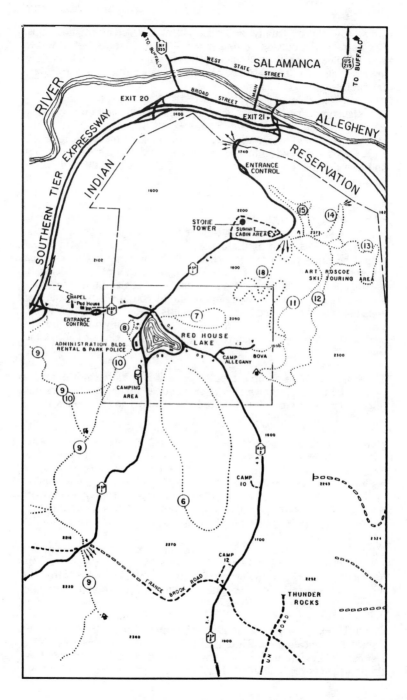

front porch, green roof and fire pit. A small general store serves the Quaker Area. The small gray and tan stone store has walk-up windows for ice cream and grill foods, a patio, and an inventory of basic camping supplies, toys, soft drinks and snacks. Picnic tables, pay phones and a bulletin board are also at this remote little store. Across from the store is the rental office (park office) where you can pick up brochures and register. Firewood, fishing permits and other services are offered.

The premiere cabins in the Quaker Area are the Ranger Trail Cabins, 2 and 4. Each of the green cabins has a porch with bench and fire pit, they are perched along the mountainside. A pit toilet and water hydrant serve these remote and private cabins. A big flat boulder in front of cabin No. 2 is a favorite gathering spot.

The Barton Trail Cabins, 1-22, are secluded and at the foot of a hill. This older colony of vertical-side cabins is used less than others in the park. Cabin No. 5 is near the road and Nos. 21 and 22 are above the roadway along a narrow ridge. These are rustic and remote cabins that face away from each other, offering excellent privacy and a backwoods experience. Cabins 15 and 16 are along a ridgeline above the road. Inside these cabins are a gas cook stove, small refrigerator, gray tables and chairs, and four cots. Cabin 12 is the most private. Cabin 13 is oversized and in a more open area near the showerhouse. Cabins 4, 5,

6 and 7 are in the best condition in this colony. These are getaway cabins.

The best way to pick one of the hundreds of cabins is to drive around, deciding if you want to be near the developed areas or in remote locations in the park. The decision is a difficult one!

Day-use areas: The main day-use area surrounding the lodge has fine picnicking sites complete with pedestal grills, tables, modern playgrounds and open fields. Many day-use attractions including mini-golf, bike and boat rental and game courts are at the busy beach. The day-use areas can be packed on holiday weekends.

Mini-golf: Try your luck at the popular putty golf course in the main day-use area. Large fiberglass animals like tigers, hippos and elephants are incorporated into the course. The neat, kid-friendly course is lighted for night play.

Red House Inn: Tudor-style and made of carefully placed greystone brick in 1928, the massive lodge has a wonderful gift shop that is well-stocked with cards, sweatshirts, hats, toys, windchimes, wooden boxes, plush animals, beach toys, film, ice cream and cold drinks. The stately inn has beam ceilings and wood floors and there are many brochure racks and soft drink machines in the lobby and hallways. Cabins can be rented at the customer counter. When outside the building, notice the wrought-iron latches on the bulky window shutters. The lodge, which has a wooden interior, has a lake and mountain view.

The upstairs restaurant has pine ceilings with coach lights that cast subtle illumination on diners. A large fireplace also warms the cheery restaurant that offers excellent cuisine.

Natural history museum: A large wing of the scenic Tudor inn is dedicated to a natural history museum, where hundreds of bird and mammal mounts are displayed in glass-front cases that have brilliant white backgrounds. Mounts include raptors, broad-wing hawk, saw whet owl, great horned owl, Eastern red-shouldered hawk, marsh hawk, many types of waterfowl and songbirds. Also in the well-lighted museum are a skeleton of a snapping turtle, diorama of a beaver, bird skeletons, the skull of a black bear, a red fox and other mammal mounts. Other natural collections on display include study skins, pressure wildflowers, butterflies, insects, rocks and minerals, a relief map of the Allegany State Forest and a small sitting room. Some outdoor seating and a playground are behind the beautiful lodge.

The lodge room that the museum occupies originally was a skiers' dormitory. Today, the museum is often the focal point for many natural history programs. It also contains considerable interpretive information about the huge park.

Swimming beach: The view from the Red House beach includes mountains and lush woodlands. The beach, along the manmade lake, has more lawn area than gray sand. The facility has a diving platform and the water is sectioned-off in front of the lifeguard chairs. Amenities here include sand volleyball, modern timber play equipment, mini-golf, three tennis courts, bike path, boat and bike rentals, fishing bait and a wooden bathhouse. A walk-up food concession at the bathhouse next to the game room serves simple grill foods, ice cream and cold drinks.

The Quaker Beach (on Quaker Lake, off NY 280), near the Cain Hollow Camping Area, is also open seasonally. The 200-yard-long beach is sandy. A small stone bathhouse with orange doors serves swimmers. The beach area has lots of mowed open spaces, small playground and picnic area. A small gravel boat launch is near the swimming beach.

Hiking/biking: The Red House Bike Path is a hard-surfaced trail that connects park amenities has a yellow center line much like a highway. In-line skaters, bikers and hikers share the multi-use trail. The bike rental offers bikes, helmets and toddler trailers. Also from the rental are boats and fishing poles. The park has 23 miles of mountain bike trails. An 18-mile-long link of the Finger Lakes Trail crosses the state park.

The huge state park has 135 miles of marked hiking trails and many more unmarked spurs and connector trails. Hikers sometimes call the park the "matriarch" of all destinations in the state. Most hiking trails are marked with a blue disc with an image of a hiker with a hiking stick. Backpacking and overnight camping on designated trails are permitted.

With too many trails to detail here, you'll need to pick up a map from one of the various contact stations in the park. First-time visitors may want to start hikes from the Red House area, where many of the trails are easy loops.

Hiking the many trails in the park is an exercise in history. You will cross lands that the Erie, Susquehanna and Senecas once lived in. The Senecas were sometimes called the "keepers of the Western door" for their stewardship of the land. Years later, during the 19th and 20th centuries, the rugged tract that is now the park was homesteaded by Quakers. During this period the Red House was believed to have taken its name from a small Indian community where a house stood that had a bright red door.

With each step along the trail you are covering a lot of history. Four glaciers advanced and retreated through this region, reshaping the land with each pass. Today, the forests have thickened and are mostly American beech, red and sugar maple, and black and yellow birch; on the south-facing slopes are white pine, aspen, white ash, hickory, cucumber and tulip trees. You'll also have a chance to see some of the 160 bird species that have been recorded including many types of waterfowl like tundra swan, hooded merganser, American coot, double-crested cormorant, greater scaup and great blue heron. Hawks commonly seen include Cooper's, red-shouldered, sharp-shinned, rough-legged and goshawk. Evening hikers may spot some owls like barred, screech, barn, or great horned.

For mammal watchers, look for deer, flying squirrels, black bear, porcupine, gray and red fox, long-tail weasel, beaver, deer and lots of others.

Boating: There are many places where you can hand-load boats or use a single-lane launch. The sloping shorelines also allow canoeists to slip their craft into the weedy lake. Yellow and blue rowboats and paddleboats are rented from a small concession at the beach. The rental is on a quiet cove of the 110-acre Red House Lake and is ideal for family boating.

Friends Boat Launch has a user fee and accesses the Allegany Reservoir. The steep, single-lane launch is heavily used by bass anglers. This area is an excellent birding area. A portable toilet and courtesy dock are at the ramp.

A gravel boat launch accessing Quaker Lake is best for cartop boats. Bring your canoe for some pleasant paddling in the Allegany Reservoir, river and tributaries.

Fishing: A small square fishing pier with a guardrail is near the boat rental, where trout and panfish are taken on live bait and spinners. Bait is sold at the beach concession. Please obtain permit at park police headquarters.

Anglers may also shoreline fish Quaker Lake. The lake has lots of structure, standing trees, fallen shoreline trees, weedbeds and, best of all, it is not heavily fished. Many anglers also fish near the road. Quaker Lake is fed by the Allegany Reservoir. Many anglers wade Quaker Lake casting spinners.

Anglers will find excellent walleye fishing in the well-known Allegany Reservoir. Most fishermen use minnows, jigs and twister tails. Use light colors in the spring. Northern pike are also abundant.

Nature: The park is mostly northern hardwoods of mixed oak and maples, and old field environment and wetlands.

Winter: Skiing (27 miles of marked trails) and groomed snowmobile trails are open. Bring your skis to experience the nearby Art Roscoe Ski Touring area that offers 28 miles of trails. There are also 60 miles of groomed snowmobiling trails.

Hunting: Deer and small game hunting are permitted in designated areas of the park. You may obtain a permit at the police headquarters. There is no hunting allowed on Sundays.

Special events: Mountain and road bike races, birding weekends, classic car cruise, arts and crafts, artist in residence, concerts and annual summer naturalist and camper's programs are planned.

Insider tips: Plan a visit to the small Red House chapel (open Saturdays and Sundays during the summer) and the annual bike races and antique show. The park offers many programs; a schedule is available at contact stations throughout the park. The city of Salamanca is the only city in the U.S. that is entirely inside an Indian reservation. It will take several days to get to know the park. A three-day weekend is barely a start. Plan a trek to the bear caves. Also plan to visit the old quaker store museum.

Long Point on Lake Chautauqua

Land: 320 acres   Water: Lake Chautauqua

Long Point is the biggest inland marina in the state and a terrific access point to the boating and superior fishing on Lake Chautauqua. The 18-mile-long lake is a top fishing destination offering shallow water, deep water, rocky shoals and shoreline structure, submerged gravel points and islands, weedbeds, docks, humps and bumps. The serious fisherman or the weekend angler can do well all season on the lake.

Tucked in the scenic southwest corner of the state, the natural lake is fertile, near Lake Erie and often busy. But this wasn't always the case. The lake was carved by a glacier and Long Point is actually part of a moraine now covered with thick woods of beech, maple, spruce, poplar and oak. Thousands of years later, according to a 1956 newspaper account, the region was discovered: "On the 'Great Map of Franquelin' of 1684, most remarkable of the early maps of the interior of North America, it locates two Indian villages, called Oniasonthe or Oniasonke, supposed to have been situated where Long Point and Bemus Point jut into the lake. Relics and remains of Indian habitation have been found at these points from time to time.

"In the days of the first white settlers in this section, it is recorded that the Holland Land Company sold Long Point to John Thompson on September 2, 1809. However, the place is mentioned prior to that period, when in 1806, Jeremiah Griffin (of Griffin's Point) moved his goods and chattel down the lake from Mayville, with his wife and children following on a sled over the ice. They were caught in such a terrific blizzard that they were forced to stop on Long Point and build a shelter for the night."

Since this time Long Point has been a favorite place to visit. In fact, during the late 1800s, in the days of silk hats and horse and carriage, steamboats once pulled up to the docks hourly, bringing up to 10,000 visitors to daily events on the point. Evidence of the area's popularity can still be seen in the many estates and summer cottages that dot the lake.

Chautauqua is an Indian word meaning "bag tied in the middle." The middle of the bag is Bemus Point, a land point that divides the lake in half.

Information and Activities

Long Point on Lake Chautauqua
Route 430, RD #3, P.O. Box 160
Bemus Point, NY 14712
(716) 386-2722

Directions: The park entrance is off NY 430. One mile west of Bemus Point.

Marina: The marina began operation in 1971. The blond-brick marina store sells ice, oil, gasoline, fishing tackle, rope, basic marine supplies and safety equipment, grill foods, toiletries and snacks. A pay phone is available. A lake chart is also wall-mounted inside the small store. There are no boats rented at the park, but there are boat rentals around the lake. Outside of the stores are a few picnic tables and attractive landscape elements. Benches next to planters are also scattered in this busy area from which you can watch the colorful boats bob at their moorings.

Boat launch: Near the main marina, a five-lane hard-surfaced launch is adequate for most pleasure or fishing craft. Lots of fishermen depart from the well-designed ramp.

Day-use areas: Gazebo-style picnic shelters, handicapped accessible picnic tables, grills, play equipment and rolling open spaces are along the jutting point. Near the beach and in the picnic area is some new play equipment.

Swimming: The large attractive white bathhouse has a walk-up concession stand and a second story that looks over an often busy timber-style group of play equipment. The bathhouse was built in 1967 and the park was opened in 1968 during the Rockfeller Administration. The guarded beach has some sand, but is mostly grassy. There is access to the beach for visitors with disabilities.

Fishing: Fishing is diverse and good from shoreline or boat. The upper half of the lake is deep, averaging about 30 feet. The bottom structure in this area is gravel, sand and rubble with some thick weedbeds. Here you will find game fish hiding during the summer's heat.

The lower end of the lake is shallower, averaging about 15 feet, and

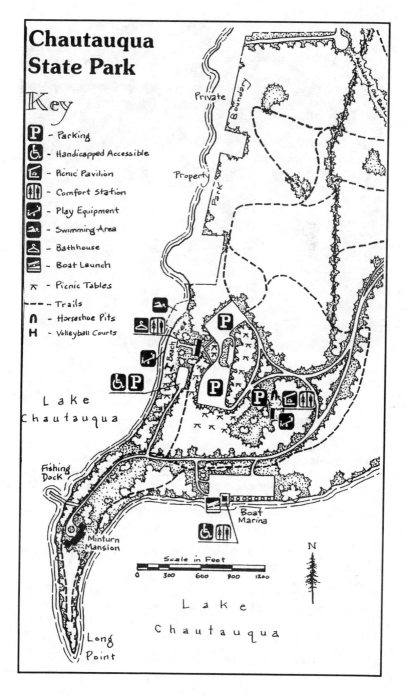

Chautauqua State Park

Key

- P — Parking
- ♿ — Handicapped Accessible
- 🏠 — Picnic Pavilion
- 🚻 — Comfort Station
- 🛝 — Play Equipment
- 🏊 — Swimming Area
- 🛕 — Bathhouse
- 🚤 — Boat Launch
- ⊼ — Picnic Tables
- --- — Trails
- ∩ — Horseshoe Pits
- H — Volleyball Courts

Private

Property

Park Boundary

Beach Area

Lake Chautauqua

Fishing Dock

Minturn Mansion

Boat Marina

Scale in Feet

0   300   600   900   1200

N

Lake Chautauqua

Long Point

the bottom is mostly featureless. The extreme lower end near Jamestown is thick with aquatic plants and several gravel shoals are evident. Bass, crappies and walleye often hold on some of the bars including Lakewood, Middle Lake shoals and Asheville Bay. Some of these shallow areas are marked with buoys.

All of these habitats are why muskie action in the lake is so good. The toothful denizen loves to patrol the deep spots, fruitful weedbeds and points where his next meal might be hiding. But because muskie can be so difficult--and time consuming--walleye, bass and crappie are the most popular species fished at Chautauqua Lake. In fact, three-pound crappies are trophy-size, while smallmouth bass average about two pounds and 11-13 pound walleyes are reported each year.

Good muskie fishing lasts from opening day to late June, declining during the summer and picking back up in early October. Like most muskie lakes, trolling large stickbaits is the common pattern. Try trolling at night and adjust the lure to run in the wake of the motor every few minutes. For more fun, try casting big spoons at the shore-line early in the morning or in the evening. The lake's record muskie is 51 pounds. Please, release your muskie.

Both large- and smallmouth bass share the lake. Smallmouth will hang near rocks and points during the spring, while largemouth will move in and out of the weedier areas and often hit spinners, grub bodies, jigs and topwater baits. The most productive times for bass are early morning or evening.

Early season walleye action is hot. Anglers typically cast Rapalas in three to eight feet of water at dawn and around dusk. This action lasts through May, and you might pick up a muskie in the process. Night fishing for walleye is very popular and productive. Most anglers use perch or chartreuse crankbaits slowly trolled in three to eight feet of water. Hot trolling locations are reported to be in the upper lake north of the Bell Tower; off the mouth of Dewittville Bay southward to Mission Meadows; and off Prendergast Bay. Weed growth in the lower lake makes trolling difficult after May.

By June, walleye are hiding in the weeds and have moved to the coolest waters in the upper end. Try the upper lake holes during the heat of the summer for all game fish. You can also try gently jigging in the weeds to bring up some fish. As the days cool off in the fall, the walleye fishing can be hot. Try vertical, barbless jigs during this time of the year. Local experts say white and yellow are good color choices.

In the winter look for vertical drops around deep holes and use a jig and minnow for walleye. If the fish are nibbling, try adding a stinger treble hook. Jig slow.

Crappie fishing is at its best just after ice-out when the scrappy crappies swim up the channels and begin to congregate around underwater structure. Use a live minnow hooked through the lips or small bright jigs or twistertail. Cast and retrieve slowly, stopping several times as you work the bait back. Yellow, white and black jig tails are recommended. For summer crappies, work along the weedlines, in deeper water with a slip bobber.

Hiking: North of the beach are a few easy hiking trails.

Winter: Cross-country skiing and snowmobiling are allowed at the park.

Insider tips: Nearby is an amusement park. Bring your own bait, and don't forget the excellent ice fishing. The lake is a very good crappie and muskie fishery.

ALLEGANY REGION

PHONE	PARK
716-354-9101	ALLEGANY REGION
716-354-2182	Allegany: Quaker
716-354-9121	Red House
716-792-9214	Lake Erie
716-386-2722	Long Point on Lake Chautauqua

▷ Availability of service or facility   ► Handicapped accessible

Facility	Allegany: Quaker	Red House	Lake Erie	Long Point on Lake Chautauqua
Tent/trailers sites (h = hookups, e = electricity)	A·e	A·e		
Trailer dump	►	►		
Showers	►	►		
Camper recreation	►	►		
Cabins	►	►		
Food	►	►	►	
Store	►	►	►	
Picnic tables	►	►	►	
Shelters (• reservations)	►	▷	►•	
Swimming beach (• bath house)	►•	►•	►•	
Swimming pool (• bath house)				
Recreation programs (• performing arts)	►•	►•	►•	
Hiking	▷	▷	▷	▷
Biking	▷	▷	▷	▷
Nature trails	▷	▷	▷	▷
Fishing	►	►	►	►
Playground	►	►	►	►
Golf (•clubhouse)				
Tennis		▷	▷	
Pond or lake (• power boats ok)	►•	▷	▷	▷•
River or stream (• power boats ok)		▷	▷	
Launching site (• hand launch only)	►•	▷	▷•	▷
Boat rental		▷		
Marina (• anchorage)				▷•
Pump out				▷
Ice skating (•rentals)				
Cross-country skiing (• rentals)	▷	▷•	▷	▷
Snowmobiling	▷	▷	▷	▷
Sled slopes		▷		

19

Central Region

This is the heartland of New York. Here are lush valleys and crystal clear lakes that offer recreation for everyone.

The region is steeped in history and offers wonderful places to visit and learn about James Fenimore Cooper, the Revolutionary era and mid-19th century military life at forts and museums.

The Central Region's 21 state parks and historic places offer a variety of things to do for the entire family. Children will enjoy beaches, playgrounds and shoreline fishing, while other members of the family can take hikes, camp, cross-country ski, ice fish, snowmobile, square dance, visit a nature center or take in a concert.

The area was shaped by glaciers, in fact, Clark Reservation has huge cliffs of five million year old bedrock that hold rare plants. One of the best beaches in the state is at Green Lakes State Park.

Central Region

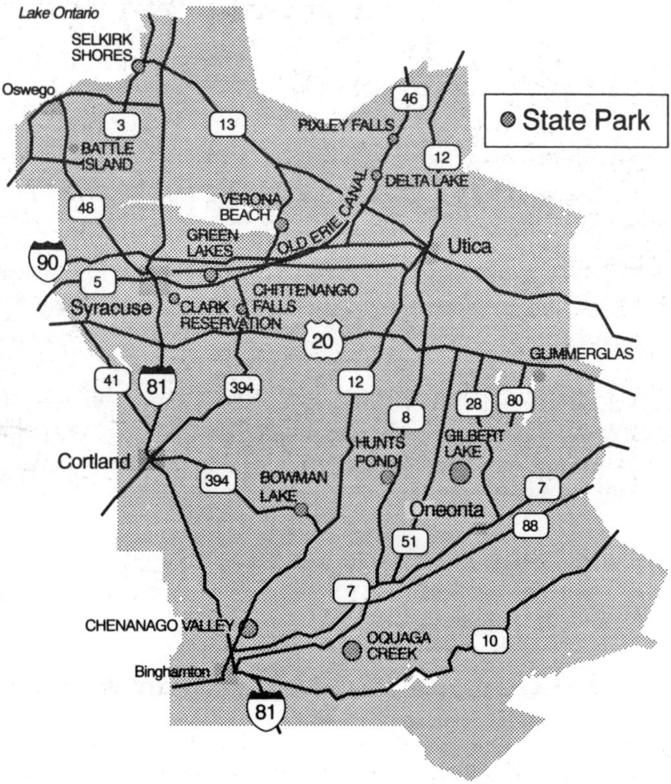

Lake Ontario

SELKIRK SHORES

Oswego

3

BATTLE ISLAND

13

PIXLEY FALLS

46

12

DELTA LAKE

48

VERONA BEACH

OLD ERIE CANAL

GREEN LAKES

Utica

90

5

CHITTENANGO FALLS

Syracuse

CLARK RESERVATION

20

GLIMMERGLAS

41

81

394

12

28

80

8

GILBERT LAKE

HUNTS POND

Cortland

394

BOWMAN LAKE

Oneonta

7

51

88

7

CHENANAGO VALLEY

OQUAGA CREEK

10

Binghamton

81

⊚ State Park

Chenango Valley
State Park

Land: 1,071 acres Water: Lakes and rivers

During the last ice age, a mile thick glacier transformed Central New York on both its punishing advance and wet retreat. The moving mountain of ice dug long, narrow, deep lakes and sculpted large hills of dirt and gravel. Some of these round hills now lie between Chenango and Lily lakes. The glacier left behind large chunks of buried ice which melted and formed the two beautiful "kettle lakes" as well as the natural bog and stream that can be seen from the nature trail. Chenango Valley is the southernmost state park in the Central Region.

In 1927, the New York Parks Commission acquired the rugged tract from the executors of the Warners' estate and by 1930 the state park was opened to the public. Three years later the Civilian Conservation Corps undertook many projects, including construction of the dam to enlarge the lake, building a 9-hole golf course, planting trees and other amenities. In 1946, additional lands were acquired and an extra nine holes were added to the golf course in the 1960s.

The park has been blessed with an active group of volunteers known as the Friends of the Chenango Valley State Park. The active nonprofit group fund-raises for park improvements, staffs the nature center's interpretive building and helps coordinate a variety of public programs and services. The long-term sustainability of quality state parks depends on volunteers and friends groups like this one. If you'd like more information about this group, pick up a flier with membership information or contact the park office. Also, consider joining or starting a state park friends group in your area—the quality of the parks depends on you.

Chenango Valley State Park is a clean, well-maintained, family-oriented park with a variety of amenities and some special activities. They include the bluebird nesting box program (including boxes on the golf course), a bat shelter building project, programs on wildlife rehabilitation and winter outdoor recreation opportunities.

Information and Activities

Chenango Valley State Park
153 State Park Road
Chenango Forks, NY 13746
(607) 648-5251

Directions: In Broome County. From Syracuse, take I-81 South to the Whitney Point exit, Route 79 East to Rt. 369 South to the park. From New York City, take Route 17 West to Rt. 7 North to Rt. 369 North. The shady park office is 100 yards away from the stone check-in station at the gate. A kiosk with a map is outside the park office. Inside the small office is a small sales area (sweatshirts, T-shirts, mugs, etc.) and brochure rack.

Emergency numbers: 911 system; park police, (607) 648-3662.

Campground: The sprawling park has three camping areas and a total of 216 sites (51 sites have electrical hookups). Chipmunk Bluff, the largest camping area, is non-electric, while many sites in Page Brook and all sites in Pine Bluff offer electrical hookups. Water and sewage hookups are not available in any of the camping areas. Pine Bluff is above the lake. Many sites in all of the loops are spacious and quite private.

Page Brook Camping Area: Sites are in a valley and many are along a winding creek. A small sandy play area and open spaces with mowed

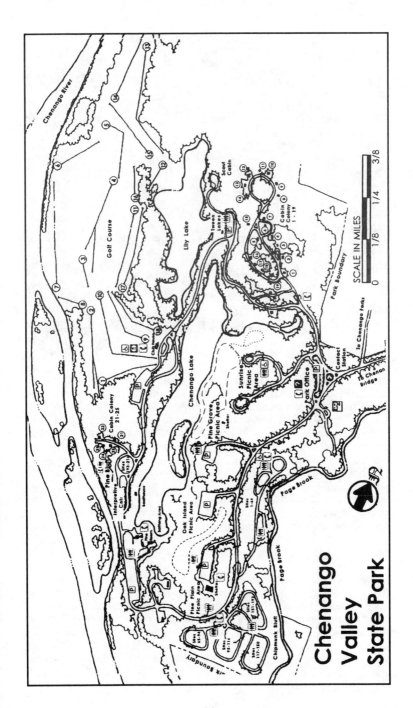

Chenango Valley State Park

SCALE IN MILES

0   1/8   1/4   3/8

24

grass offer children and campers an impromptu place for field games. Sites are evenly spaced with a thin wall of shrubby vegetation that separates them. Recommended sites include 3, 4-6 (for larger RV rigs), 7 and 9. Page Brook is about 50 percent shady. Sites 14, 16 and 17 are along the winding low banks of a creek and close to a small day-use area and bathhouse. Shade lovers will want to inspect spruce tree-shaded sites 18 and 19. Loop 22-36 offers shady sites, with many great for popup campers. Sunny sites, backed up against a veil of vegetation are 29-31. Site 31 is oversized. Site 36 is firmly packed, almost hard-surfaced and close to the bathhouse. Sites 12 and 15 are under mature trees with a caliper of 18 inches and at the base of a hill. A small loop, sites 52-64, are open and grassy. Site 53 is a semi-shady pull-through. Sites 59 and 60 are the most private in the entire park. Sites 61 and 64 are plenty shady and near the open day-use area.

Chipmunk Bluff Camping Area: Loop 65-150 are generally grassy with sparse gravel pads and many pencil-straight pine groves scraping the sky overhead. Each of the sites has a fire ring and picnic table. A quarter-acre open space is mowed and available for field games in front of sites 72-74. Chipmunk Bluff has an ideal mix of full sun and shade from pines and hardwoods. Sites 80-82 are the best tent sites in the park. These and other nearby sites are notched out of the open woods and separated by a thin wall of brush. Sites 91-93 are excellent sites for families with small RV units or tents. These sites are near the play area.

At the entrance of the small loop 95-116 is a half-acre mowed spaces were volleyball nets are often in use. Sites 148 and 149 are near this inviting passive recreation space. Sites in the 140s are backed up against a wooded tract. Sites in the 117-143 loop are on slightly higher ground with gravel and grass pads. If you want to be near the open space area consider sites 123 and 124. Site 128, on a knoll, is a terrific tent camping location. Sites 135, 137 and 138 are oversized.

If privacy is your goal, consider sites 140 and 141 that are on-the curve of the somewhat bumpy hard-surfaced park road and not far from the bathhouse. Loop 151-192 is shady, fairly well separated, private and often busy with family campers. Sites 156 and 158 are oversized and near the bathhouse. In this loop, tent campers will want to carefully inspect the high and dry site 162—it's a great one. Sites in the 170s are heavily wooded and large. Site 177 is near a mowed area and ideal for tent-camping families. Sites in the 180s are well separated by vegetation.

Pine Bluff Camping Area: This is the preferred loop for small RV units. The rolling loop has two-foot thick spruce, shade and electrical hookups. The scenic blufftop camping area also has plenty of room for large RV rigs, and there are views of the beach and lake. This popular camping area is within walking distance of the swimming area.

Cabins: The park operates 24 modest cabins that are dark brown wood clapboard with stone chimneys and screened porches. Most of the rustic units are shady and nestled along a wooded hillside at various elevations. Cabins also have a picnic table and fire ring. Units 1-19 are three-room models with a kitchen area, small bedroom, and one large room usually with a double bed, tables, chairs and heat source. Cabins 21-25 have two rooms, a kitchen, large room with beds and source of heat. This group of cabins is in the Pine Bluff Camping Area. Cabin 22 is the most private. Cabins 1, 3 and 8-14 have fireplaces and all others have a wood stove. Each unit has electricity, cold running water only, a full-size refrigerator, LP gas cooking stove, table and chairs. Bring your own linen and cooking utensils. There is a flush toilet at each cabin; hot showers are in the campground areas. Cabins are not available from mid-October to April. There is a two-night minimum stay.

Cabin 8 has an interesting porch and small sideyard. Cabins 12 and 14 are perched near a ridge with a view of a wooded valley. Families with small children may want to consider cabin 15. It has a sideyard and is along the quiet hard-surfaced road where children may ride bicycles or other pedal toys.

Golfers will want to reserve cabins 21-25, which are near the 18-hole course.

Day-use areas: The Pine Grove Picnic Area is a large mowed space with a baseball backstop and scattered picnic tables. The Oak Island day-use area is served by a large hard-surfaced parking lot. The Pine Plain Picnic Area features a beautiful stone and timber rentable pavilion. The Tween Picnic Area also has a scenic stone shelter and fine amenities for family reunions and other group outings. From this day-use area is one of the best views of the lake and lush wooded hills that roll off into the hazy distance sky. The park has three reservable picnic shelters.

Swimming beach: Skirted by a beautiful fieldstone and timber day-use building, the beach is also near a large parking lot. The low, tan-colored clapboard bathhouse has men's and women's changing rooms and showers. Unique to New York, the swimming area is actually a level concrete bottom of the lake that is corded off by yellow and white rope and buoys. Wood park benches surround the clean manmade swimming part of the lake. Various planting pockets, knee-walls, fences and walkways outline and define the busy swimming area. No fishing is allowed at this hybrid area that is part natural beach and lake and part cement swimming pool. A small supervised diving area is also at the clean swim site. A food concession, picnicking area and WPA-built shelter are behind the mostly hard-surfaced swimming area. This wonderful WPA building was used as a bar and a hotel during the canal-building days.

Golf: Eat breakfast (or lunch) at the clubhouse before your 18-hole round. The clubhouse is of stone and flanked by a flapping American flag, rail fences and heavily wooded fairways. Banquet and catering services are available for outings; call (800) NYVENDING. The course is medium length. From the blue tees it measures 6,271 yards long. A small pro shop sells a few golf clubs, hats, shirts and golf balls. The clubhouse restaurant and bar have terrific pine walls, wood tables and a wonderful aroma of grilled foods and golf chatter in the air. The 18-hole course has a slope rating from the blue tees of 70.6/124.

Carts are available and often pulled up near the outdoor eating area near the clubhouse. Holes 3, 6 and 12 have water hazards and 10 is a strong dogleg to the right to a small green. Birdhouses along the fairway mark the 150-yard length to the center of the green. The course has two practice greens near the clubhouse.

Hiking: Edge Trail is a .6-mile loop with 11 learning stations which are indicated by green numbers on a white background. There is a rest room accessible by persons with disabilities at the Sunrise Picnic Area. Along the trail, hikers will learn about the edge effect (transitions between forest and field or lake and wetland, etc.), white oaks, pin oaks, ironwood, blue beech and American hornbeam trees, as well as white and blue spruce trees, birds of the area and plenty of interesting facts about other trees including white cedar, black cherry, scotch pine and white pine. In addition, you'll learn how wildlife use this special habitat, how food is transported, how charcoal was made, and that oily extracts from the black cherry tree were once used as sedatives and as a flavoring for rum. You might spot some wildlife on the hike too. For excellent views of the lake, hike the Woodland Trail.

Boating: The small boat rental near the beach has four small concrete docks where aluminum boats launch from.

Fishing: Shoreline anglers try their luck along the cove near the swimming beach. The lake is stocked with trout. Other species in the lake include sunfish, bluegill, rock bass, yellow perch, pickerel and black bass.

Nature Center: The small stone interpretive center is behind the boat rental concession near the swimming area. It has double front doors that are often swung wide open. Inside the well-lighted, single-room center is a small library, a sample roosting bat box, various bird nesting boxes, a touch table with bones and skulls to examine, fossils, information about the old canal, CCC Camp SP-13, Company 236 and WPA program, flags, black and white photographs of CCC workers and tools, and the early use of the park which dates to the mid-1820s. Also in the center is information about the founders of the lake, Indian activity, a topography map, bluebird nesting program, VCR and television. The center is open seasonally and usually staffed by volunteers. Wildlife in the park includes deer, rabbit, coyote, beaver, waterfowl and many types of woodpeckers, kingfishers, herons, warblers and thrushes.

The active Friends of Chenango Valley State Park, a non-profit volunteer group, contributes services to the park including outdoor education programming like bird hikes, slide shows, fly tying workshops, wildlife rehabilitation, history programs, mountain bike clinics, crafts and nature walks.

Winter: Cross-country skiing is encouraged when conditions warrant. Sledding is also offered at the park during the winter.

Insider tips: Many park visitors are repeaters. According to staff, several generations of the same family use the park annually. Bike races and a craft show are only two of many annual activities. The annual arts and craft show is held near the beach on Memorial Day weekend and vendors sell jewelry, woodworking items, plants, photographs and barbecue food. The park recently acquired a lock on the Chenango Canal, which may be restored in the future to better interpret the canal history.

Chittenango Falls
State Park
Land: 194 acres Water: Chittenango Falls

Just south of the village of Chittenango and five miles north of Cazenovia is the picturesque 167-foot falls that is the focal point of the quiet Chittenango Falls State Park. The waterfalls were also the focus of considerable industry in the mid-1800s. Traces of factories, including stone foundations, can still be seen of an old water canal and buildings.

In 1866, 40 acres around the tall waterfalls were offered for sale at a public auction and sold to the Rev. George Boardman, who gave the tract to his son, Derrick. It wasn't long until young Derrick was approached by a gunpowder maker to sell the scenic land. Derrick said he would sell for $2,000, but would reduce the price by $500 if Mrs. Helen L. Fairchild, a local Cazenovian, would purchase the land and dedicate it for public use.

Nature-loving Mrs. Fairchild had a strong desire to protect the dramatic falls and quickly raised $2,250 toward the purchase and preservation. During the fund-raising effort she formed the Chittenango Falls Park Association in 1887. From 1887 to 1922, the park was under the direction of the association, remaining open for the general public.

In 1922, worried about the possibility of accidents around the rushing falls, she proposed that the state take over the park. Today, the small park features quiet camping, fishing, short trails, unique habitats and scenic day-use areas.

About 100,000 people visit the park annually.

Information and Activities

Chittenango Falls State Park
2300 Rathburn Road
Cazenovia, NY 13035
(315) 655-9620

Directions: The rushing creek along Rt. 13 guides you to the park. The stair-step falls can be seen from the road. Inside the small park office is an interesting 1870s photo of the falls. In the picture are ladies with hoop dresses and big hats. Winter scene photos from 1895 and 1919 are also inside the tiny office that is attached to the maintenance building.

Emergency numbers: Park police (315) 492-6422; State police (315) 363-4400.

The waterfalls: From the parking area past the check-in station is a walkway to the cascading falls. On your way to the falls you'll pass a wonderful Civilian Conservation Corps-built stone shelter and walk along a flagstone path.

The magnificent waterfalls were created after the retreat of the most recent continental glacier about 12,500 years ago. The falls resulted from a glacial diversion of the stream over a wide terrace of limestone. The charming Chittenango Creek descends the north margin of the Allegany Plateau.

Today, the clear waters of the creek flow north, from Cazenovia Lake toward Oneida Lake and Lake Ontario, cascading over these ledges. The gorge below the falls was cut through Onondaga limestone that was formed from sediment in the sea that once covered the area.

Chittenango Falls and the surrounding area have undergone many changes in the last 200 years. The falls were originally purchased by John Lincklaen, founder of the village of Cazenovia, and resident agent of the Holland Land Company, in 1797. The property was sold in 1813 to Studson Benson. During these years the property was part of a booming industrial center. The falls were critical to the development of manufacturing. A few of the companies in the area included William's Stone Quarry, H. L. Jones Paper Mill and Foster's Sawmill.

By the end of the Civil War, industry disappeared from the falls area. At that time, the acreage passed to the state for permanent park use.

Today, large slabs of stone form steps that take visitors to the base of the rushing falls. The wide falls are best viewed from the base, where crashing water spills into the rocky creek and a light spray fills the air.

Campground: The campground has 22 sites on a single loop. Trailer size is restricted to 22 feet, due to a small campground access bridge. According to staff, site 9 is the most private. It is heavily used, slightly oversized and near the pedestrian bridge. The campground attracts mostly tent and pop-up campers.

The open campground is high, dry and intimate. All of the grassy sites have a picnic table and steel ground-mounted fire ring. Sites 13 and 14 are backed up against natural vegetation, as are most of the sites on the outside perimeter of the loop. Site 16 is oversized. Site 9 is best for the maximum-size 22-foot-long trailer. The gray showerhouse has an exterior utility sink. The small but clean showerhouse has only one shower per side.

A tetherball court and drinking fountain are near sites 6 and 8. A sand volleyball court is also in the campground. Site 22 is by itself and below the showerhouse.

Firewood is sold at the park office.

Day-use areas: At the top of the falls are a wonderful stone CCC shelter and benches scattered along a hillside. Plenty of picnic tables and play areas are offered in a mowed open space next to the parking lot. A ball field is behind the check-in station. The park has one picnic shelter and a single basketball goal at the park office.

Hiking: The Chips Trail (.75 mile round-trip) and the quarter-mile Gorge Trail are moderate in difficulty and heavily used. From the Rt.

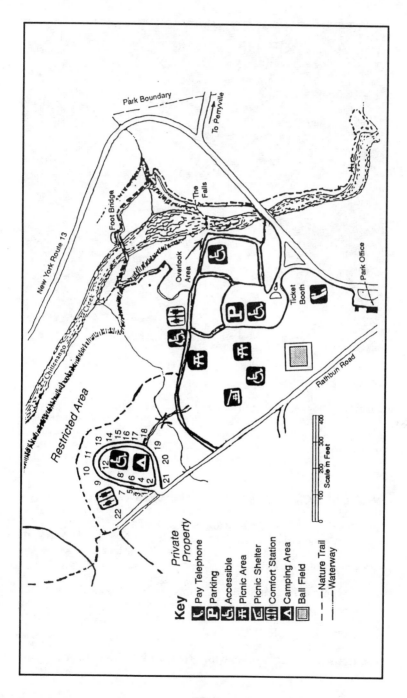

Key

Private
Property

📞 Pay Telephone

🅿 Parking

♿ Accessible

🎇 Picnic Area

Picnic Shelter

🚻 Comfort Station

⛺ Camping Area

Ball Field

- - - Nature Trail

······ Waterway

Park Boundary

To Perryville

The Falls

Foot Bridge

New York Route 13

Chittenango Creek

Overlook Area

Park Office

Ticket Booth

Restricted Area

Rathbun Road

Scale in Feet
0 100 200 300 400

9 10 11
8 12 13 14
7 15 16 17
6 5 18
4 3 2 19 20
22 1 21

13 bridge there is a spur that is often used by anglers. A dry falls is also at the end of the short spur.

Fishing: Try fly fishing or use red worms or salted minnows in the fast-running creek that bisects the park. Above the falls, the creek is stocked with brown trout; below the falls, landlocked salmon have been placed. Indians once maintained a salmon fishery at the base of the falls. Fish biologists are hopeful the salmon will do well in the creek.

Nature: The Chittenango Ovate snail was discovered here in 1905 and lives nowhere else on earth. Originally these snails occurred in great abundance, but now are rare. Competition for habitat by a pest species of snail is a major factor affecting the Ovate snail's survival. Access to the snail's habitat is restricted. It is uncertain whether the species will survive or fade into extinction.

Another unique resident of the falls area is the roseroot. The plant has thick succulent leaves and is known in only three locations in the world. It survives here by clinging to the high sheer ledges away from disturbance by people.

The Harts-tongue fern is known in New York to fewer than 10 sites,

including Chittenango Falls State Park. Disturbance to its habitat has nearly eliminated it from the park.

The park has about 170 vascular plant species and 13 species of ferns. While in the park look for whitetail deer, gray squirrel, Eastern chipmunk, woodchuck and many birds, including cedar waxwings that love the falls area. The local Audubon Society has identified 93 species of birds in the park including Northern and Louisiana waterthrush, five types of swallows, northern harrier, Eastern wood-pewee, rufous-sided towhee, four types of vireos, common warblers and several types of hawks.

Some natural history and recreation programming is offered. According to staff, face painting is one of the most popular summer activities.

Insider tips: Waterfall enthusiasts will want to visit this tall cascade. Record attendance at the park is 1,530 on Memorial Day in 1994. The unit is a quiet, low-energy park with a small campground. Ask about the wood sculpture of a grizzly bear. The smiling bear, holding a trout in its paws, was carved from a large stump.

Clark Reservation
State Park
Land: 310 acres   Water: 10 acres

The clear, deep lake at Clark Reservation State Park was formed by the rushing rivers of glacial melt water 10,000 years ago. The bedrock of the park is up to 400 million years old, having been laid down under ancient shallow seas. The creatures living in the sea were trapped and slowly, molecule by molecule, their bodies were replaced by mineral, forming fossils we see today. The fossils can be found in the park or in the Nature Center. Fossil examples in the nature center include horn coral, trilobites, honeycomb coral, brachiopods and others.

The interesting park is world famous as one of the country's few locations of the delicate Hart's tongue fern. This rare fern, one of 26 species found in the park, requires a special habitat that is cool, moist woods, limy soils and a northeast-facing slope. Because it is in inaccessible places in the park, the special fern is hard to find, but most of the other bright green ferns can be seen from the trail. These ferns go back about 300 million years in the evolution of the plant kingdom.

Ferns were one of the earliest plants with vascular tissue, i.e., a system of tubes to transport water and nutrients to the plant. Algae and mosses are examples of plants without a vascular system. You'll also find 100 species of interesting mosses, a carpet-like pioneer plant that protects the ground from erosion and paved the way for development of permanent plant communities.

Clark Reservation, with its deep, quiet lake and looming cliffs near Jamesville, had its start as a park in 1915, when Mary Clark Thompson of New York City purchased the 108 acres surrounding the lake. She believed that this land near the edge of the northern escarpment of the Appalachian Plateau on the divide between Onondaga Valley and Butternut Valley was important, scenic and valuable. In fact, her purchase probably saved the area from being quarried. She donated the land to the state as a memorial to her father, Myron Clark, who had been governor from 1855 to 1857. The tract was dedicated as a state park in 1926.

Long before Mary Clark Thompson owned the lake, much of central New York was occupied by Algonquin Indians until the end of the 13th century. At one time, the lake had an Indian name, *"Kal-yah-koo,"* which means *"satisfied with tobacco."* According to legend, an Indian woman who lost a child in the 62-feet-deep lake would come each autumn to cast tobacco into the water. This would appease the evil spirits and encourage the Great Spirit to watch over the child.

Information and Activities

Clark Reservation State Park
6105 E. Seneca Turnpike
Jamesville, NY 13078
(315) 492-1590

Directions: In gently rolling Onondaga County five miles southeast of Syracuse. From Syracuse, take Rt. 481 South to the Jamesville Exit. Follow Jamesville Road to Rt. 173 and Rt. 173 West 1.25 miles to the park entrance. There is no rock climbing or rappelling at the park.

The New York State Parks Central Region administrative office is here at Clark Reservation, housed in a wonderful fieldstone building with a flapping flag in front and a small covered bridge nearby that arches over the craggy Dry Lake Creek. It's open 8 a.m. - 4:30 p.m. weekdays.

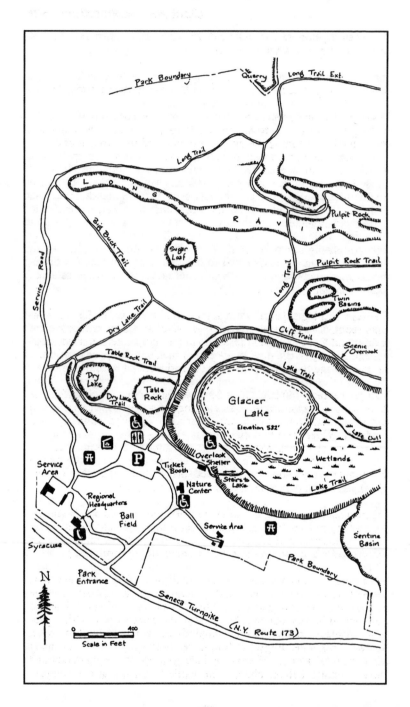

Park Boundary

To Quarry

Long Trail Ext.

Long Trail

LONG

RAVINE

Pulpit Rock

Big Buck Trail

Service Road

Sugar Loaf

Pulpit Rock Trail

Long Trail

Dry Lake Trail

Twin Basins

Cliff Trail

Scenic Overlook

Table Rock Trail

Lake Trail

Dry Lake

Dry Lake Trail

Table Rock

Glacier Lake

Elevation 582'

Lake Outlet

Overlook Shelter

Wetlands

Service Area

🅿

Ticket Booth

Nature Center

Stairs to Lake

Lake Trail

Regional Headquarters

Ball Field

Service Area

Syracuse

Sentinel Basin

N

Park Entrance

Park Boundary

Seneca Turnpike (N.Y. Route 173)

0   400
Scale in Feet

37

Emergency phones: Park police, (315) 492-6422; state police, 911. A telephone is near the nature center.

Day-use areas: Two pavilions, playgrounds, playing fields, picnic tables, open spaces, rest rooms and trailheads entertain visitors.

Hiking: The hiking trail is accessed from the northeast side of the parking lot, not far from the ridge-side nature center. The trail rises above the lake, skirting the cliff that is outlined by a four-foot chain-link fence. Along the twisting walk are rock outcrops that are shaped by the never-ending forces of water and weather. Worn smooth, broad Table Rock rests above the cold glacial lake and is the first major geological feature along the many trails such as Table Rock Trail, Big Buck Trail, Cliff Trail, Lake Trail, Saddle Back Trail, Pulpit Rock Trail, Long Trail and others.

This undulating and wide trail takes you past car-size boulders and rocks that are smooth and pillow-like. From this rocky trail that circles the lake, you will have terrific vistas and views of the steep lake and rock outcroppings that catch the sun.

Fishing: Fishing is permitted, but the action is modest. The lake contains rough fish, pickerel and sunfish. Anglers report catching other species and lots of painted turtles along the shore, and songbirds nesting and singing in the trees nearby. For pickerel try spoons and spinner baits in the transition zone from lake to wetland in the spring.

Nature center: The CCC-style stone and clapboard building is flanked by a demonstration garden, ridge top view, open spaces and pedestrian walkway. Inside the seasonally operated environmental education center are a variety of fauna mounts including gray and red squirrel, great blue heron, raccoon, woodchuck, opossum, snapping turtle and songbirds. Also in the small facility with a beam ceiling is a touch table loaded with nature objects that children and other visitors can explore with their senses.

Other educational elements include samples of tree leaves, a display on the geology of New York and the glacial history of Clark Reservation, fossils, seeds pods and a large relief map that depicts the rugged terrain and the roads and amenities of the surrounding territory.

In a corner of the nature center is a small display of a fossil-filled cave, which teaches about fossils and general geology. Fossils are the remains or traces of organisms that lived in ancient geological time and were buried in rock that accumulated on the earth's crust. Other geologic displays include information about Moorehouse limestone, Nedrow limestone, Edgecliff limestone, Springvale chert and many other types of stones. Fossils include gastropods, cephalopods and other examples behind glass. The earliest fish are also displayed.

These early fish-like fossils, called ostracoderms, and were found in the Silurian age strata. There, fascinating organisms were much like today's fish, except they were characterized by bony body plates.

Outdoor education: The Council of Park Friends and state park staff conduct a number of outdoor education programs including pond life, woodland wonders, swamp tromp, the big picture (ecosystem), reptiles and amphibians, botanical hikes, tree identification, plants and medicine, edible wild plants, birding, spring wildflowers and more. The center also has a small library of regional field guides, an insect collection, brochures and preserved specimens including northern water snake, red-bellied snakes, frogs and salamander. You can join the friends group and learn more about their activities by writing CPF, P.O. Box 153, Jamesville, NY 13078. Check the window of the nature center for hours of operation.

Nature: The park's land has 80 species of trees, 26 types of ferns (some rare) and 100 types of moss that adorn magnificent limestone outcrops. Visitors might also see some of the 140 species of birds, including winter wren, pileated woodpeckers, ruffed grouse, tanager, cedar waxwing and bold-looking kingfishers that eye the lake, ready to plunge into the water for a fresh fish dinner. The park also has white-tailed deer, chipmunks, flying squirrels, gray fox, mink, skunks and cottontail rabbits.

Nearby state parks and attractions: Chittenango Falls State Park (Rt. 13, four miles north of Caznovia); Green Lakes State Park (Rts. 290 and 5, 10 miles east of Syracuse) Old Erie Canal State Park (Oneida, Chittenango, Fayetteville, Rome - this park is a linear canal-side trail); and Verona Beach State Park (Rt. 13, seven miles northwest of Oneida).

Insider tips: Rolling and pretty, the clean park is great for a day of rocky hiking, learning about the round glacial lake and having a picnic. The 10-acre glacial lake is one of the few meromictic (non-mixing) lakes in the United States. In other words, the warmer surface waters and cold bottom water of the lake do not mix. Geologists speculate that the glacial meltwater and waterfall into the lake once contained a volume of water greater than the American Falls at Niagara. This torrent of water lasted about 2,000 years.

Stop by the Central Region park office for additional information about area state parks. For fern watching, try the Lake Trail south or Long Trail. Spring wildflower enthusiasts should hike the easy Long Trail. Geology buffs will want to traverse the Cliff Trail, which is difficult hiking.

Green Lakes State Park
Land: 2,104 acres   Water: Green Lake and Round Lake

At the ribald turn of the century, small steamboats brought excited passengers from Syracuse and Fayetteville on the Erie Canal to Green Lakes Landing, where they enjoyed the beautiful lakes they had read about in national magazines and newspapers.

In 1928, during the Roaring Twenties, the two intriguing glacial lakes near Fayetteville were preserved as part of an initial 500-acre tract acquired by the state and named Green Lakes State Park. Much of the land the state purchased was a military tract granted to soldiers of the Revolutionary War. Today, the park boasts some of the cleanest and finest park facilities in the state including camping, cabins, a sandy beach, picnic shelters, hiking trails, 18-hole golf course, play fields and large day-use areas.

Visitors will surely ask, "why is the lake green?" The answer is complex.

The longer wavelengths (e.g. the red end of the light spectrum) are the first to be absorbed by the water and hence only blue and green light is transmitted to the deeper waters. Light is dispersed and reflected back to the surface by suspended materials in the water. If the water is turbid, containing much suspended material, the mean depth from which light is dispersed is small.

However, if the water is very clear, as is the case with Green Lake, then the mean depth from which light is dispersed is much greater, and therefore, contains much more blue and green light. Most of the suspended material is unproductive. Consequently most deep, clear, unproductive lakes, such as Green Lake, tend to have a deep blue or green color. In Green Lake, about the only suspended material in the water to disperse the light is suspended calcium carbonate.

In some lakes the suspended material itself can be pigmented and impart color to the water. Lakes with heavy phytoplankton blooms will cause a green color. Another factor is the presence or absence of dissolved humic materials which tend to act as a yellow filter. The presence of calcium carbonate, however, coagulates humic material, shifting the color of the light being transmitted toward the blue end of the spectrum.

In short, Green Lake is green because it is deep, unproductive (little phytoplankton), clear (so the observe "sees" light which has been dispersed from a great depth) and it contains lots of suspended calcium carbonate which reflects blue-green and dissolves humic (organic) materials.

Interestingly, scientists found that the water at 75-foot depths in Green Lake is rosy pink. This unique three-foot layer is due to purple bacteria.

Information and Activities

Green Lakes State Park
7900 Green Lakes Road
Fayetteville, NY 13066-9658
(315) 637-6111

Directions: In upscale Fayetteville, visitors can enter that park off NY Route 290, or the golf course from Route 5. The park is 11 miles east of Syracuse. The park office has information about the park and surrounding attractions.

Campground: The campground has 137 sites (42 electric) in two areas. According to staff, many campers are repeat customers who often stay on the same site year after year. A new playground is behind site 103.

The Pine Wood camping area, sites 1-56, is along two delightful loops that surround a showerhouse and small nature center. Properly trimmed trees are scattered throughout the rolling campground, offering just the right combination of shade and sunlight. The trimmed trees also allow RV units to back under them.

Green Lakes has correctly installed ground-mounted fire rings flush to the ground. Picnic tables are at each site. Site 19 is on a grassy knoll and is a perfect site for a tent or pop up camper. Sites 20 and 21 enjoy lots of midday sun. Sites 31-38 are private, on a breezy knoll and under a grove of skyscraping pines. If you enjoy the morning sun, consider grassy sites 38-42, near cabin No. 1. A small sandbox and water hydrant are near these open sites. Behind sites 43 and 44 are some tall pines that offer ample shade. Site 45 receives midday sun. All of the sites in the 40s are grassy. Sites in the 50s are shady, neat and clean.

Sites 63 and 64 are hard-surfaced. Many conifers help outline the clean, rolling campground.

Rolling Hills Camping Area, sites 65-128, has a newer playground and clean showerhouse convenient to all sites. This loop is about 70 percent shady. Sites 105 and 106 are near the showerhouse that has a bulletin board near the entrances. Most of the sites are grassy; some have thin gravel pads. If you enjoy sunny sites, consider sites 113 and 114. Many of the sites are backed up against natural vegetation and are private. Sites 116 and 117 are under a grove of maples on a level above other sites.

Sites 115-125 look down from a ridge upon sites 105-110. Site 125 is against some cedars, but also enjoys some midday sun. Sites in the 130s are ideal for medium to large RV rigs. Site 101 is at the end of the loop, private and overlooks a grassy day-use area. Sites in the high 80s are on a knoll above sites in the low 80s. Site 84 is next to a wooded ravine. Some sites in the 70s are private, with no camping sites across from them. There are excellent trails that connect the campgrounds to the day-use areas and beach.

Register for camping at the main park office. The campground is often full on weekends throughout the summer.

Cabins: The park's seven cabins have three rooms, a flush toilet, and are popular. There is a two night minimum stay required. Cabins are scattered along a steep tree-lined embankment above the lake. The cabins are pleasant and have a small side yard. Hot showers are available in the campground.

New York State Parks

Cabin 1 is near a ridge and fence and comes complete with a ground-mounted fire ring, pedestal grill and picnic table. The cabin has a screened porch.

Cabins 3-5 are closer to the road than the others. They are perched above Round Lake and shady. The entire cabin colony is quiet and within walking distance to the campground.

Cabin 6, 7 and 8 are near the fence and ridge line with a wonderful view just steps away. These cabins have stone chimneys and brown rough-sawn siding. A huge stump in front of cabin 6 is a great place to sit and relax. Each cabin has a lantern-style light above the front door and the inviting screened porches are outfitted with chairs and a small table.

Inside the cozy cabins are a simple sink, electric stove, refrigerator, bunks, small fireplace and a table. Cabin guests need to bring their own soap, towels, linen, blankets, firewood, and eating and cooking utensils.

Day-use areas: No in-line skating is allowed at the park. A Frisbee golf course is available to visitors. Each day-use area is separate and self-contained having a rest room, shelter, drinking fountain, volleyball net, open spaces and ball field nearby. Some of the shady day-use areas have picnic tables with wonderful stone legs.

Beach: The attractive beach has a jumbo hard-surfaced parking lot where throngs of people converge on hot days. The expansive fine sandy beach has elevated lifeguard chairs and is serviced by a brown showerhouse and a walkway that skirts the sandy edge. A full basketball court is behind the showerhouse. The sand is groomed daily and the lake's water is clear. There are many benches that outline the beach that has firm, easy to walk on sand.

The water is gentle, allowing small children a chance to safely play and cool off on hot days. Large white buoys section off the water into guarded zones. The showerhouse has coin-operated lockers, lifeguard offices, colorful painting, a trophy case, wall thermometer and snack concession. The walk-up concession stand features coffee, ice cream, pretzels, grill items, cold drinks, chips, French fries, pizza slices, candy and lots more. The bathhouse was built in 1960.

The beach also boasts a diving well and bike rack. The end of the supervised beach is marked by a green sign.

Golf: Robert Trent Jones designed the testy 18-hole course. Up to 50,000 rounds are played on the scenic course annually, with many golfers cursing the hilly, difficult back nine. The front nine is more open than the tight, rolling back nine. The course was built from 1933-

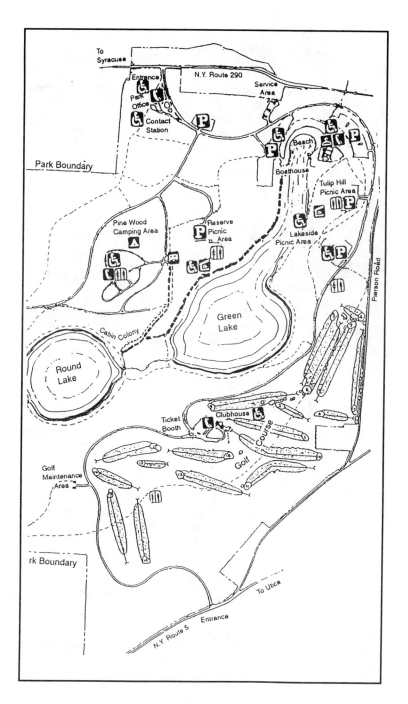

To
Syracuse

Entrance
Park
Office

N.Y. Route 290

Service
Area

Contact
Stabon

P

Park Boundary

Beach

Boathouse

Tulip Hill
Picnic Area

P

Pine Wood
Camping Area

Reserve
Picnic
Area

P

Lakeside
Picnic Area

P

Green
Lake

Cabin Colony

Round
Lake

Pierson Road

Ticket
Booth

Clubhouse

Golf
Maintenance
Area

Golf Course

rk Boundary

To Utica

N.Y. Route 5   Entrance

44

1936. The course is rated at 68.4. About 38 percent of golfers use carts.

The course, a good test for the low handicapper, gets a lot of play and can be slow at times. The fairways are plush and the putting is tough on undulating greens that have huge slopes. Green Lakes' golf course is one of Jones' finest.

The hilltop pro shop has a large practice green in front of it. The attractive stone building houses a bar that serves alcoholic drinks and a cafeteria-style restaurant that serves salads, light lunches, breakfast and hot and cold drinks. There are seven tables inside the restaurant. An oil painting of Robert Trent Jones hangs over the fireplace in the cozy bar. Jones has a glint in his eye, as if to say, "go ahead, try to beat my course..."

The concession and bar have a patio with six orange umbrella tables that overlook the park. The patio is connected to the beautiful stone clubhouse and restaurant.

Next to the clubhouse is the starter shack and gray pro shop that features clubs, clothes, balls, putters, caps, cart rental and information. Tee times are required Friday through Sunday.

Hiking: The hiking distance around Green Lake is 2.3 miles and Round Lake is .8 mile. The Green Lake Trail is made of gravel, smooth and easy, while the quiet Round Lake Trail is wood-chipped. The park has 17 miles of trails.

A long hard-surfaced biking trail winds through the park, connecting the clean and green spaces and amenities. Trails around both lakes are great for first-time hikers. It takes about two hours to hike around both scenic (and colorful!) lakes.

Boating: Along the cove, next to the beach, is a tiny boat concession that rents row- and paddleboats. Boats are rented by the hour and you must be at least 15 years old to take one for a spin. A yellow bike rack is behind the small boat rental building.

Fishing: The nearest bait shop is about 1.5 miles from the park. Green Lake is annually stocked with rainbow trout. The stocked trout range in size from seven inches to three pounds. Powerbait is the most popular bait. The clear lake is fished heavily. Other fish in the lake include yellow perch, smallmouth and rock bass. Both of the lakes are up to 200 feet deep.

Nature: The park has recently expanded. One recent parcel came from the estate of Betsy Knapp. This area of land adjoining the park was added in 1995 and is known as Indian Oven. Miss. Knapp, a sixth generation resident of Fayetteville, owned the Indian Oven Farm established in 1870 by her great-great grandfather, David Collin. Local Onondagas told this early settler that their ancestors camped here and baked bread in the ovens, which were crevices in the rocks in the hills. These crevices were created 12,000 years ago when waters from the melting glacier uplifted the rocky basin of the ancient sea. The gift of this and other lands makes possible the preservation of unusual geologic features of the region.

Some environmental education and recreation programming is offered during the summer from the brown nature center. The small building houses displays, hands-on natural objects, wall posters, information about water and geology, insects, birds and bird's nests, wildflowers, nests, honey bees, animal footprints, a goose mount, nature photographs, small library of field guides and a touch table complete with furs, bone samples and more. The nature center is in the Pine Wood camping area. Check the small bulletin board for details about programs and hikes.

More than 200 species of vascular plants exist within the park, along with more than 60 kinds of trees and shrubs. The park also features 25 species of ferns and 100 herbaceous flowering plants. Common trees include American beech, sugar maple, Eastern hemlock, yellow birch, tulip poplar and American basswood.

Wildlife watchers may see whitetail deer, red or gray foxes, minks, flying squirrels, skunks, raccoons, woodchucks, shrews, weasels or cottontail rabbits. More than 100 species of birds have been recorded at the park including pileated woodpeckers, wood thrush, many warblers, raptors and a few waterfowl visitors.

The southwestern part of the park is an excellent place to see upland forests in a natural state with all of the typical spring flora. The woods near Round Lake contain huge tulip poplars and stately hemlocks, sometimes referred to as "lords of the forest" by early settlers.

Winter: Cross-country ski on the park's 17 miles of trails.

Insider tips: Green Lake is the closest—and nicest—beach to Syracuse. The beach gets mobbed on hot days. Round Lake is a National Natural Landmark registered with the U.S. Department of the Interior.

The park has recently acquired an additional 404 acres of land (yet another 150 acres might also be bought soon!). Staff is extra professional at the park, making all visitors and golfers feel welcome. The scenic—and difficult—golf course is one of Robert Trent Jones' best efforts. During World Wart II, the park was a German prisoner-of-war camp. Remnants of their gardens are still identifiable.

Old Erie Canal State Park
Land: 851 acres   Water: Erie Canal

The 363-mile Erie Canal flows quietly today. But its romance, drama and exciting history are alive and well preserved by canal parks, fascinating museums, aqueducts, towpath, drydock and weighlock. The tale of the canal is told along the 36-mile state park trail system.

The Erie Canal played a major role in development of New York and the United States. The cities of Albany, Utica, Rome, Syracuse, Rochester and Buffalo developed in the late 1700s due to their strategic location along heavily used wagon routes to the west. About the same time, a few pioneering companies believed that water transportation was a more effective way to move cargo than overland horse and wagon. As a result, by 1793, minor canals were being developed by connecting area waterways in the Mohawk Valley.

In 1817, the state of New York backed the canal concept and broke ground for the watery link near the city of Rome. Construction continued from 1817 to 1825—using mules and manpower. Lateral canals, constructed to accommodate heavy traffic, were abandoned by 1873 when trade did not develop as anticipated. With the scheduled opening of the more efficient Barge Canal, as well as increasing competition from railroads, the Erie Canal became commercially inactive in 1918.

Fifty years later a segment of the abandoned canal was transferred to the state and the towpath trail was established. The Old Erie Canal has been designated as a National Recreation Trail by the U.S. Department of the Interior and the Interior's National Park Service. The gentle trail runs from DeWitt (near Syracuse) to Rome, providing excellent recreational opportunities including hiking, horseback riding, bicycling, canoeing, fishing, picnicking and snowmobiling. The linear park's proximity to Green Lakes and Verona Beach state parks offers tremendous outdoor recreation opportunities.

Information and Activities

Old Erie Canal State Park
DeWitt-Rome, NY
(315) 687-7821 Office
(315) 492-6422 Park Police

Directions: Old Erie Canal State Park may be accessed from Thruway exits 33, 34 and 34A.

Emergency number: 911 system.

The trail: Mile markers are placed along the smooth gravel path that winds along the banks of the murky canal. Hikers, bikers and horseback riders will pass some wonderful small communities that offer restaurants, shopping, history and other services.

Facilities: Poolsbrook (near Fayetteville) and Cedar Bay (near DeWitt) picnic areas have rest rooms, footbridges, parking and access to the towpath where visitors can view the remnants of stone aqueducts. A branch of the Erie Canal Museum near Cedar Bay is open during the summer. Erie Canal Village (west of Rome) and Canal Town in Canastota provide visitors a wonderful chance to experience turn-of-the-century life along the Erie Canal.

Canal water is suitable for non-contact recreation only. Wash thoroughly after contact.

A number of three-sided shelters with benches and trail maps along the

Chittnango Landing Canal Boat Museum.

trail offer shelter and information.

Historic sites: There are many points of interest along the canal.

Chittenango Landing Canal Boat Museum: (On Boatyard Street in the village of Chittenango) The museum is in a board-and-batten-style building that houses a blacksmith shop, woodworking tools, sawmills, historic photographs and other work stations. The mission of the museum is to interpret canal boats and the interesting repair methods and techniques used to keep the boats and cargo moving.

The boat landing was built in 1935 and consists of three dry-docks, sawmill, stable, warehouse and woodworking shop. Hundreds of canal boats were built and repaired by the facility. Since 1986, volunteers, with the help of some state funding, have been rebuilding and renovating the historic repair facilities. Many school groups visit to learn about the dry-docks, tools and machinery that keep the grand boats navigating the Erie Canal.

Eventually, there will be full-sized boats at each of the dry-docks and

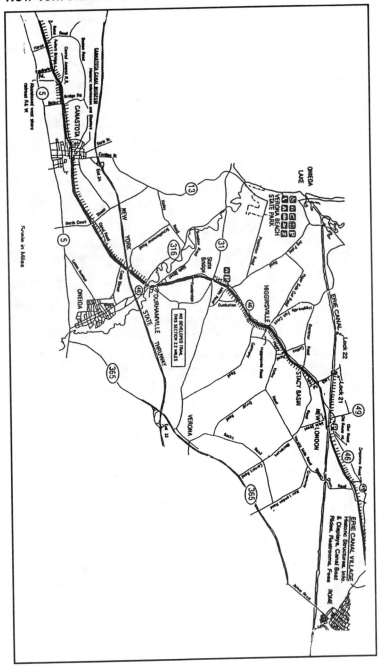

replica boats on display. This was the only drydock serving the entire Erie Canal.

Notice how each of the dry-docks is at a different depth and how gravity drains them, allowing workmen access the boat hulls. Look for interpretive signs that explain how the boats were handled once in the dry-docks.

Inside the museum are information about the lifestyles of the boat builders and their families, examples of maritime tools, small replica boats, a diorama about life on the Erie Canal, checkerboard on a keg, bits and pieces of artifacts found on the sites, small sales counter and porch that overlooks the canal. Some of the books for sale include The Best of American Canals, Canaler's Songbook and others. A full-size harnessed mule is also on display that details how the canals were made.

Town of Camillus Erie Canal Park: At the mid-point of the canal, between Albany and Buffalo, this 300-acre park includes a restored section of the waterway, nine miles of trails and two picnic areas. Within the park is the 1844 Nine Mile Creek Aqueduct, the Sims Store Museum and outdoor operating lock and exhibit. The museum is also a departure point for boat rides and a weekly dinner cruise. Call (315) 672-5110 for more information.

Erie Canal Museum, 318 Erie Blvd. in East Syracuse. The museum is one of the country's leading maritime museums and is housed in a National Register landmark—the 1850 Weighlock Building, the only surviving canal boat weighing station. The museum features a full-size canal boat, theater, exhibits, demonstrations, artifact collection and gift shop. Call (315) 471-0593.

Canastota Canal Town Museum in Canastota is housed in an 1860s canal-era building filled with exhibits. Call (315) 687-3451.

Erie Canal Village is a re-creation 1840-1850-era outdoor living history museum managed by the Rome Historical Society. It is located on an original, exposed portion of the Old Erie Canal. Fifteen historic structures have been relocated in the area. Interpreters and crafts people further enhance the experience. The village is at 5789 New London Road, Rome, NY. Call (315) 337-3999.

Canal Center, operated by the Erie Canal Museum, is on the towpath across from the DeWitt's Cedar Bay Picnic Area. The exhibit introduces visitors to the many canal-related features they will see along the trail. Call (315) 471-0593.

Boating: Bring your canoe; the gentle canal is a great place to paddle.

Fishing: The warm waters of the canal are best for rough fish including brown bullhead and carp. Other species that will take live bait include bass, pike, chain pickerel and assorted panfish.

Nature: Canal users will discover a mixture of hardwoods and conifers along the path. Major tree species include sugar and red maple, black willow, quaking aspen, sycamore, sumac, arborvitae, white and Scotch pine. Honeysuckle and several dogwood species are also along the famous waterway.

Lands that adjoin the canal are home to white-tail deer, woodchuck, raccoon, beaver, muskrat, weasel, and red and gray squirrel. Bird species include warblers, catbirds, waterfowl, herons, woodpeckers, kingfishers and raptors.

Insider tips: Explore the canal with a bike or canoe. The Chittenango Landing Canal Boat Museum is an interesting attraction that details the boat repair work conducted during the heyday of the Erie Canal.

Selkirk Shores
State Park

*Land: 980 acres Water: Lake Ontario,
rivers*

Nearby Port Ontario is one of the earliest settlements in this beautiful area of the state. Established prior to 1836, the Port Ontario
Land Company was the first to survey the tract for development—
which came and went quickly. A 1,000-acre section of this land later
became the state park that fronts Lake Ontario on the west, bounded on
the north by the Salmon River and on the south by Grindstone Creek.

Once busy Port Ontario gave way to the faster developing city of
Oswego, which had good harbor facilities and best met the increasing
demand for shoreline access to Lake Ontario. By 1925, development
of the park area was underway. From 1925 to 1963, the state increased
the park size and facilities. The region is now known for excellent fishing, boating and vacationing.

Selkirk Shores, built largely during the Depression, has some of the best examples of Civilian Conservation Corps construction in this part of the state. CCC Company 1204 worked in the park from 1933-1940, building terrific wood and stone buildings, retaining walls and public facilities. One of the finest examples of log construction is the shelter in the Bluffs Area. It is often used for weddings and other functions that demand a quality site.

The adjacent Salmon River is well-known for top fishing. Both the Salmon River and Grindstone Creek give up 20-pound trout, coho, chinook, lake trout, Atlantic salmon and others. Sport fishing is a major attraction in the lake and rivers that pass by the park. In addition, the lower ends of both streams can be canoed and Lake Ontario is a wonderful body of water to sail across.

The park's other assets include a swimming beach, bluff-top camping, wildlife viewing, picnicking and relaxation along its many shorelines. Near the park office is an outdoor information board about the Seaway Trail. The trail, which outlines the lake on the U.S. side, has details about state and national historic sites, the War of 1812, state boat access locations and significant places to visit.

Information and Activities

Selkirk Shores State Park
Route 3
Pulaski, NY 13142
(315) 298-5737

Directions: In Oswego County, near Port Ontario. From Rochester take Rt. 104 east to Rt. 3 north to the park entrance. From Syracuse, take I-81 to Exit 36 (Pulaski), proceed west on Rt. 13 through Pulaski, then 1.5 miles on Rt. 3. The park is 238 miles from Buffalo, 196 miles from Niagara Falls, 94 miles from Rochester and 96 miles from Morristown.

Emergency numbers: Park police, (315) 298-5534; ambulance, (315) 298-6515.

Campgrounds: The park operates 148 camping sites, 88 with electric hook-ups. Loop C is the most popular camping area, with sites 98-111 the most heavily used campsites. Other popular sites are the inner part of Loop A (5, 7, 9, 11, 13, 15, 17, etc.) due to the shade in the afternoon and sun in the morning. There is also a small play area for children in this area of the rolling campground. The campground is often full on mid-summer weekends. Electric sites are 1-19, 28, 43-79, 80-95 and 98-111.

Sites 1-18 are sunny, while sites 21-25 are shady and privately located at the end of a spur. Sites 27, 29, 32, 34, 36 and 39 are backed up against a natural area of cedar and shrubs. The sites in the 30s are open and grassy. Sites 43 and 44 are near the bathhouse and have a firm pad that can accommodate large RV rigs. A basketball goal is near this loop. Bring your Nikes.

Sites in loop B, sites 62-79, have 12-foot by 12-foot cement pads and oversized fire rings. The handy cement pad is a perfect place for a picnic table. Near site 65 is a sign that says "Caution: Poison Ivy."

Loop C, sites 80-113, are lightly shaded, private and also have cement pads at each site. Sites 80 and 81 are two excellent places for a large family to share. All of the sites are backed up against natural vegetation. A play sandbox and drinking fountain are in the middle of the loop. Try site 98 if you would like to be next to the camp store and on the bluff. Many of the level grassy sites in this loop are sunny and have a obscured view of the lake. Site 113 is a terrific site for a small pop-up camper.

Loop D has several sites along the bluff that have water views. One of the best is site 142. A basketball goal is in this loop. From some of these sites you will see and hear the breaking of the waves on the gravel and coarse sand shore.

The wood-frame camp store sells firewood, insect repellent, cold drinks, bottled water, T-shirts, flashlights, toiletries, diapers, cereal, plastic toys, floating swim toys, snacks and ice. A picnic table, pay phone and bulletin board are out front.

Cabins: Most of the cabins are behind camping loops C and D. A trail connects the cabins and campground. Cabins 1-16 sleep four; cabins 17-24 sleep six people. Cabins are rented for a minimum of two nights and up to two weeks. All of the units have a gas stove, refrigerator, flush toilets, fireplace, screened porch and beds. A four-person cabin will have a double bed in a bedroom and two singles in the living room. The six-person cabins have two bedrooms. One bedroom has a double bed and the other two singles. Two more single beds are in the living room. Bring your own cooking and eating utensils, linens, towels and so on. *To make a reservation, call (800) 456-2267.* A deposit is required. Household pets are allowed, but you must bring written proof of a current rabies inoculation.

The cabin colony is in a gently rolling area above the campgrounds. Cabins have stone chimneys and rough-sawn brown clapboards. Each cabin has a small gravel parking space for two cars. The cabins have

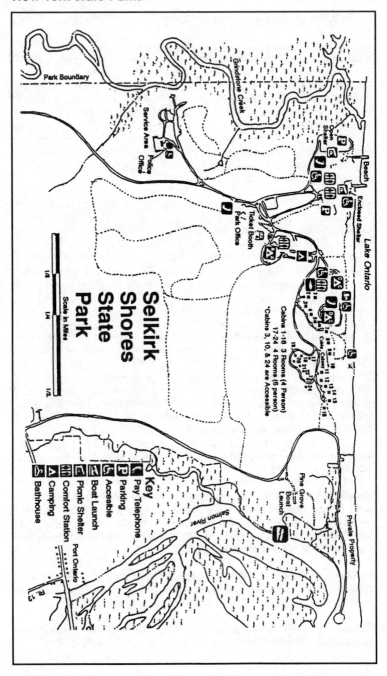

Selkirk Shores State Park

Cabins 1-16 3 Rooms (4 Person)
17-24 4 Rooms (6 person)
*Cabins 3, 10, & 24 are Accessible

Scale in Miles

Key

Pay Telephone
Parking
Accessible
Boat Launch
Picnic Shelter
Comfort Station
Camping
Bathhouse

Park Boundary

Grindstone Creek

Service Area
Police Office

Ticket Booth
Park Office

Open Shelter

Beach

Enclosed Shelter

Lake Ontario

Pine Grove
Boat Launch

Private Property

Salmon River

Port Ontario

Rt. 13

comfortable porches, picnic tables and grills.

Cabin 3 is on a rise and cabin 5 has five steps up to the door, from which you have a partial view of the lake. Cabins 4-7 are in a mostly open area. Cabin 7 is shady and private. Cabins 17-24 have working shutters and are built on block piers. Each of these cabins is separated and private. Cabins 20 and 21 are close to a low, marshy area. Site 22 is extra private. Cabin 23 has a small yard where children play. Cabin 24 has a ramp to help visitors access the unit. Sites 15 and 16 are the prettiest cabins, and they are private and have a partial view of Lake Ontario. Cabin 14 faces out over the high bank and has a mossy roof. The most private cabins and the ones closest to the shoreline are 8, 9 and 10.

Cabin 30 is a two-story cabin (house) that can sleep six. It has a half-bath upstairs, front and back porches, kitchen, dining room, living room, hot water, full bath with shower and wood stove. Cabin 29 has a loft and full hot water bath.

Day-use areas: The park has two picnic shelters; one is enclosed and holds 200 people. The lovely enclosed log shelter is on a lake bluff and has a kitchen and two fireplaces. The park has more than 400 picnic tables and 80 cooking stations in the wooded day-use area near the beach. The park maintains a quality baseball diamond that is literally carved out of the woods. Some serious games take place on this field of dreams.

The shady Bluff Picnic Area is on the towering bluff, shady and popular. Some beautiful log and stone Civilian Conservation Corps buildings are in many of the day-use areas. The reservable shelter here has thick logs 18 inches in diameter that hold up the grand sloping porch. The cozy porch is also supported by massive timber columns. The scenic building has fireplaces, glass doors and a wonderful view of the sparkling lake. A volleyball court and sandbox are behind the massive log building.

Recreation hall: Limited programming is offered from the recreation hall. Inside the CCC-built stone hall are a few game tables. A bench near the recreation building is positioned to have a quiet view of the lake. Youth nature programs and recreational programs for campers are sometimes offered from the building.

Swimming beach: The beach is gravel and grass and used mostly by campers. A single volleyball net is heavily used at the beach. A stone retaining wall outlines the area that is scattered with benches.

Hiking: Most of the 15 miles of hiking trails are easy to moderate. Part of Loop 4 is difficult.

One of the best hiking trails is actually a marked cross-country ski trail that is a combined 3.5-mile loop that traces near the entrance road and on the Red and Green trails. Most of the hiking trails are through hardwoods and stands of Scotch pines and near park roads. Use your imagination to combine short loops into longer day hikes.

Boating: The two-lane launching ramp is at Pine Grove and includes a floating dock. Mexico Point's four-lane boat ramp off Rt. 104B is managed by Selkirk Shores State Park. There are lots of marinas and lake access points in the area.

Fishing: Salmon and walleye is a big draw from shore, charter boat or drift boat. A few 10-pound walleye are taken from the pier near the swimming beach. When planning a trip on the Salmon River, call the hotline, (315) 298-6531. The recorded message talks about water levels. Plenty of charter boats operate in the area.

The east branch of the Salmon River is the crown jewel of New York's rivers for salmon and steelhead. In Oswego County, the river meanders through mixed hardwoods and has a gravel bottom. This section of the river gets moderate fishing pressure and produces 4-8 pound brown trout. The mouth to lower reservoir section of the river is the best stretch. It is stocked by the nearby hatchery. Hundreds of thousands of salmon and trout that are planted in the river return each year to find heavy angling pressure. The best fishing is in the fall, beginning in September. Snagging is the primary way fish are taken when they are concentrated in the narrows of the river.

Other methods include using Hot N' Tots or Little Cleo-type spoons. Lake trout can be taken on minnows or a slip-shot floating rig. Spawn bags can also be productive.

Oswego County is remote and has lots of quality streams where brook trout, bass and northern pike can be taken.

A fish cleaning station is open and has a water hose near camping Loop C.

Nature: In part because hunting or trapping are not permitted in the park, wildlife viewing is excellent. Visitors may see ruffed grouse, varying hares, red and gray foxes, white-tailed deer, migratory hawks and some of the 200 birds that have been recorded in the park. Tree species at the park include American beech, white and yellow pine, Eastern hemlock, sugar maple and red oak. The park also has an excellent plat of wildflowers, mosses and ferns.

The park is on the southeast shore of Lake Ontario, which puts it on a leading line of the spring migration as northward-bound birds swing east to avoid flights over the large lake. In addition, the park's proximity to Derby Hill allows additional spring hawk-watching opportunities. Extensive trails and a mixture of habitats including wetlands and mixed woodlands offers a wide variety of species to be observed.

Species of particular interest include pine warbler, black tern, pileated woodpecker, sharp-shinned hawk and ruffed grouse. Autumn hawk flights are best observed from September through November with north or northeast winds. In years when the water level is low in Grindstone Creek, many species of shorebirds many be seen between August and November. A handy five-panel bird checklist is available at the park office.

Over the years, 27 species of waterfowl have been recorded, as have the common loon, 10 types of hawks, six species of bitterns and herons, 10 types of kinglets and thrushes, brown creepers, 28 warblers and many more.

The park is on the Erie-Ontario lake plain. The tract was at one time the bed of an ancient glacial lake, the ancestor of the present day Lake Ontario. One of the most significant Great Lakes dune systems adjoins the park. Such dunes prevent shoreline erosion and afford shelter to marshes and ponds, protecting rare plants and delicate ecosystems. Visitors are asked to refrain from walking on the dunes.

Winter: Snowmobiling (access to Tug Hill) and cross-country skiing on groomed trails are offered.

Insider tips: Plan a stop at the ice cream shop near the main entrance to the popular park. Almost all of the park buildings were built by the Civilian Conservation Corps. Spring and fall, anglers use the park heavily. During the summer, most of the visitors are family campers. About 30 percent of the visitors to the park are from out-of-state. Ron Brown, U.S. Commerce Secretary who was tragically killed in an airplane crash in Bosnia in 1995, loved to camp with his family at Selkirk Shores State Park. The park is known for great sunsets.

Nearby attractions include Fort Ontario, Oswego Speedway, NYS Salmon Hatchery, historic villages of Mexico and Pulaski, Sunset Bay Park, golf at Daysville and many marinas.

CENTRAL REGION

PHONE	PARK
	CENTRAL REGION
315 492-1756	Battle Island
315 593-3408	Bowman Lake
607 334-2718	Chenango Valley
607 648-5251	Chittenango Falls
315 655-9620	Clark Reservation
315 492-1590	Delta Lake
315 337-4670	Gilbert Lake
607 432-2114	Glimmerglass
607 547-8662	Green Lakes
315 637-6111	Hunts Pond
607 859-2249	Old Erie Canal*
315 687-7821	Oquaga Creek
607 467-4160	Pixley Falls
315 942-4713	Selkirk Shores
315 298-5737	Verona Beach*
315 762-4463	
	STATE HISTORIC SITES
315 428-4522	John Burroughs Memorial Field
315 343-4711	Fort Ontario
315 823-0398	Herkimer Home
315 492-1756	Lorenzo
315 492-1756	Oriskany Battlefield
315 492-1756	Steuben Memorial
315 831-3737	

Amenity columns (rotated headers, left to right):
Tent/trailers sites (h = hookups, e = electricity); Trailer dump; Showers; Camper recreation; Cabins; Food; Store; Picnic tables; Shelters (• reservations); Swimming beach (• bath house); Swimming pool (• bath house); Recreation programs (• performing arts); Hiking; Biking; Nature trails; Fishing; Playground; Golf (•clubhouse); Tennis; Pond or lake (• power boats ok); River or stream (• power boats ok); Launching site (• hand launch only); Boat rental; Marina (• anchorage); Pump out; Ice skating (•rentals); Cross-country skiing (• rentals); Snowmobiling; Sled slopes

State Historic Sites descriptions:

John Burroughs Memorial Field — In a quiet field surrounded by the Catskill Mountain, visit the grave of this famous literary naturalist.

Fort Ontario — Watch the guard unit reflect the activities of the troops at this star-shaped fortress in the late 1860s.

Herkimer Home — Recapture colonial days at the Mohawk Valley farmstead of Gen. Nicholas Herkimer.

Lorenzo — Admire the furnishings of the Lincklaen family in this 1807 mansion overlooking Cazenovia Lake.

Oriskany Battlefield — Gen. Herkimer's troops were ambushed in the bloodiest battle of the American Revolution.

Steuben Memorial — Visit the replica cabin and the final resting place of the 'Drillmaster of the Revolution.'

△ Availability of service or facility   ▶ Handicapped accessible   * Bridle paths

61

Finger Lakes Region

More than 10,000 years ago, the last great glacier scraped across New York sculpting the Finger Lakes Region. As the wall of ice receded, it left behind steep valleys which were to become deep, clear Finger Lakes and led to the formations of the area's spectacular gorges.

Some of the largest and most beautiful waterfalls are in the region including the towering 215-foot Taughannock Falls. Taughannock Falls is one of the highest in the East. Buttermilk and the falls at Watkins Glen are also dramatic.

There is no more dazzling gorge and series of waterfalls than at Watkins Glen where visitors can walk on meandering trails or take in the celebrated *"Timespell"* laser show.

The Finger Lakes Region offers year-round escapes including 200 square miles of world-class boating and fishing waters.

Four of the parks have natural swimming pools and most are near the rolling hills that are often lined with vineyards, charming restaurants and inns.

Finger Lakes Region

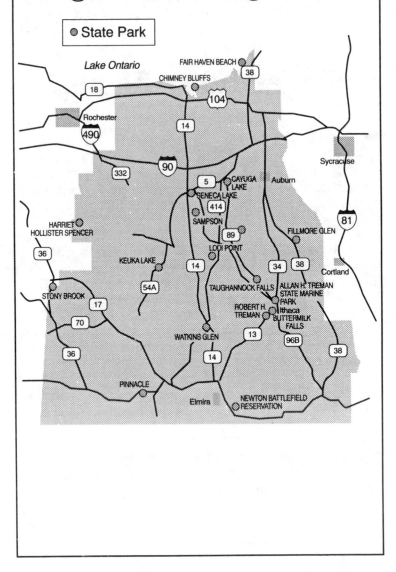

State Park

Lake Ontario

FAIR HAVEN BEACH
38

CHIMNEY BLUFFS

18
104

Rochester
14

490

90

Sycracuse

332

5   CAYUGA
         LAKE   Auburn

SENECA LAKE
414   81

SAMPSON
                                FILLMORE GLEN
HARRIET
HOLLISTER SPENCER   89

36   LODI POINT

KEUKA LAKE   14   34   38
                                            Cortland
54A   TAUGHANNOCK FALLS ALLAN H. TREMAN
STONY BROOK   STATE MARINE
17   PARK
                         ROBERT H.   Ithaca
70   TREMAN   BUTTERMILK
                                     FALLS
36   WATKINS GLEN   13   96B   38

14

PINNACLE

                  Elmira   NEWTON BATTLEFIELD
                             RESERVATION

Buttermilk Falls
State Park
Land: 762 acres Water: Falls,
Buttermilk Creek, Treman Lake

If you ever wanted to leap into a cold pool at the base of a cascading waterfall on a hot summer's day, then Buttermilk Falls State Park is your place to visit. The water does indeed look a bit like buttermilk as it tumbles over the rocks that stair-step and descend to the deep pool below. The falls are as gentle as falls can be. A refreshing sound and scenic views will further enhance your swim in the waters of refreshing Buttermilk Creek.

It started about 12,000 years ago during the last glacier's meltdown and retreat that Buttermilk Creek began pouring down the steep slopes, forming the long cascade from which the park takes its name. Over these many years, day by day, season by season, the rushing stream has eroded the native shale and sandstone of the valley side, creating ripple pools, high cliffs, falls and Pinnacle Rock.

These cool woods and shady glens have been the home to the Cayuga Indians, who once lived in 25 cabins near the town of Coreorgonel. The surrounding lands were then cultivated, often with groves of apple and plum trees. Sadly, the Coreorgonel inhabitants had to flea the area before the arrived of the Continental Army, which burned the town Sept. 4, 1779. Soon early Europeans settled the scenic area, constructing mills and dams along the creek. In 1872, Van Orman's Dam was constructed above the main falls and supplied water to the city of Ithaca until 1903. Scott's Dam was built for a grist mill in the upper park in 1875. Today there is no evidence of these structures that were once so important to the development of the region.

In 1924, Robert and Laura Treman donated 154 acres in Buttermilk Glen to the state. The park has since been enlarged to 751 acres. Once famous as a site for movie making, the park now has a unique swimming hole, a scenic gorge trail, camping, picnic areas, playgrounds and cabins for rent.

Information and Activities

Buttermilk Falls State Park
c/o Robert Treman State Park
R. D. #10
Ithaca, NY 14850
(607) 273-5761, summer
(607) 273-3440, winter

Directions: In Tompkins County, on Route 13, at the southern edge of Ithaca. A refreshment center, with vending machines and nearby phone, is near the park office at the main gate. Inside the park office is brochure rack.

Special notes: In-line skating is restricted, see office for further information. No bikes are allowed on pedestrian trails. Swimming is allowed in guarded and designated areas only.

Emergency numbers: Park police, (800) 255-3577 or (607) 387-7041; medical, (607) 273-2671.

Campground: Buttermilk Falls State Park operates 60 campsites, none with utility hookups. The hilly campground usually has lots of tents and smaller RV units. Sites 7-14 are up against a natural area and face a wooded narrow valley. Most of the sites have mixed gravel and grass pads, picnic tables and fire rings. Site 28, one of the more pri-

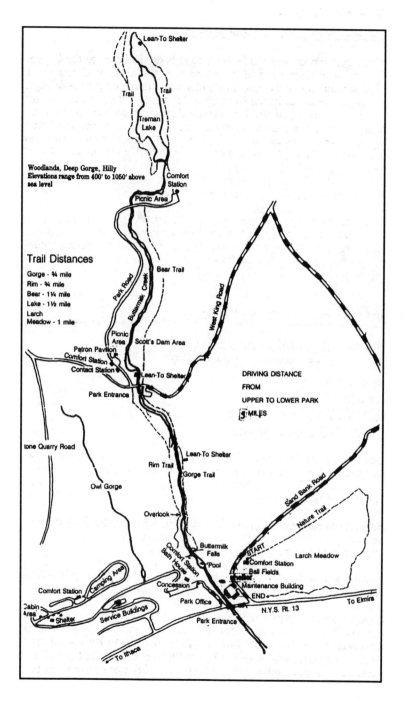

Lean-To Shelter

Trail

Trail

Treman Lake

Woodlands, Deep Gorge, Hilly
Elevations range from 400' to 1050' above
sea level

Comfort Station

Picnic Area

Trail Distances

Gorge - ¾ mile
Rim - ¾ mile
Bear - 1¼ mile
Lake - 1½ mile
Larch
Meadow - 1 mile

Bear Trail

Park Road

Buttermilk Creek

West King Road

Picnic Area

Scott's Dam Area

Patron Pavilion

Comfort Station

Contact Station

Lean-To Shelter

Park Entrance

DRIVING DISTANCE

FROM

UPPER TO LOWER PARK

5 MILES

tone Quarry Road

Lean-To Shelter

Rim Trail

Gorge Trail

Owl Gorge

Overlook

Sand Bank Road

Nature Trail

Larch Meadow

Buttermilk Falls

START

Comfort Station
Bath House

Pool

Comfort Station

Ball Fields

Concession

Maintenance Building

END

Comfort Station

Camping Area

Cabin
Area

Shelter

Service Buildings

Park Office

Park Entrance

N.Y.S. Rt. 13

To Elmira

To Ithaca

66

vate sites, is notched into the woods and is excellent for a larger RV unit. Up on the hill next to it is a terrific high and dry tent camping site (No. 26). Sites 27, 28 and 32 are on the curve and have a view of towering pines and large-diameter mixed deciduous trees. The campground is at least 70 percent shady, and drinking water hydrants are evenly spaced through the area. Sites in the 40s are near the bathhouse that is near a small set of children's play apparatus. Site 48 is accessible for campers with disabilities.

Because of the sites being on different elevations and the larger trees, there is a good feeling of visual privacy throughout most of the campground and cabins. The campground is more than a mile from the base of the falls.

Cabins: Along the edge of the shady campground is the seven-cabin colony. Cabin 4 may be the nicest of the group, complete with a small grill, porch, gravel parking and picnic table. This cabin faces a densely wooded valley. A small brown pavilion with a stone chimney also serves the small colony of rustic cabins.

Rough-sawn sided cabin 7 is also a pleasing cabin that has a a woodland view. These tiny cabins are on the edge of the campground, neatly mixed in with campers and tents. The cabins are on varying elevations and are mostly shady. Some cabins have more than one picnic table in their side yards.

Day-use areas: At the base of the falls, near the swimming area, are a number of picnic tables and pedestal grill and rest rooms. A lifeguard office and first aid station are also near the pool at the bottom of the famous falls. Many visitors merely park, then wander up and look at the falls, barely using the day-use areas.

Swimming: Two red lifeguard chairs and a diving platform are at the base of the falls overlooking the designated swimming area. A section of the pool beneath the milky falls is segmented with a rope and orange and white buoys. From the popular swimming area, across a narrow footbridge is the Gorge Trailhead that leads hikes near the falls—so near, you'll feel the spray coming off the rapidly cascading sheets of water. The swimming area is only 50 feet square and the water can be cold and refreshing.

The improved shoreline and grassy day-use area behind the swimming area can be busy with sunbathers and children. The falls are about 80 feet wide, and plant materials seem to cling for their lives where the water plummets over the rocky ledge. Bring your suit and take the plunge near these popular falls.

Hiking: From the waterfalls, the moderately difficult Gorge Trail runs along Buttermilk Creek. The creek is in a deep gorge with elevations ranging from 400 to 1,050 feet above sea level. The Gorge Trail, which is closed in the winter, is .75-mile long. Other trails include Rim Trail (.75-mile), Bear Trail (1.25 miles), Lake Trail (1.5 miles) and Larch Meadow (1 mile).

Fishing: Angling is possible in the creek in Treman Lake. Thompkins County has more than over 102 miles of trout streams and 28 miles of warmwater streams. Or fish in the 42,496-acre Cayuga Lake with its dozens of tributaries. The lake is famous for lake trout, salmon, brown and rainbow trout. Call the DEC fishing hotline at (607) 753-1551 for updated area fishing reports.

Nature: Limited outdoor education and camper programs are offered as funding and volunteers permit. Nature lovers should hike the self-guided interpretive Larch Meadow Trail. The one-mile-long loop begins at the comfort station by the ballfields in the lower park, next to the bend in Sandbank Road at the bottom of the hill. The interpretive trail is marked with numbered posts; a brochure that details the 19 learning stations is available at the park office.

Larch Meadow is a 200-acre natural area bounded by hills, a floodplain, woodlands and a wetland. Hikers will learn about the larch tree, whose bark contains tannin which is used in leather making, an old farm road and old farmsteads, a few remnants of the "Great Swamp," a network of wetlands that extend to Cayuga Lake, water purification, flood control and ground water springs.

You'll also read about and view poison ivy and sumac, and other more benign swamp plants including alder, dogwood and skunk cabbage. This wetland area is an excellent wildlife viewing tract. Be ready to spot wild turkey, woodcock, salamanders, turtles, waterfowl, snakes and deer. Larch Meadow is one of the last known areas where the eastern bog turtle, an endangered species, can be seen in Tompkins County. Hikers will also learn about gray shale and the sandstone gorge of Buttermilk Flats, and a boulder that was transported from Canada on the glacier thousands of years ago. Speaking of geology, did you know that Cayuga Lake was carved by a glacier and that south of it is a terminal moraine which partly filled the valley?

Also along the educational walk you will learn about soil types, old pastures and their modern day wildflower inhabitants, a stream called Cayuga inlet that flows north, Ostrich ferns (one of the biggest in the state), the sycamore tree that has jigsaw like bark, huge black walnut trees that are still in demand by furniture makers, whip-like willows that frequent the floodplain and green ash trees that make perfect baseball bats and hammer handles.

Winter: Some of the trails are open year-round.

Nearby state parks: Robert H. Treman (Rt. 13, south of Ithaca); Allan H. Treman (Rt. 89, north of Ithaca); and Taughannnock Falls State Park (Rt. 89, eight miles north of Ithaca).

Insider tips: Some segments of the The Perils of Pauline were shot at the park (many movies used the gorges in this part of the state a backdrop during the 1920s and 1930s). Try driving the Sand Bank Road for a five-mile drive to the upper end of the park. This is a urbanized park, often filled with university students. It's a high-energy day-use destination for Ithaca residents also.

While camping at Buttermilk, take the kids to Cornell's campus, Science center (607-272-0600), Cornell Plantation or the Cayuga Nature Center on Rt. 89. Ithaca is also well-known for wineries and antique shopping. Contact the Convention and Visitors Bureau at *(800) 28-ITHACA*.

Cayuga Lake State Park
Land: 142 acres Water: Cayuga Lake

Cayuga Lake State Park is the smallest park in the Finger Lakes region that offers camping, swimming, boating and day-use facilities. The small park is on the largest Finger Lake, Cayuga Lake, but some official sources argue that Seneca Lake is a tiny bit bigger. We do know one thing for certain; Cayuga Lake is a terrific boating and fishing lake, and Cayuga Lake State Park is one of the most popular camping destinations in the region.

The park is in the heart of the Finger Lakes, where thousands of visitors annually come to nourish themselves on the spectacular scenic beauty, learn about historical events and enjoy world-class water sports. From wineries and antique shops to the birthplace of the women's rights movement, this part of the state offers plenty of opportunities for day trips from your campsite or cabin in the park.

Cayuga Lake derives its name from the Iroquois Indians who once lived and farmed along its temperate shores. The Cayugas were the

"Gue-u-gweh-o-no" or "people of the muck land." It's thought many of the Native Americans lived near Montezuma Marsh. They called the adjacent lake *"Tiohero"* or *"clear water."* During the Revolutionary War, General John Sullivan led part of the Continental Army through the region to throttle the Iroquois nations that had sided with the British. The north end of the lake, including the park, was part of a Cayuga reservation in the late 1700s.

Soon settlers began clearing the region and construction of the Erie Canal system helped develop the village of Seneca Falls. For a time, the area was a busy shipping center, but it is best known as the birthplace of the women's rights movement. Plan a trip to the nearby Women's Rights Historical Park and the National Women's Hall of Fame in Seneca Falls.

The park opened in 1928 along the 38-mile-long lake.

Information and Activities

Cayuga Lake State Park
2678 Lower Lake Road
Seneca Falls, NY 13148
(315) 568-5163

Directions: Route 89, three miles east of Seneca Falls. The park office has a small brochure rack.

Emergency numbers: Park police, (800) 255-3577; medical emergency, 911.

Campground: The 286-site campgrounds are relatively flat, sprawling, grassy and mostly shady. Only 36 sites have electricity. Most of the trees in the west campground are 10 inches in diameter and they do a good job of shading sites that are equipped with picnic tables and ground-mounted fire rings. Site numbers are printed on the hard-surfaced driveway, not on posts that is more typical in New York parks. Clapboard bathhouses have showers, toilets and outdoor sinks. Be careful of low, wet sites. The campground is often full on weekends during July and August. The electric sites are full much of the summer. Lots of bass fishermen use the campground, especially in the spring and early summer.

Sites 1-9 are private, grassy and dotted with flowering shrubs. Loop 10-38 has high, dry, wide and grassy sites that are ideal for tent camping. Site 15 is the best in this loop. It has a gravel parking spot and is near a shrubby strip. You'll also see many RVs in this small loop that has some gravel parking pads. Be careful about sites in the 30s; they are close to the road.

Loop 39-55 has sites that are on varying elevations, including sites 43 and 44 that are on top of a knoll. Sites 50 and 51 are near the rest room and play area. There are terrific family camping sites. The rest room building has a telephone and soft drink machine.

Loop 114-128 is a grassy loop with cement fire boxes. Sites in the 120s are more open, catching sunlight much of the day. Site 128 is a perfect, wide RV spot. Site 143 is oversized, near quiet sites 145 and 146. Sites in loop 78-113 are more sunny and compact. The loop has a small playground with swings, teeter-totter and nearby bathhouse at its entrance. Sites in the 90s are backed up against Seneca Falls Country Club. Site 102 is an easy site to back in to.

Loop 160-237 has some good sites for larger RV units, including 199 and 201. For tent campers, inspect wide and grassy site No. 200. Some of the sites in this loop are perfect for sun-lovers, especially the wide open sites 204, 206, 237, sites in the 240s and others in this section. For privacy, consider veiled sites 209, 210, and 239 that are notched out of the young deciduous woods. Sites 212-220 are low and can stay wet for a period after heavy rain.

Electric camping sites are off of Route 89 west of the camp office and are booked solid all summer. These high and dry sites are popular with RVers. Reserve them early.

To order firewood, call 568-0919.

Cabins: Cayuga has 14 popular cabins, with many on a hillside above the park office. Cabins 1 to 7 (one-room units) go sequentially up the shaded hill with a view of the lake. Cabin 8 is bigger and one of a kind with a stone fireplace and double front doors. The park was privately operated at the turn of the century and when the state took possession of the park, its first job was to clear burned buildings and trees. The cabins were built for the CCC crews that did much of the work.

Cabins 9-14 are just off the road with little space around them. Next to cabin 8, somewhat private cabin 7 is the next best choice for a relaxing weekend along one of the most popular of the Finger Lakes.

The cabins are booked virtually all summer.

Day-use areas: Horseshoe courts, swimming beach, open spaces and boat moorings are in front of the park office. Near the beach, along the flat lakeshore, is a large brown building (known as Pavilion No. 1) that was once a concession stand and is now rented out as a public hall and also serves as the bathhouse for the swimming area. Weddings and

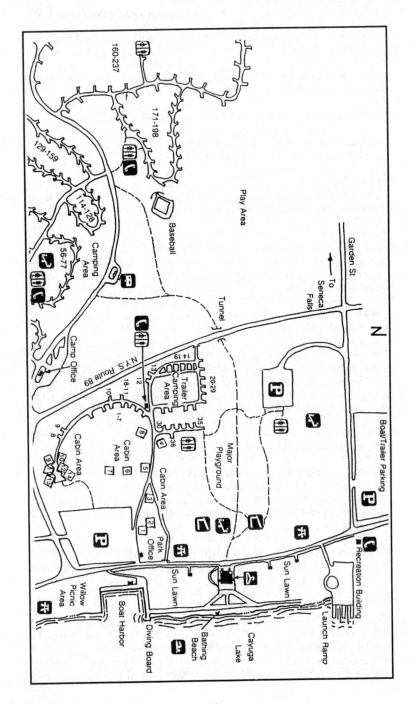

160-237

171-198

129-159

114-128

56-77

Camping Area

Baseball

Camp Office

Play Area

Tunnel

To Seneca Falls

Garden St

N

N.Y.S. Route 89

Trailer Camping Area

14-19

20-29

10

18-11

1-7

9

8

8

6

5

4

3

2

1

7

30

36

35

Major Playground

Cabin Area

Cabin Area

Park Office

Boat/Trailer Parking

P

P

P

Willow Picnic Area

Boat Harbor

Diving Board

Sun Lawn

Bathing Beach

Sun Lawn

Cayuga Lake

Launch Ramp

Recreation Building

other events are often conducted in the huge timber-frame structure. Inside the building are rest rooms, solid wood floors, dark wood wall panels, vaulted beamed ceilings, historic milk glass light fixtures and an old elk head mount. The second floor has a porch with a blue stone balcony that overlooks the lake and nearby beach.

Near shelter No. 2 and 3 are a pair of basketball goals and a small group of play apparatus. The park has three pavilions (two with walls), four pay phones, good handicapped accessibility, a small recreation building and picnic areas with grills and tables.

Swimming: The small swimming beach in front of the bathhouse is surrounded by a pleasant grassy sunning lawn. The water in front of the beach is sectioned off by white buoys and guarded.

Boating: In front of the park office is a mooring dock and improved shoreline where anglers often gather to cast for warmwater species. A mid-lake channel is maintained for larger boats. Most boating on this section of the long lake is by small craft. It is possible to get to the Atlantic Ocean via the adjoining Erie Canal, down the Hudson and Mohawk rivers, and out to sea. The park's boat ramp has two concrete lanes with nearby mooring spaces.

Fishing: Much of the lake near the park is only six feet deep. About three miles down the lake, the depths change dramatically. Crappie, perch, some bass and other panfish are the popular warmwater fare near the park, where the waters are shallow and warms up quickly in the spring. Anglers will find lots of aquatic vegetation that will grow to the surface. Cayuga Lake has an average depth of 181 feet and about 67 miles of shoreline. The state park offers anglers the perfect place to camp and explore the lake. Many anglers consider Cayuga one of the best fishing lakes in the state.

Elsewhere in the lake are northern pike, smallmouth bass, lake trout, landlocked salmon, sunfish, smelt and yellow perch. You must travel south to Canoga before the water starts getting deep. Lake, brown and rainbow trout and landlocked salmon are planted in this, the longest of the well-known Finger Lakes.

Nature: State park interpreters visit the park during the heart of the summer to conduct natural history programs and other recreational activities. Look for program fliers posted on tackboards throughout the park or ask at the park or campground offices.

Although the small rectangular park has limited wildlife viewing, nature lovers can travel a short distance to the Montezuma National Wildlife Refuge which is rich in bountiful marshes and is considered an important nesting and resting site for many species of migratory birds. Careful management of the 3,500-acre natural area, and its diked pools, ensures a suitable mix of emergent and submergent plants to go along with the mudflats and open water that attract many birds—and bird watchers.

The refuge was established in 1938. The refuge has been the site for the release of 28 bald eagles over the years and tens of thousands of Canada geese. Various waterfowl annually visit. The unit has a visitors center, trails, observation deck, three fishing areas, boat ramp, hunting, trails and programs. Call (315) 568-5987 for details.

Insider tips: Make reservations early for the electric camping sites. Cabin No. 8 is the preferred hillside unit. Most wineries in the area are open year-round and offer great values.

Fair Haven Beach
State Park
Land: 740 acres   Water: Lake Ontario

The Cayuga and Seneca Indians called Little Sodus Bay *"Date Kea-shote"* and *"Little Seadose."* This was long before French traders came to the area in the 1600s and dubbed the scenic bay *"Chroutons,"* meaning a passage that leads to the Cayugas.

Over the next 200 years, shipping and trading increased in the area to the point that a harbor was built in 1872 to support the railroad industry. As a result, the area became a hub for shipping wood products, building supplies, stoves, apples and potatoes. During this time, trains hauled huge amounts of coal and milk to fuel the industry and people building New York state. A large ice industry also grew near the park in response to the demand for cooling railroad cars full of milk. Fair Haven ice was considered the finest during this period.

All of this commerce spawned the village of Fair Haven. The village crackled with life as new industries, ideas and lifestyles emerged and flourished. As transportation improved by the early 1900s, the lakeshore was dotted with handsome cottages and the village became a popular resort.

From this popularity, a parks commission was formed in 1923 and the idea and energy for park development reached high gear. Work started in 1927, on roads and basic infrastructure. In the 1930s the park was a work site for the Civilian Conservation Corps. More than 200 laborers built stone buildings, winding walkways, hilltop campsites and beautiful retaining walls from local natural materials. The park was also used as a POW camp in 1944 and 1945. German prisoners were put to work on local farms.

Information and Activities

Fair Haven Beach State Park
Route 104A
Fair Haven, NY 13064
(315) 947-5205

Directions: On the south shore of Lake Ontario. The park entrance is off of Rt. 104A. Inside the park office is a bulletin board that details many area attractions and services.

Emergency number: Park police, (800) 255-3577; medical emergency, (315) 252-7242.

Campground: The park has 191 campsites (44 electric, 147 non-electric). From mid-June to Labor Day the campground is full on weekends. This scenic park attracts many campers from throughout the region, including Pennsylvania and New Jersey. Firewood is available from the office. The campgrounds are open from mid-April to the end of October.

The small camp store offers ice, simple food items, concession foods and soft drinks. Try a Beach Bum (corn chips and chili).

The Bluff Camping Area has electric, no water hook-ups. From the road along the top of the bluff north of the campground is a beautiful view, especially at sunset. Once in the camping area guests will find plenty of bluff-top shade and firm pads to park an RV rig on. Sites have fire rings and picnic tables. Site 68 is near the showerhouse. Sites along the outside perimeter are backed up against natural areas. The lack of understory plant growth offers good breezes. From site 77 on, in the back of the loop, camping sites are on higher ground. The sites

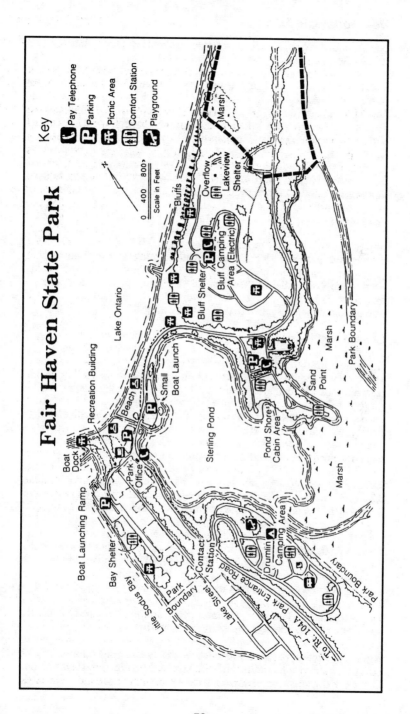

Fair Haven State Park

Key

☎ Pay Telephone
🅿 Parking
🛈 Picnic Area
🚻 Comfort Station
🛝 Playground

0 400 800'
Scale in Feet

Lake Ontario

Bluffs

Overflow

Lakeview Shelter

Bluff Shelter

Bluff Camping Area (Electric)

Recreation Building

Small Boat Launch

Beach

Boat Dock

Park Office

Sterling Pond

Pond Shore Cabin Area

Sand Point

Marsh

Marsh

Park Boundary

Boat Launching Ramp

Bay Shelter

Little Sodus Bay

Park Boundary

Contact Station

Drumlin Camping Area

Lake Street

Park Entrance Road

To Rt. 104A

Park Boundary

on the high bluff are well above the shimmering lake. A basketball goal is at the end of the loop.

The Drumlin Area is a popular tent camping area. Some of the most requested sites are 165-185 and 242-247, which are larger sites. Sites 106-113 are also heavily used, according to staff. This campground is grassy and shady. Sites from 110-120 allow campers to get behind the park road about 30 yards. High and dry site 198 is great for a medium-sized RV rig.

Sites in the 170s are near the marsh, where waterfowl can often be seen dipping for food and quacking randomly. At the end of this area is a small playground. Bring your fishing pole and insect repellent if you camp along the water's edge.

Site 188 is perched on the hillside above site 187, which is also above the marsh area. Site 185 is a short walk-in site that has a view of the acres of cattails that punctuate the murky marsh water. Mostly shady sites in the 220s and 230s are best for small popup campers. Be careful of site 215; it can be wet. Spacious sites 200 and 204 are excellent grassy tent sites along the curve of the narrow road.

Cabins: Fair Haven has 33 cabins, eight of which are open year-round. This is one of best cabin colonies in Central New York. Cabins 34-36 sleep six with two sleeping rooms. They have hot showers, toilet and appliances. Cabin 9 sleeps four with inside wood stove, gas stove and refrigerator. Cabins 1, 2, 4 and 33 have two sleeping rooms, center room with stove, refrigerator and electricity. Other cabins are spartan, outfitted with four bunks and electricity. Cabins 13 and 17 are four-person with gas stove, refrigerator and propane space heater. Cabin 12 is a six-person cabin with three sleeping rooms and inside woodstove, gas stove, refrigerator and hot and cold running water.

Cabins 7-9 are among shallow cover near a grassy peninsula. Cabins 31 and 32 are along the marsh. A small courtyard-like area in front of cabins 10-16 and 26-29 is equipped with playground equipment. Cabin 13, below the larger cabin 12, is perfect for a family with a canoe. The gentle shoreline along the cabin colony is a terrific place for kids to fish and play. Cabins 19-22 are grouped together toward the end of the loop near the marsh, which is choked with cattails and the occasional honking of a Canada goose. Bring your fishing pole when staying in the waterside cabin colony.

Day-use areas: The park has interesting arch-style reservable picnic shelters, and you can rent the recreation building.

Recreation center: Staff stationed at the center offer many types of public programs including hikes, arts and crafts, and recreation. Games and recreation equipment can also be rented here. Kickball games and family films are popular with campers during the summer.

Swimming beach: Open only when lifeguards are on duty. Fair Haven's beach is sandy and one of the nicest in the park system. There are two adjacent beach areas, east and west. A small bridge connects the two sandy sections of lakefront. Two diving boards are along the narrow channel near the bridge. If you can swim across the channel, lifeguards will let you use the diving boards.

Hiking: The Bluff Nature Trail (.8-mile) is accessed from the Bluff Camping Area and forms a loop. Pick up a green five-panel self-guided interpretive brochure from the park office. A pavilion and rest room are along the easy trail that has 10 numbered posts that correspond to brief write-ups in the brochure. Park elevations range from 245 feet to 360 feet above sea level.

Hikers will learn about many places and types of animal houses that exist in nature, the importance of water and the marsh, forest growth. You'll learn what a "drumlin" is and that you can stand on it, nature's way of recycling, the sounds of the forest and many great quotes from famed nature writers and poets. One of my favorite quotes is by Nessmuk: "We're not out here to rough it. We're here to smooth it. Things are rough enough in town."

The Lakeshore Trail (3 miles) follows the lakeshore and through the marsh at the east end of the park.

Boating: Small rowboats are rented by the hour and paddle boats are rented by the half-hour for use on the quiet pond. Come to the park office to rent a boat and pick up personal flotation devices and oars.

The two-lane, hard-surfaced launch is busy with both pleasure boaters and anglers heading out onto Lake Ontario. Overnight mooring is available for a fee; register at the park office. A picnic shelter and small playground are near the modern ramp under a canopy of mature maple trees.

Fishing: Bait and fishing information are available at nearby bait and tackle shops. A wooden fishing pier is on the pond near the park office and beach. There are plenty of shoreline fishing access points around the edge of the murky pond. The pond often has thick aquatic weeds and fallen trees along the shore. It also has lots of peaceful picnic tables along the water's edge where anglers can relax and enjoy good panfishing. Minnows and slip bobbers are the top producing method.

Nature: In the spring mayapple and trillium are everywhere. Because of plentiful standing dead timber, woodpecker populations are high. Nature lovers should try paddling around the marsh for chances to see many types of wildlife including muskrat, shorebirds, reptiles, amphibians and songbirds.

Winter: The park is open year-round (including eight cabins) for snowmobiling, ice fishing, hiking and cross-country skiing.

Nearby state parks: Cayuga Lake (Rt. 89, 3 miles east of Seneca Falls) and Selkirk Shores (Rt 3, 3 miles west of Pulalski) are not far away.

Insider tips: The wide sandy beach often is busy on warm summer weekends. The park has many drinking fountains that are boxed in with wood panels and conveniently scattered throughout the day-use areas. The long sandy beach is a great place for an evening walk. From the beach you can easily view distinctive bald-face bluffs in the distance. Bring your bikes or canoe; there are lots of places to explore in the scenic park.

The park is a good blend of natural areas, high-energy beach, fishing and quality camping and cabins. A nearby nine-hole golf course is popular with campers.

Fillmore Glen State Park
Land: 941 acres Water: Dry Creek, Owasco Lake Inlet

Fillmore Glen State Park can be very cool—during a hot summer, that is. The long narrow gorge is a refreshing natural respite from the summer's heat. Towering hardwoods and green pines also offer shady trails, camping and day-use areas near a strong running creek. About half of the people who visit Fillmore Glen are from less than 50 miles away; the other half can be from most anywhere, including Canada, all 50 states, Europe and Asia.

The park was named for Millard Fillmore, the 13th President of the United States. Fillmore, who was born in a crude log cabin just five miles from the park, succeeded President Zachary Taylor who died in office on July 9, 1850. Fillmore completed Taylor's term, but was not nominated by the Whigs at the end of the term. Four years later, however, he was nominated for the presidency by the "Know Knothing" party (an appropriate name for modern parties, too), but was defeated. Fillmore died in Buffalo in 1874.

He served three terms in the New York state legislature and was elected comptroller. Fillmore was also a member of Congress for eight years, and vice president before succeeding Taylor. Active in all levels of politics and civic matters, Fillmore was the University of Buffalo's first chancellor and founder of Buffalo Hospital. Fillmore is best remembered for signing the Compromise of 1850, which attempted to forge a compromise between pro-slavery and anti-slavery interests. Because the measure established a stricter fugitive slave law, he lost critical northern support. Since 1975, the historic village of Moravia has conducted an annual festival called "Fillmore Days" in honor of its native, cabin-born president.

The park's trails were dedicated in 1921. In 1925, a 39-acre site was transferred to the state. Since it has grown to 941 acres complete with campground, hiking, pavilion, cabins and more.

Information and Activities

Fillmore Glen State Park
RD #3, P.O. Box 26
Moravia, NY 13118
(315) 497-0130

Directions: One mile south of Moravia on Rt. 38. Inside the park office, which is the entrance booth, is a set of A-frame brochure racks with visitor information and various black and white photos of the Civilian Conservation Corps. facilities and members.

Emergency numbers: NYS Park police, (800) 255-3577; medical emergencies, (315) 252-7242.

Campground: Maybe the best camping sites are in what is called the overflow area, which is open, bordered by trees and near a volleyball court. The campground is open mid-May to mid-October. It's full on holiday weekends and is often full by Friday afternoon on summer weekends. It's just inside the main park entrance.

Sites 1-8 are flat, shady and oversized near the creek. Most of them are grassy with some gravel mixed on the pad. Each is equipped with a fire ring and wood picnic table. If you like being near the creek examine sites 24 and 25. Loop 9-23 is shady and great for smaller units. Site 13 is backed up against the service area, but it would be quiet in the evening. From site 23 to the end of the loop, there might be some road noise. Campers with small children might want to choose site 1; it's near the rocky creek, park office, stone bridge and sprawling day-use area.

Loop 26-46 has mature trees dotting the tract and many of the sites are backed up against shrubby and wooded natural areas. For those who like more open, sunny sites, consider 29, 31 and 35. Site 44 is nestled under a small grove of pines and near the rest room. Site 46 is framed by a wonderfully flowering lilac and close to the brown brick shower and rest room building. This site also overlooks the small campground play area that is equipped with three toddler swings, six regular swings, slide, four teeter-totters, grills and picnic tables.

Site 70 is at the base of a hill, private and near the children's play space. Sites 47-68 are mostly open, facing a one-acre mowed open space. Site 68 is the most private in this loop, with sites 64 and 65 having some shade. All of the sites back up against a wood line, but they are open and sunny through the entire day. Large RV's would like this open, flat section of the campground. There are no hooks in the campground.

Cabins: Fillmore Glen has three small cabins that can be rented by advance reservation.

Day-use areas: Two ball diamonds with backstops and five acres of open space are next to the park office near the entrance to the pleasant campground. The park has three rentable shelters, a playground and play fields. The large pavilion at Fillmore Glen is one of the finest in

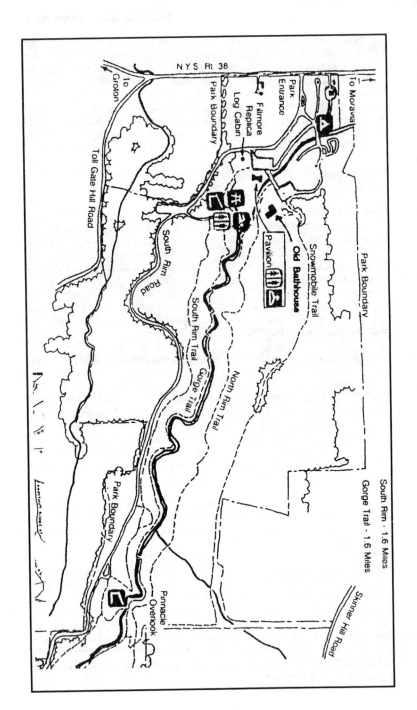

the park system. It has small six-over-six Colonial windows, light brown clapboard siding, beam ceilings, stone columns and a wide day-use area that stretches to include the tiny Millard Fillmore log cabin. The lovely and well-tended CCC building was constructed in 1932 and has terrific interior lights that are suspended from black chains over the clean varnished picnic tables. From the pavilion you can barely hear the rush of a small stream as it cascades over boulders. Notice the temperature change as you walk back to the falls, over the stone bridge. The park also has a fordway bridge that connects day-use areas.

Swimming: Stream-fed swimming is open during the summer in Dry Creek.

Millard Fillmore: The log cabin president was the only chief executive born in central New York and the first born in the 19th century. A small log cabin, much like the one President Fillmore was born in about five miles from the park, is near the large day-use area near the pavilion. The cabin (the original was torn down in 1852) is outfitted with historical interpretive signs and period furnishings including a rough wood table, two chairs, crude cooking and fire tending tools, kettle, candle making supplies and a creaking wood floor under foot. Notice the low ceiling and short door opening. The replica cabin was built by area history buffs in the 1960s.

Near the cabin a boulder and plaque commemorate FDR's *"Tree Army,"* as the Civilian Conservation Corps was sometimes called.

Hiking: Moderate hiking, the steep glen, "Cowshed" ledges and waterfalls are the along the three walking trails. All of the trails (North Rim, South Rim and Gorge Trail) are 1.6 miles long. The Gorge Trail cross the gorge on eight bridges. Sections of the trail are rugged. Next to the Lower Falls, near the beginning of the glen, is the "Cowsheds," a huge recess in the cliff where weaker shale has weathered away under a broad ledge of limestone.

Roadways around the park are rolling, but there are gentle places to walk or bike ride. South Rim Road is the best road to explore. It parallels the gorge and lies near lush farm fields. The Pinnacle Overlook is off this road.

Near the park's upper corner is the Summer Hill State Forest, where you can explore a deep, botanically rich gorge and a high, level forest. The Wisconsin Glacier leveled this area as it scraped across New York more than 15,000 years ago. Vast quantities of water pouring off the glacier and down the steep hills cutting into the underlying sandstone and limestone beds forming the linear glen you will view along the hike. The best hike in the park is a nearly four-mile loop comprised of the Gorge Trail and the South Rim Trail. These trails form a loop with a vertical rise of 350 feet.

Meandering through the state park is the misnamed Dry Creek, which has its source in a low drainage area on the top of Summer Hill; a dam nearly two miles away holds back the waters in a pond. The backed-up waters are control-released, flowing downhill through the steep gorge to the park's day-use areas, where it is dammed a second time to allow swimming. Along the trail you'll discover five "joints" in the rock layers that form falls and a short spur that takes you to the "Cowsheds," a deep recess carved by post-glacial water action. Local lore says that cows actually used the cool and shady shelter-like ledge to escape the summer heat.

There are eight bridges along this cool, streamside hike. A number of other spurs also lead from this trail route including a footpath to the three-story Upper Falls and the Pinnacle Overlook near the seventh bridge.

Fishing: In nearby Owasco Lake, the fishing can be better than average. The coldwater lake fishery is supported by heavy annual trout stocking (up to 40,000 fish each year). The average rainbow trout taken is two pounds; browns are about four pounds and landlocked salmon are typically three pounds. The south end of the lake nearest the park can produce good smallmouth bass catches. The lake is deep and can be windy.

For lake trout try still fishing with a spinning rod, a one-ounce barrel sinker, snap swivel, rubber band, English-style bait hooks, a bait needle and smelt as bait. Thread the bait over the long-snelled hook until the hook points are at the bait's eye. The free-moving barrel sinker and swivel allows the trout to pick up the bait and move away without feeling any resistance. Use the rubber band in front of the open-bail reel to hold the loop of line so that you can tell if the trout is moving with your offering. Set the hook when the line moves the second time. For larger trout, try trolling in 130-140 feet, above the thermocline. Troll small spoons in green or green and silver colors. Seventeen-pound lake trout are taken each year from the relatively small lake, and 20-pounders are sometimes boated.

Winter: Fillmore Glen has two snowmobile trails and opportunities to cross-country ski or hike the moderate trails. The gorge trail is closed during the winter months.

Insider tips: Bring your mountain bike and ride old South Rim Road to Pinnacle Overlook. From the lower park, the overlook is 1.5 miles away and mostly uphill. Giant white trillium are abundant in the spring along South Rim Road also. Fillmore Glen is a terrific family park, complete with a safe feeling, medium-sized campground and many amenities. Historic Moravia is only a mile away. A privately operated golf course is adjacent to the rolling park.

New

Keuka Lake State Park
Land: 621 acres Water: Keuka Lake

The champagne center of America is concentrated around Keuka Lake. Nine wineries, six of which offer public tours and tasting, are delightfully scattered across the temperate valley. Hundreds of acres of vineyards flourish under the moderating influences of the lake, winds and rich soils.

Keuka Lake is the only branched Finger Lake. Like the others, Keuka was formed by the great continental glaciers that invaded from the north more than 10,000 years ago. But unlike the other Finger Lakes, the mighty glacier excavated a river that had a deep branched valley. This action left behind a Y-shaped trough dammed at the ends by debris which filled with water to form the crystal-clear lake. Keuka Lake is also known as *"Crooked Lake."*

Some of the best fishing in the country is in the lake, and the state park's access and camping make it a perfect destination for trout and salmon anglers. The waters are extraordinary clear. Both the deep lake nd the orientation of the valleys have a moderating effect on winter weather, making the surrounding lands ideal for vineyards and tourists. Aside from many fine wineries, the area also has historical and aviation museums, charming shops and budget-busting antiquing.

Over the years the scenic area has seen many groups of settlers use the fertile lands. One early settler was Jemimah Wilkensen, a Native American who founded a religious settlement known as the Universal Friends. Some years later the Pennsylvania Dutch and New England Yankees settled the area and compromised on the name of their town, nearby Penn Yan.

Information and Activities

Keuka Lake State Park
3370 Pepper Road
Bluff Point, NY 14478
(315) 536-3666

Directions: In Yates County, the park is south of Penn Yan off Pepper Road from SR 54A.

Emergency number: Park police, (800) 255-3577; medical emergenices, 911.

Campground: The campground, built in 1969, has 150 sites on three loops; 53 sites have 30-amp electrical service and are always the most popular with RV campers. The mostly open campground is up a hill, with sites placed along level tracts. Many trees have been planted that will someday provide plenty of shade. Each loop has a modern brick showerhouse. Staff says about half of all campers come to the park to boat or fish. The campground is filled on holidays and July and August weekends.

The Twin Fawns Loop, with sites 1-50, is open and mostly flat. The sites on the outside perimeter of the loop are backed up against a natural area. The inside sites have a screen of vegetation. Sites 9 and 10 are shaded by two big willows and are near a trail. The back of this loop offers shadier grassy sites. Site 17 is private, walled-off by a thick growth of shrubbery at the base of a small hill. Sites are wide throughout the loop. Sites in the 40s have firm gravel pads. Site 29 offers plenty of room to maneuver a larger RV unit into. Electric sites are 18-28, 30 and 38-50.

All sites in the Deer Run Loop are grassy and have steel firerings and wood picnic tables. Views from this loop include farmlands, woodlands, sloping hillsides and hazy mountains that roll off into the distance. A few mature trees are scattered around the generally open camping area. Sites in the 60s are along a grove of young pines and evergreens. All of the sites are wide, firm and deep, big enough for medium to large RV units.

Sites 101-150, called the Esperanza View, have high ground and more relief than these in other loops. RVs like the loop that has many electrical hook-ups. Strips of dogwoods help buffer sites and the views of the campground. Site 137 is surrounded by shrubs. If you enjoy sunny camping, try this loop with a good view of the green rounded mountains. This is the nicest loop and it's often filled with families with small children. Electric sites are 102-114, 130-141 and 148-150.

Day-use areas: The day-use area slopes down to the lake. Other facilities in the park include play equipment, two enclosed picnic shelters and a swimming beach.

Swimming beach: The mostly gravel and coarse sand beach is flanked by a sunning lawn. The water is sectioned off with orange and white buoys in front of lifeguard chairs. A low brick bathhouse, which has an open-air changing room and showers, is 100 yards from the shoreline of the lake. Plenty of picnic tables, which are shaded by mature trees. A pay phone and sand volleyball courts are also at the beach. The beach is open only when it is guarded.

Hiking: Hiking trails are moderately difficult and color-coded. The trails run from the camping area to the lakeshore which is a significant elevation difference. In the fields, the trails are mowed to define them. The Orange Trail is open and all the trails are open for cross-country skiing.

Boating: A three-lane concrete launch with wooden courtesy docks offers excellent access to the lake. Boaters (bass anglers!) should remember there is a 45 mph speed limit on the lake. There are 10 mooring docks and a rest room at the ramp. Check other boating restrictions. Boats can be rented from any of the four marinas on the lake. Check the list of marinas posted in the park office. Lake charts are also sold at nearby marinas and bait and tackle shops.

Of the Finger Lakes, Keuka may be the most pleasant to canoe. There are plenty of access points that can put you on the water to enjoy 700-foot cliffs (Bluff Point), enchanting cottages that dot the shoreline, vineyard views and usually smooth water. The lake can be windy, so choose your course accordingly. Canoeists should also try the Keuka Lake outlet, with access in the nearby community of Penn Yan.

Fishing: Trout and bass fishing in the area is very good and the shoreline access from the park is excellent. Some old-timers say there are

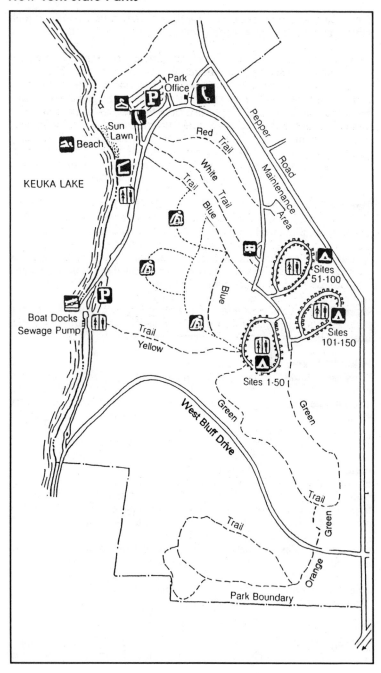

KEUKA LAKE

Park Office

Sun Lawn

Beach

Pepper Road

Red Trail

White Trail

Trail

Blue

Maintenance Area

Blue

Sites 51-100

Boat Docks
Sewage Pump

Trail

Yellow

Sites 101-150

Sites 1-50

West Bluff Drive

Green

Green

Trail

Green

Trail

Orange

Park Boundary

some real "meat holes" in Keuka Lake—places where a single hook spoon can still bring in the day's meal.

Keuka is the third largest of the Finger Lakes, offering more than 18 square miles of surface. The branched shape of the lake offers more shoreline than any other Finger Lake, nearly 59 miles. The lake has an average depth of 101 feet and some bottom humps that hold fish. There are places in the 22-mile-long lake that are 180 feet deep. The cold lake is best known for lake trout, having the third highest harvest rate in the state. The cold waters and steep-sided shoreline also make it an ideal smallmouth bass and perch fishery. The exceptionally clear lake has good numbers of northern pike, largemouth bass and pickerel. Fishing for these species is best at either end of the lake.

Lake trout are native to the waters and reproduce naturally. The average laker will weigh 3.5 pounds and landlocked salmon weigh two to four pounds. Lake trout frequent all the deep spots in the lake and anglers can often have good success night fishing or casting a 1/8-ounce jig during the day. In front of the park is an excellent place to try. Once summer is in full swing, trolling is the most productive method. Troll slow and try a vibrating lure.

Some of the best hot spots for browns and rainbows are off Hammondsport and Cold Brook. These species look for the warmer water found here in the colder months of the year. In the fall, fish the creek mouths.

Smallmouth action is best in June and July, when casting crankbaits and jigs in the shallows off rocky points can product results. Hot spots include Willow Grove, Keuka College, Eggleston, and Bluff and Marlena points. If you can't pick up the smallies with deep-running crankbait, try drifting a crayfish. In the summer smallmouth often suspend at 50 feet and are most often caught while fishing for trout or salmon. Use Mr. Twisters along the shoreline in the fall.

Yellow perch from Keuka are delicious. They have extra firm meat that is the best tasting of any species (in my humble opinion, anyway). Drift with minnows or a jig in the same places as you would for smallmouth bass. There are plenty of 10-12 inch perch in the lake. Other panfish, including rock bass and crappies, are found in the springtime shallows. For largemouth bass, fish the weed lines using spinners, plastic worms or topwater plugs at night.

During the summer the lake can get busy. Anglers are advised to fish in the morning or on weekdays.

Winter: Open year-round, the trails are popular with cross-county skiers.

Insider tips: The world's largest pancake was made in nearby Penn Yan (the record stood for two years). The whopper flapjack measured 27 feet in diameter and was made using a cement mixer to mix the batter and a crane to flip it.

Also in Penn Yan is Doug's Meaner Wiener food shack near the go-cart track. Keuka offers good passive outdoor recreation; bring your bike, walking shoes or in-line skates. Keuka is a quiet retreat park, with a great view and a great base camp to explore the region's wineries and other attractions.

The Esperanza Mansion, built in 1838, which is the largest structure in the county, and can be seen on the hillside from the park, is now open to the public. Over the years the mansion—which was intended to resemble a pre-Civil War southern plantation—has been the county poorhouse, an art gallery and a winery. A large two-story dinner boat that can hold 350 for evening meals operates on the lake. Also while in the area, consider a trip to the nearby Windmill Farm and Craft Market.

Sampson State Park
Land: 1,905 acres   Water: Seneca Lake

The park has a military look softened by a wonderful view and access to Seneca Lake. From the 90-degree roads to cannons and barracks-like buildings, the old Navel and Air Force training base has been transformed into a popular and pretty state park.

Sampson State Park touches the eastern shore of Seneca Lake, where a million years ago a river flowed. Throughout the ice age powerful continental glaciers bulldozed their way from Canada, digging lake basins up to 600 feet deep. Another melting sheet of ice filled the lakes more than 10,000 years ago. Following the last glacial event, nomadic hunters settled the fertile area as stone-age cultures slowly developed. Later, as Europeans also explored the region, hunted and eventually settled, they encountered Seneca Indians who had long led a settled agrarian life. The Senecas are one of the Six Nations of Iroquois Confederacy.

During the Revolutionary War, the Continental Army forayed into

Central New York to destroy many Iroquois towns. History-minded visitors may want to find the state historical marker along the highway south of the park entrance that notes the burning of the Seneca town Ken-dai-a. Much of the land between Seneca and Cayuga lakes was ceded to soldiers as payment for their war service. Homesteaders soon flocked to the area, including the tract of land that is now the state park.

About 150 years later, with the outbreak of World War II, these quiet farming areas made way for the second largest naval training installation in the country. The bustling center was named for Rear Admiral William T. Sampson of Palmyra, N.Y. After the war, the facilities became Sampson State College and educated thousands of returning veterans. It was also used as an Air Force base during the Korean War, and in 1960, Sampson became a state park.

Information and Activities

Sampson State Park
6096 Route 96A
Romulus, NY 14541
(315) 585-6392

Directions: On the east side of Seneca Lake, off 96A northwest of Ovid. The park office is in a huge dark brown building that has a large indoor recreation area outfitted with game tables, tables and other equipment.

Emergency number: NYS Park police, (800) 255-3577; medical emergencies, 911.

Campground: The busy, shade-tree, grassy campground has 245 electric sites along five loops. The most popular are those sites near the lake. The campground fills up on summer holiday weekends, while about 175 sites are typically used on all other summer weekends.

Day-use areas: Bluebird boxes dot the sprawling open spaces that are criss-crossed by hard-surfaced roads that were once part of the Naval training station. Other day-use amenities include basketball goals, ball diamonds, a recreation building, two tennis courts and scattered play apparatus.

Military buildings have been removed and some roads were adapted in the transformation to a state park. Old fields are growing grasses and wildflowers, and soon, these fields will support increasing numbers of shrubs and trees. Eventually a mature forest will emerge, hiding the war training fields.

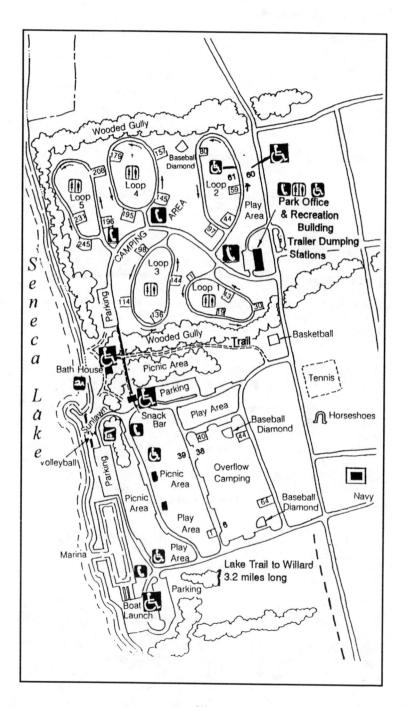

Wooded Gully

179   157

208

Baseball
Diamond

80

Loop 4

61 60

59

44

Loop 5

145

Loop 2

Play
Area

195

23

196

CAMPING AREA

97

Park Office
& Recreation
Building

Trailer Dumping
Stations

245

98

Loop 3

Loop 1

43

144

30

114

136

19

Wooded Gully

Trail

Basketball

Bath House

Picnic Area

Tennis

Parking

Snack Bar

Play Area

Horseshoes

Sunlawn

volleyball

Play Area

Baseball
Diamond

40

44

Picnic
Area

39 38

Parking

Picnic
Area

Play
Area

Overflow
Camping

64

Baseball
Diamond

Navy

6

Play
Area

1

Marina

Lake Trail to Willard
3.2 miles long

Play
Area

Boat
Launch

Parking

S
e
n
e
c
a

L
a
k
e

Swimming: Near a cove and sunlawn, the guarded beach is open during the summer. It's close to camping loop 3.

Museum: Housed in a red brick building with white trim and surrounded by a tall fence (the old "Brig") and examples of old cannons, the Sampson Navy Memorial Museum is operated by volunteers. The impressive building is at the main entrance to the park. The museum has historical photographs, displays and lots of information on the lifestyles of the men and women who trained and lived at the base. In the future, the Air Force will occupy another area of the building to display memorabilia from their time at Sampson.

Sampson Sailor: An imposing monument of a sailor dominates the entrance of the park. It is dedicated to the 411,429 naval recruits and untold thousands of ship company workers, service school graduates, waves and nurses who were assigned to the Sampson Naval Station. Sampson was opened Oct. 20, 1942 and operated until the end of World War II. The marker says: *"To our shipmates who made the ultimate sacrifice for their country and to those who survived, we the Sampson W.W. II Naval veterans dedicate this memorial."* It also says: *"To the living: Smooth sailing, fair weather, and favorite waves and tides."*

Hiking: Park roads are good for biking and in-line skating. The Lake Trail to Willard is an easy three mile walk.

Boating: The modern marina has 123 seasonal and transient berths and a launching ramp. Seneca Lake is a popular place for fishermen.

Fishing: Aside from the Great Lakes, Seneca Lake is the deepest inland lake east of the Rocky Mountains. It is up to 618 feet deep and averages 291 feet. The significant depth also makes it one of the coldest and best fishing lakes in New York. The 66-square-mile lake has 75 miles of shoreline and is fed by two major tributaries, the famed Catharine Creek at the south end and the Keuka Outlet on the west side at Dresden. The bottom of Seneca is rock, sand and muck. The water is clear to slightly cloudy. The deep lake has frozen over only once in the last century.

First-time anglers will be overwhelmed. Because Seneca is big water, it needs to be broken up into manageable areas of water—which will help you to understand what types of fish and patterns are best for a particular section.

Seneca Lake is best known for lake trout, and lake trout derbies. The lake also has good numbers of rainbows and browns. An average lake trout is about 3.8 pounds, browns 4.4 pounds and rainbows are typically three pounds. Lake trout, like all salmonids, are temperature-oriented fish. Therefore, no matter what type of fishing you do—still fishing, trolling, or from the shoreline—the objective is to present the lure

in the 48-degree water. If you can put that lure near a structure at that temperature, you will catch lots of lakers.

Sampson State Park, with its many modern berths, is ideally located for anglers. It is especially appealing because it is across the lake from Dresden, a year-round hot spot. Nine miles south of Sampson is Lodi State Park, which has seasonal dockage and two launching ramps, but no camping. There is a small boat access site at Severne Point on the west side.

In the spring and fall, lake trout anglers will want to fish at about 90 feet. Most of the lures used are silver-plated fished from big rods and sturdy level-wind reels. Some lakers are also taken still fishing in the shallows in April and May. Live bait anglers need to remember to not be anxious when they feel a nibble. Wait for the fish to pick up the bait and move off, then stop and swallow the bait. It on the second tug that you set the hook.

For smaller excitement, try for perch across the shoreline at Dresden. Try 15-18 feet of water in the spring and fall. Try quietly working the weedlines casting jigs and minnows with an ultralight rod and reel. Hook the minnows through the eye with a gold No. 6 hook. In the rest of the lake, look for good populations of smallmouth bass. Use

crankbaits around the rock rubble. Some anglers enjoy drifting a crayfish or minnow in 18-30 feet of water in the summer. Getting your lure
or bait deep is one of the tricks in catching smallies. Largemouth bass
are hard to find in the lake.

Most brown trout are taken with stickbaits (Rapalas) from shore or
while trolling. Try the south end of the lake or the warmwater dis-
charge near Dresden. While trolling, you'll pick up some rainbows
using stickbaits or spoons. During the spring and early summer
explore creek mouths, and as the water warms, retreat to the deeper
portions of the lake. Lots of shoreline anglers at the park cast simple
red and white spoons or jigs and minnows.

Intrepid anglers might also want to try for some northern pike. They
are usually found in weedbeds during spring and early summer and will
chase 4-6 inch chub minnows, big suckers or traditional spoons and
Rebel- and Rapala-type lures. Local experts say the clear water and
spooky nature of Seneca's northern pike can make them difficult prey.
Nevertheless, long casts can help.

Nature: Several wooded ravines can be informally explored where
you might see deer, foxes, rabbits, raccoons, opossums and a good variety of songbirds. About 20 species of waterfowl also use the lake.
Many of the small natural areas are of willow and poplar trees that have
taken over some of the shoreline.

Other nearby state parks: Cayuga Lake State Park (Rt. 89, 3 miles
east of Seneca Falls); Seneca Lake State Park (Routes 5 and 20, 1 mile
east of Geneva); Lodi Point (Lodi Pt. Road off Rt. 414, 2 miles west of
Lodi); Taughannock Falls (Rt. 89, 8 miles north of Ithaca) and Watkins
Glen (at the village of Watkins Glen).

Insider tips: Some visitors will enjoy visiting and learning about the
locks and the Cayuga-Seneca Canal system. For canal information,
call (800) 4-CANAL-4. Neighborhoods in nearby Geneva have many
Federal-style homes that are more than 200 years old. Bring your bike
or in-line skates.

Stony Brook State Park
Land: 568 acres   Water: Stony Brook

Stony Brook State Park is a wonderful scenic park established in 1928, just before the Great Depression. Many of the lovely buildings and early park development were done by laborers from the Civilian Conservation Corps. The men built a lodge building, swimming areas, shelters, stairways through the gorge and roads. During World War II Italian prisoners of war were housed in the Transient Camp and also worked on a variety of park projects.

Indians were the first to notice natural gas bubbles rising from the water in the lower park. In 1882 a driller unsuccessfully tried to locate oil by sinking a well near the bubbles. The gas, however was captured and fueled cooking, lights and ongoing development of the scenic area.

In the late 1800s, the glen became a popular resort, or "summer garden" as it was called. Both entrances to the park were developed. The popular retreat included a large dance hall, well-kept paths, rustic bridges, gardens, outdoor theaters, swings and seating for hundreds.

The theater was often used for the performance of "The Legend of Red Wing." According to local lore, Red Wing was an Indian maiden who leapt to her death in the glen following a fatal struggle there between two rival suitors.

At station No. 8 along the Gorge Trail, you will see a great train trestle abutment that once brought visitors from as far away as St. Mary's, Pa. Imagine the spectacle of a locomotive pulling passenger cars across the gorge on a high iron bridge supported by huge pillars, 239 feet above the brook.

By the 1920s the prosperity of the resort declined, and it was abandoned briefly until the state rescued the pristine 250-acre tract in 1928. The state expanded it to 577 acres over the years.

Information and Activities

Stony Brook State Park
Route 36
Dansville, NY
(716) 335-8111

Directions: On Route 36, three miles south of Dansville, or Exit 4 off of SR390. A small brochure rack and pay phone are in the reddish-brown park office.

Emergency numbers: Park police, (800) 255-3577; medical emergencies, 911.

Campground: The campground has 125 non-electric sites, with the most popular sites scattered along the Stony Brook. Sites 93-104 and 103-115 have a premium fee. No alcohol is allowed in the campground. According to staff, site 53 is the most private and requested site in the campground. Families with children will love sites 87-92, which are near the playground and open space. The clean and neat campground is at the south entrance to the park. Campers must register before occupying a site.

Sites 1-53 are shady and served by a showerhouse with an outdoor slop sink and small swing set. Sites in the 40s are along a gentle ridge, tucked into the hillside. Sites are compact and on varying elevations. Sites 40 and 41 are deep and grassy, while site 39 is notched out of the woods. Sites on the outside of the loop are backed up against natural areas. A new showerhouse serves this loop.

Sites 54-130 are along the hard-surfaced park road that has a speed

limit of 15 mph. Most sites are under a broad canopy of mature trees. Sites along the babbling brook (sites 93-115) are popular and well-worn. Across the stream from these sites, the rock wall goes straight up. Although the some of these sites are small, camping near the stream is pleasant. Sites 87, 91 and 92 are under overhanging trees and near the playground. These are excellent sites for pop-up campers. Sites 117-120 are great for two families to reserve for a relaxing weekend.

Day-use areas: The park has a wood basketball goal, tennis courts, horse shoe pit, soccer fields, stone and pedestal grills and plenty of picnic tables. The park rents picnic shelters.

Swimming: Each summer the staff carefully dams the brook to form a beautiful natural swimming pools that typically opens in mid-June. The gorge is up to 250 feet tall in this area and the scenic swimming area is up to eight feet deep. According to staff, gorge hiking and swimming are the main attractions at the park. The super-clean snack and gift shop located on the rim of the gorge features soft drinks, video games, grill foods, candy, small toys, charcoal and hand-dipped ice cream. It's near a small playground and drinking fountain. The handsome deck at the snack bar offers visitors a scenic and cozy place to enjoy the spectacular view and listen to the rushing of the water. There

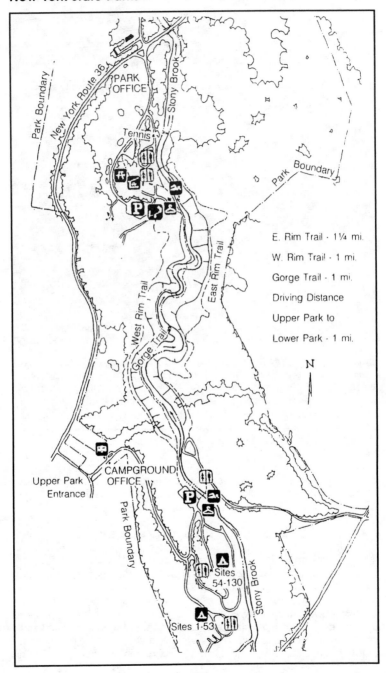

E. Rim Trail - 1¼ mi.

W. Rim Trail - 1 mi.

Gorge Trail - 1 mi.

Driving Distance
Upper Park to
Lower Park - 1 mi.

Stony Brook State Park

are also many benches and a viewing platform at the gorgeside day-use and swimming area.

Behind the concession stand is the bathhouse, with lockers. The showers do not have hot water. The view from the swimming area is of sheer rock walls and the rushing stream.

A second natural pool is near the campground and has a bathhouse and day-use area equipped with picnic tables and grills. A wooden walk and seating are along the edge of the seasonal natural pool.

Hiking/nature: The concrete abutments along the Gorge Trail are all that remain of an old railroad bridge. Originally the bridge was wood, but because steam engines kept catching it on fire, a steel bridge was put in its place and operated for many years. The steel bridge, which at one time was the tallest east of the Mississippi, was dismantled in the early 1940s. Two 40-foot waterfalls are along the gorge trail.

Gorge Nature Trail: The ruggedness of Stony Brook seems out of place in this otherwise gentle and rolling part of the state. The glen is actually very young geologically, as least compared to the ancient hills it bisects. The elements have not had time enough to round its features to equal those of contours of surrounding lands. The nature trail, which is in two sections, allows visitors to experience the gorge and learn about the wonderful ecology and geology of the deep glen.

The Gorge Trail is .75-mile long and ascends 250 stone or wooden steps. Stony Brook emerges from the gorge and flows into the Canaseraga Creek in the main valley. Its waters eventually reach the Genesee River and Lake Ontario. About 10,000 years ago, Stony Brook was young, there was no gorge. The rushing stream flowed down the hillside in front of a huge glacier that was melting and gradually moving northward. The enormous glacier left behind giant piles of earth and rock called moraines. Some of these long slopes can be seen from the highway near the park. Since the glacier receded, Stony Brook has slowly eroded its rugged chasm in the ancient rocks of the rolling hillsides.

Along the trail are some varied and interesting natural communities that have adapted to the shady steep slopes and cool temperatures. As you walk the gorge, notice how some plant roots have adapted to spread out and cling to the walls and hillside allowing them to flourish in the terrain. Yellow birch, hemlocks and many smaller plants are doing well in this 400-million-year-old sedimentary rock. Some plants have also found ways to grow in the crumbly layers of shale that was once a muddy sea bottom.

Some astute hikers might ask: Why is there a grove of trees on this side of the brook while the opposite side is a rugged, bare cliff? The

104

answer: Streams wander as they flow, which is called meandering. Erosion of the bank is typically greater on the outside of the curve or meander. The cliff opposite is being undercut by the stream during high water, and stones that fall from above are swept away. The grove on one side of the gorge is inside the meander and rarely floods. Slowly rocks and soils that have been deposited or fallen from above have accumulated and trees have been able to establish themselves. Hemlock, yews and cedars are found here.

At station No. 7, Hourglass Falls flows. Here hikers should notice the straight cracks in the rocks around the waterfalls. This entire region is criss-crossed by joints where floodwaters sometimes get behind and break off large slabs of rock.

On some of the walls are primitive plants similar to those that grew millions of years ago to the size of trees. Some of these include bulbet ferns that produce small bulbets under their leaves that drop off like a seed in late summer, helping to spread the plant. Carpet-like moss also clings to the minimal soil and holds moisture in its tiny stems. Strange, flat liverworts, with no true leaves or stems, hug the rock in many moist locations along the trail. Among other plant life is the light green lichen, a combination of alga and fungus, which gets its nutrients directly from the bare stone. All of these plants produce spores—tiny

105

dust-like particles that can float on the wind.

At station No. 11 are some boulders that are of different stone than the layered rocks of the gorge walls. They are hard and rounded and are found scattered about the landscape. These boulders, called "erratics," were brought here from the north by the great continental glaciers that once bulldozed the landscape. When the glacier melted, these boulders and others things like silt, sand, gravel and cobbles were left behind. This debris is called "till" and forms a base for soil.

If you are observant, you'll notice that conditions on the rim of the gorge and the bottom are quite different. The rim is sunny, dry and warm compared to the depth of the cool glen. In the transition zones maples, beech, basswood, hemlock, yellow birch and oak grow. At the southern end of the trail, pine and oak thrive.

Hikers who take the West Rim Nature Trail will find stations marked with letters, not numbers. Visitors will learn about pileated woodpeckers and their huge holes, white pines, scouring rushes (which have particles of silica that pioneers used to clean their pots and pans), cedar groves and some old woodland areas filled with slow-growing hemlocks that once provided railroad ties. Look for water thrushes, juncos, phoebes and many types of woodland mammals along these terrific trails. Pick up a brochure on these two trails from the park office.

Fishing: A few trout make it to at least one of the pools in Stony Brook.

Insider tips: Stony Brook is one of the cleanest state parks in New York. The gorge trail is super; bring your comfortable hiking boots. Don't miss a swim in the cool natural pools made from damming the flowing brook.

Taughannock Falls State Park

Land: 745 acres   Water: Cayuga Lake

Taughannock Falls is 215 feet tall---higher than the more famous Niagara. The park has wonderful contrasts. From wide, flat open spaces to thundering waterfalls, the shimmering lake and patches of woodlands offer visitors lots of things to see and do.

Taughannock (pronounced *tau-han-nock*) is probably derived from the Native American word "Taghkanic," which means *"great falls in the woods."* A more dramatic explanation of the name also comes from Native Americans. The Cayugas and Senacas are two nations of the Six Nation Confederacy of the Iroquois who once controlled all of central and western New York. Legend says that a rebel Iroquois chief, named Cannassatego, insulted the council of chiefs concerning a land dispute with the Delaware tribe. Usually the Delaware Indians yielded to the Iroquois, except for one proud chief from an ancient line, called Taughannock, who vowed revenge.

Chief Taughannock led 200 warriors north into Iroquois territory and west up the side of Cayuga Lake. The Iroquois drove the warring party to the north bank of the lake near a stream that is now named Taughannock Creek. Outnumbered, they fought valiantly before succumbing. Chief Taughannock killed the local chief and inflicted mortal wounds on Canassatego before he was slain. His ravaged body, legend says, was thrown over the falls and thus denied a proper funeral. The falls were named in his memory.

Since Indian occupation, the region has seen waves of development including a canal system that quickly fell into decline, a railroad station at the upper gorge, and luxury hotels that were built on either side of the abrupt gorge near the falls. For many years during this golden age, urban visitors came to the area by ornate steamboat and lodged at the gilded hotels.

The park was only 64 acres when it first open in 1925. Since, it has grown to 745 acres and has seen development of foot trails, a campground, cabins, beach and marina that were built in the 1920s and 1930s.

Information and Activities

Taughannock Falls State Park
P.O. Box 1055
Trumansburg, NY 14886
(607) 387-6739

Directions: On Cayuga Lake, Route 89, eight miles north of Ithaca. The park office has rest rooms and is open 9 a.m. - 9 p.m. most of the summer.

Emergency numbers: Park police, (800) 255-3577; medical emergencies, 911.

Campground: Sites 34 and 61 are the most requested sites in the hilly 76-site campground. Sixteen sites have electrical hook-ups. The hard-surfaced campground road has speed bumps and winds through the mostly shady tract where sites are grassy. All of the camping spots have a fire ring and picnic table.

Sites 1-16 are ideal for pop-up campers. Up the hill, near site 19, are a small play area and picnic shelter. A site for campers with disabilities is also maintained in this area. Sites in the 20s are on higher, grassy ground and perfect for tent camping. Site 32 is under a canopy of trees near equally attractive site 34. Sites in the high 30s are shaded and have a distant view of the long lake. Sites in the 40s also have a view of the handsome lake from a ridge. Sites 55, 56 and 57 are private tent camping sites. Site 61 is the best site in the park for a large RV. Many of the sites in the 60s have gravel pads, but they are uneven.

Cabins: The park has 16 cabins with electricity. The cabins are rustic, a bit like camping in a wood tent. The single-room cabins have four cots and a refrigerator. Cabin 1, sometimes called the "honeymoon" cabin, is secluded and often requested. Two of the cabins at the park are accessible to persons with disabilities. The charming cabins are rough-sawn with tan trim and shingle roofs. Units along the higher elevations have a partial view of the distant lake. Cabins 2 and 3 are along a high ridge, while cabin 10 has a steady lake view. Cabins have picnic tables, grills, and some have interesting bleacher-style seats near the well-used fire rings. Most of the structures have a large enough side yard where a screen tent can be pitched. Because of the slightly crowded cabin colony, you can really smell the hot dogs and hamburgers cooking at the dinner hour. A hard-surfaced walkway winds through the rustic colony.

Day-use areas: The park sprawls along the rolling Cayuga Lake shoreline offering appealing day-use areas and excellent views of the lake, vineyards and hilly shores. The park has dozens of shoreline picnic tables and adjacent open spaces that have scattered park benches for resting and viewing.

Swimming: Outlined by floating buoys and flanked by a brown bathhouse, the small grassy beach is open during the summer. There's plenty of picnic tables around the beach that offer wonderful views of the bobbing sailboats and fertile shoreline.

Hiking: Hiking the gorge to the falls, that plunges 215 feet into a 30-foot-deep pool, is inspiring, especially in the spring when the creek runs strong. When you are at the base of the falls, the 400-foot sheer walls form an amphitheater of beauty and solitude. It takes about 2.5 hours to hike around the entire rugged gorge. Along this hike you will cross a foot bridge at an unusually wide section of the gorge, see wonderful views of the steep gorge and eventually end up at the roaring falls. One of the best views is from an observation platform near the falls where hikers can see the rushing wall of white water plummeting into the pool.

About three-quarters of this trail is a self-guided nature trail that features 14 learning stations. According to the five-panel brochure available at the park office, "Had you been at this spot two million years ago, you'd have been under hundreds of feet of stone! 20,000 years ago you'd have been under half a mile of ice! And 10,000 years ago you'd have been standing on the shore of Cayuga Lake, right next to Taughannock Falls! Now the falls are three-quarter mile away along this gentle path."

While wandering through this scenic gorge it is sometimes hard to imagine two million years ago that Cayuga Lake was only a small river. Today, the lake is 38 miles long, 435 feet deep and has frozen over only a few times in modern history. In fact, the lake is so deep it retains heat, actually tempering the shoreline climate, making it conducive for vineyards—and late season fishing.

Long before the rivers that eventually became Cayuga Lake, the bluish-gray layers of limestone that make up the gorge walls were formed by an ancient sea. This limestone is composed of compressed, disintegrated skeletons of billions of ancient sea animals or lime which settled from sea water. More than 350 million years ago the rock layers in the gorge were sediments on the bottom of a sea that covered much of western New York.

The wide section of the gorge that you will pass through was made by a meandering stream that snakes through the valley. The constant eroding has undercut and widened the gorge in progress. In other places you'll notice how the shifting stream has created areas where the forest grows thick. At post seven, take time to examine some rounded boulders that were brought here from Canada during the last ice age. Millions of such rocks were torn from the landscape by the passing glacier. Lodged in the ice, they gave the glacier great scraping power, scouring the landscape and shaping the wide valleys and hills.

Once at the 215-foot-tall falls, look for two major rock formations. The bottom half of the cliff is made of weak shale. If you look closely you'll see where the texture changes to sandstone above. The shale is more susceptible to weathering and erosion and wears away more rapidly. This undermines the sandstone, which occasionally breaks off in chunks along pre-existing cracks, called joints. In this way the waterfall slowly erodes the gorge further back into the hillside.

Wallace Stegner could have been standing here when he wrote these words in Sound of Mountain Water: "By such a river it is impossible to believe that one will ever be tired or old. Every sense applauds it. Taste it, feel its chill on the teeth: it is purity absolute. Watch its racing current, its steady renewal of force: it is transient and eternal. And listen again to its sounds: get far enough way so that the noise of falling tons of water does not stun the ears, and hear how much is going on underneath—a whole symphony of smaller sounds, hiss and splash and gurgle, the small talk of side channels, the whisper of blown and scattered spray gathering itself and beginning to flow again, secret and irresistible, among the wet rock."

Toward the end of the nature trail you also learn about massive sycamore trees with mottled green, brown and whitish bark that stretch

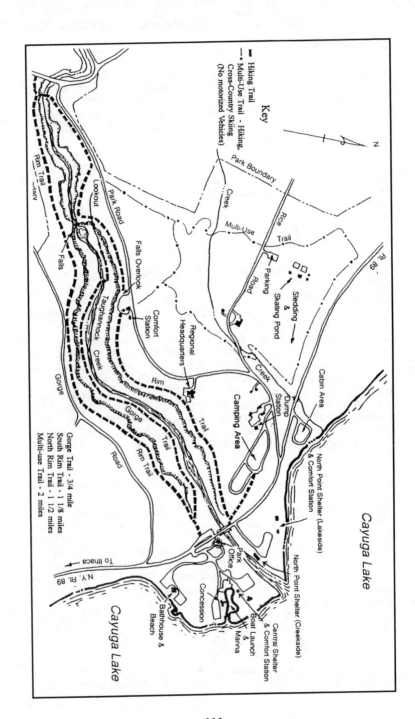

Key

▬▬ Hiking Trail
▪ ▪ ▪ Multi-Use Trail - Hiking
- - - Cross-Country Skiing
(No motorized Vehicles)

N

Park Boundary

Creek

Rice

Multi-Use

Trail

Road

Parking

Sledding
&
Skating Pond

Rt. 89

Rim Trail

Lookout

Park Road

Falls

Falls Overlook

Comfort Station

Taughannock Creek

Regional Headquarters

Rim

Trail

Camping Area

Creek

Dump Station

Cabin Area

North Point Shelter & Comfort Station

Gorge

Gorge Trail

Rim Trail

Gorge Road

Gorge Trail - 3/4 mile
South Rim Trail - 1 1/8 miles
North Rim Trail - 1 1/2 miles
Multi-use Trail - 2 miles

To Ithaca

N.Y. Rt. 89

Park Office

Concession

Boat Launch & Marina

Bathhouse & Beach

North Point Shelter (Creekside)

Central Shelter & Comfort Station

Cayuga Lake

Cayuga Lake

111

more than 100 feet to scrape the sky. Also along the hike are samples of joints in the cliff wall, quiet places of unique plant communities, and details about the special climate and tempered conditions in the region.

Boating: Narrow docks provide limited seasonal mooring in the parks marina basin. The park also has a two-lane launching ramp, day-use areas, playground structure, concession stand, gasoline pump and parking. Small fishing boats are available for hourly rental. The small concession stand also sells firewood, ice, live bait and grill items (hot dogs, hamburgers, etc.). From the clean concession window you can look west and see a huge cream-colored mansion on the hillside that was once the home of the man who donated the park. Over the years the stately building has been used as a sanitarium, and is now an elegant restaurant and inn with a panoramic view of placid Cayuga Lake.

Fishing: Shoreline fishing, especially from the piers, is popular. Lake trout, landlocked salmon and rainbows are taken from the shoreline. Most anglers use a slip-float rig with live bait. Off the end of the pier you can cast into 90 feet of water. There are three bait and tackle shops nearby.

Cayuga Lake is 42,956 acres (67 square miles) with a maximum depth of 435 feet. The 38-mile-long lake is from 1.5 to 3.5 miles wide and has steep sides at the south end and shallow flats at the north end. About 25 percent of Cayuga's total area is less than 20 feet deep. The lake's varied habitat supports many species and excellent warm and cold water fishing. Warm-water species like bass and panfish are self-sustaining through natural reproduction, while trout and salmon are heavily stocked.

Largemouth bass, which have a good population and growth rate, are one of the most sought-after species in the lake. So are smallmouth bass. Because most anglers practice catch-and-release methods, the populations are stable. Each year some five-pound smallmouth are taken. The lake has a small population of northern pike and chain pickerel, and yellow perch that tend to be well-distributed, but small. Thirteen-inch crappie and nine-inch bluegills are common in the shallower north end of the lake. Lake trout, which feed on abundant alewives and smelt, are doing well, while landlocked salmon fishing has been off in recent years. Brown trout fishing is recovering and growth rates are good, while rainbows have some natural reproduction and a stable population. The average rainbow is 17 inches and three pounds.

Fishing tips: After the ice has melted, some browns, landlocked salmon and rainbows are concentrated along the southwest shoreline and can be taken on Rapalas from planer boards. Early May in 30-foot water can also be a great time to troll for these denizens. Spring and early summer is a great time to still-fish for lake trout in shallower waters at dusk. By summer lakers suspend on the east and west shore-lines in waters from 40-90 feet deep.

Crappie anglers should concentrate efforts after ice-out in the shallow bays and coves for some fast action. Fish for pike in June; cast the weed pockets with a live chub or sucker. After spawning in late May, largemouth move deep and south. Some of the best largemouth action of the year takes place in June along weed points where fish suspend in three to four feet of water. Cast crankbaits of chrome and blue or Texas worm-rigs. As the summer wears on and the water temperatures rise, largemouth continue southward when jigging and plastic worms will work.

Smallmouth angling holds up until mid-summer and gets hot again in mid-September. They are tough to find, often hovering near deep water. In the fall, smallmouth come in to feed along the shorelines in 15-feet waters. Work rocky points with jigs and twister tails.

Nature: About 10,000 years ago this area was covered by a glacier. The powerful ice mass moved on a north-south axis, deepening several stream valleys that also run north and south. When blocked at the ends by moraines, which are gravel deposits, these glacial valleys became the Finger Lakes. The valleys oriented to the east and west were not affected as much because the glaciers ran across them, rather than through them. These valleys which were at the higher elevation than the lakes are called *"hanging valleys."* When the glaciers melted, the east-west stream immediately started carving out the Taughannnock gorge. The stream eroded tons of bedrock, cutting through the layers of shale at rates up to one foot per year, gradually moving the location of the falls westward to its present site.

The falls which occupy this vast gorge are now part of the delta where the stream and the lake meet. A hard-working stream is still moving the falls upstream. Constant wetting and drying, freezing and thawing have carved out the gorge walls to a circular shape, creating an amphitheater-like area. The 215-foot falls is higher than Niagara, making this one of the highest falls east of the Mississippi.

Insider tips: Take a scenic drive around the lake—and stop at a few wineries or the Cayuga Nature Center—when camping at the park. Fishing and the falls are the primary reasons people visit the park. Annual events at the park include a concert series. The regional office for the Finger Lakes state parks region is at the park. Camper recreation and nature programs are offered.

Allan H. Treman State Marine Park

Land: 91 acres Water: Cayuga Lake, 399 boat slips.

Allan H. Treman State Marine Park offers mooring, boating and fishing access to the southern end of Cayuga Lake, the longest of the 11 Finger Lakes.

Seasonal slips are assigned annually by lottery. Applications hand-delivered or postmarked Jan. 1 through the 15th are included in the lottery. Applications postmarked before the first of January are not considered. Obviously, seasonal slips are very popular at this marina.

The park has 30 transient boat slips, 30 dry slips rented by the season, an eight-lane launching ramp, picnic areas, playing fields, pay phone, hot showers, marine sewage pumpout and access to the Barge Canal. Many slips also have 20 or 30 amp electrical hook-ups.

Since the mid-1960s, the southwest corner of Cayuga Lake has become a recreational center. The city of Ithaca developed nearby facilities for swimming, ice skating, baseball and exercise in nearby Cass Park. In 1976, the marina was named Allan H. Treman State Marine Park to honor a distinguished former chairman of both the Finger Lakes State Parks Commission and the State Council of Parks. A memorial grove of trees was planted as a reminder of Mr. Treman's contributions to state parks and the city of Ithaca.

Information and Activities

Allan H. Treman State Marine Park
c/o Robert Treman State Park
R.D. #10
Ithaca, NY 14850
(607) 272-1460, summer
(607) 272-3440, winter

Directions: On North Route 89 (Park Road) in Ithaca.

Emergency numbers: Park police, (800) 255-3577; Ambulance, (607) 273-8000.

Marina: The park office contains plenty of marine-based information. For example, there are posters and brochures about navigational aids, boating rules, equipment requirements, the canal system, boating safety and bits and pieces of information about general boating.

An ice machine and pay phone are at the park office.

The wide marina is comprised of long wooden docks with many types of boats bobbing at their moorings. You'll find sailboats, powerboats and yachts in the marina and plying the long lake.

Near the rest room and along parts of the park are benches from which visitors can watch busy sailors fiddle with their craft or gaze at the hilly shoreline.

Also in the Ithaca area are charter-boat operators, learn-to-sail schools, marine services, boat rentals and fishing information.

Day-use areas: Patches of mowed open spaces contain picnic shelters and pedestal grills.

Nearby state parks: Robert H. Treman State Park (Rt. 13, 1.5 miles

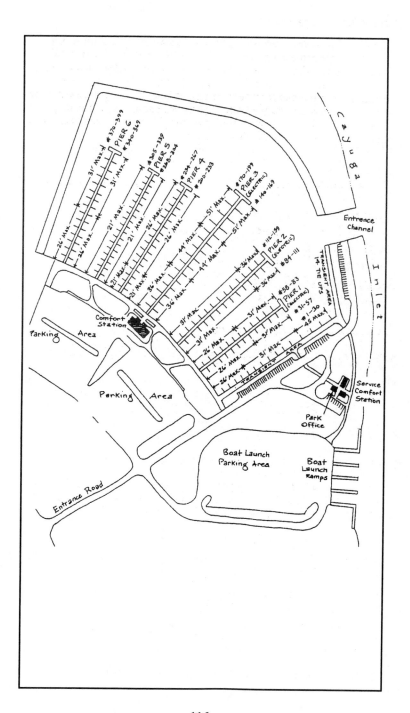

south of Ithaca); Buttermilk Falls State Park (Rt. 13, south of Ithaca); Cayuga Lake State Park (Rt. 89, three miles east of Seneca Falls) and Taughannock Falls State Park (Rt. 89, eight miles north of Ithaca).

Insider tips: Remember the narrow window of time for the slip lottery. Skullers can often be seen gliding across the lake near the shorelines.

The Cass Park ice rink, in a gray dome-like building, is near the marina. There is a fee to launch your boat at the park.

Robert H. Treman State Park

Land: 1,070 acres Water: Enfield Creek and Fishkill Creek

Deep cool gorges, a natural swimming pool, large waterfalls, grist mill and scenic hiking are the reasons thousands of visitors come to Robert H. Treman State Park. The gorge park has two main recreation areas and more than 2.25 miles of scenic trails, 12 waterfalls, numerous milky cascades, quiet pools and fascinating rock strata. The tallest of the waterfalls is the 115-foot Lucifer Falls. The most spectacular portion of the glen is in the upper quarter-mile, where the massive grandeur has been the setting of many early Western and Alaskan cinema productions. From the starting point in the upper part to the lower end and back is nearly five-miles-long.

Enfield Glen is a plunging two-mile-long gorge, more than 11,000 years in the making. Its scenic falls and sheer rock walls serve as a focal point of the park. Through the gorge rushes Enfield Creek, which makes flumes, chutes and rocky cascades over ledges and steps of rock. Along the foamy creek are three large falls and many smaller falls from the mid-section to the upper area.

The term "glen" is an old Scottish Gaelic word simply meaning valley. Typically it refers to a wide gentle valley, often of shade and gentle meadows. But used in this part of the state, glen means gorge, of which Enfield is one of the finest.

Nature buffs will enjoy Enfield Glen and its unique ecosystem. The gorge is actually two glens interwoven. The wide, deep section with forested slopes was carved by a strong flowing creek during the long period between glacier visits. The more rugged sections of the gorge were eroded by the creek during the shorter period following the last glacier. Places where the stream's course is slightly different and referred to as "interglacial" regions. This is a scenic place of complex plant and animal communities, and stunning geological features.

Information and Activities

Robert H. Treman State Park
R.D. No. 10
Ithaca, NY 14850
(607) 273-3440

Directions: In Tompkins County, five miles south of Ithaca. Both park entrances are off Rt. 327. A pay phone and drink machine are next to the park office. Special notes: In-line skating is restricted. No bikes on trails. Swimming in guarded designated areas only.

Emergency numbers: Park police, (800) 255-3577; Ambulance, (607) 273-8000.

Campground: Like nearby Buttermilk, Treman was not originally designed for camping. But by the 1950s, when campers became popular, these and other older parks squeezed in a campground where they could. Therefore, some of the camping sites are narrow, rocky and not very private.

Treman has 11 electrical sites, which are popular with RVers, among its 72 sites. Also popular is the small playground near the camp entrance that includes climbers, five swings and a teeter-totter. A picnic shelter is also near this day-use area at the campground.

Sites 9-11 are nestled under towering pines and along the hard-surfaced road. Many of the sites at Treman are wedged against the hillside on varying elevations. Sites 1-6 are best for small pop-up campers along a ridge above a pleasant day-use area and near the showerhouse. Sites 12 and 13 are also near the play area. Some sites in the 30s back up to a natural area. A few grassy and shady sites are 20-24. Site 37 is near the brick showerhouse and day-use area that has a ball diamond. Sites in the 40s are sunny and breezy. A small creek tracks behind sites in the 50s. Firewood is sold at the park office.

Cabins: Fourteen rough-sawn cabins form a small colony not far from the creek and swimming area. The cabins are available from mid-May to mid-October and the advance reservation system charges a small fee. Cabins 1-13 are one-room units with cots that sleep four people, refrigerator, outdoor picnic table and grills with the unit, and have a nearby public showers and toilets. Cabin 14 has three rooms (two bedrooms, kitchen and bathroom) and sleeps up to six people. This larger cabin has six cots, refrigerator, range top for cooking, sink, table and chairs, and a flush toilet. Hot showers are at the public shower building. Cabin 5, like all the cabins, is attractive, just off the shady roadway.

Day-use areas: One hallmark at Treman State Park is the inviting mowed open spaces perfect for informal field games, family gatherings and picnics. Volleyball and Frisbee are the most popular activities. Lush rolling hills and mixed forests outline many day-use spaces. The park operates two reservable picnic shelters.

Swimming: A section of the Enfield Stream is partially dammed each summer, creating a natural swimming pool. The designated area is watched over by lifeguards and at the lower end of the park. The swimming area opens in mid-June.

Hiking: In the spring, pink and white trillium line the Gorge Trail (2.25 miles) from which you can see and hear the rushing creek. The deep gorge has massive walls that are increasingly coated with many forms of delicate plant life. This well-used trail routes hikers up hill from the lower park to the upper end, and the Rim Trail (2.25 miles), brings hikers back along the south edge of the gorge. Much of the hike is along Enfield Creek, which is a 600-descent. With hemlock overhead and the constant rush of the creek, you will climb several stairways and pass smaller falls that are no more than 100 yards apart. Along this series of small falls, look for cracks and joints in the rock strata.

As you hike you will actually pass through two gorges. One is very old. The lower section of the glen is relatively wide and forested, the result of carving waters that occurred between two glacial periods. The upper section of the glen is more recent, having been cut by the last passing ice age. Therefore it is more rugged. The two gorges come together at the impressive Lucifer Falls. This 4.5-mile hike is one of the most scenic in western New York. All trails close Nov. 10th.

Fishing: Native rainbows and browns run up stream to the fordway. Landlocked salmon are also in the system. Cayuga Lake is nearby and offers excellent lake fishing.

Nature: Interpretive naturalists travel to the park to put on programs. Check with the park office for scheduled themed hikes and outdoor education programs.

Enfield Mill: At the upper end of the park, about three miles away, is a clapboard grist mill that was built in 1839 to replace one that burned to the ground. The large grist mill was operated until 1917 by John G. Kuhns.

Robert H. Treman purchased the mill in 1916 and his wife gave it to the state on April 2, 1920. Inside the creaking, timber-frame mill are examples of old millstones, and heavy milling equipment that was used to grind corn and wheat. Oak pins were used in the heavy frame construction and some of the main floor beams are 14 inches square and 36 feet long, each hand-hewned from a single log. The mill was part of an agricultural hamlet known as Enfield Falls, where settlers and homesteaders built a small community.

The second floor of the mill, which is next to a lovely cascade and stream, offers visitors a chance to see the large grinding mechanisms. Also here are bits and pieces of era tools, bins, shakers, separators and wide drive belts. The top floor has the heavy gears and the powertrain. From the blurry nine-over-six windows you can hear and see the small falls rushing below. An inviting creek-side day-use area is next to the bulky old mill that is open all summer.

Nearby state parks: Buttermilk Falls State Park (Rt. 13, south of Ithaca); Allan H. Treman State Marine Park (Rt. 89, north of Ithaca); Taughnnock Falls State Park (Rt. 89, 8 miles north of Ithaca); Fillmore Glen State Park (Rt. 38, one mile south of Moravia).

Insider tips: Allan H. Treman State Marine Park is five miles away, complete with 399 slips and eight launching ramps into Cayuga Lake. The combined 4.5-mile Rim and Gorge trail at Robert H. Treman makes for one of the most beautiful gorge hikes in the state. Bring your bathing suit for a dip in refreshing—make that cold!— Enfield Creek. Be sure to ask for a copy of the five-panel historical brochure entitled, "Robert H. Treman State Park: The Hamlet of Enfield Falls."

Watkins Glen State Park
Land: 764 acres   Water: Glen Creek, small lakes

Watkins Glen is one of the nation's most treasured natural features. It's also the oldest and best known state park in the Finger Lakes region. The 1.5-mile-long path through the glen has left generations spellbound as they descend 600 feet to a rocky stream, past 19 waterfalls and beneath towering 200-foot cliffs. You simply won't find a prettier place in the state of New York.

The impressive gorge is near the head of Seneca Lake, the deepest of the Finger Lakes, in the village of Watkins Glen. It was named for its founder, Dr. Samuel Watkins, a native of England. Watkins visited the area in 1788, finding the area inhabited by peaceful and civilized Iroquois Indians. The tract of land Watkins claimed included the state park and considerable surrounding lands.

The park consists of two parts. The section west of the railroad bridge extends back four miles and is the older geologic portion. The eastern section, the part most visited by tourists, extends 1.5 miles from Franklin Street to the N.Y.C.R.R., rises 700 feet in elevation and contains 832 steps. This part of the gorge was formed since the mile-thick Wisconsin ice sheet disappeared. The deep canyon and cliffs range from 100 to 300 feet high and were cut by a stream that can be seen at the main entrance.

The glen is broken from section to section into cascades and pools of great beauty. The small rocky stream is still cutting deeper into the colorful rocks. Weathering has not had time to broaden the gorge to any noticeable extent, leaving the cliff walls sheer and tall, sometimes overhanging the rushing stream. Plan to spend at least a half-day on the gorge trail looking at the stream falls and ancient rock formations that have been changing and shaping the glen for 350,000 years.

The fabulous gorge opened to the public in 1863 by Monvalden Ells, a journalist from Elmira. The area was privately owned and operated as a tourist resort until the state of New York purchased the property in 1906 for just over $46,000. Since 1924, the park has been open and managed by the state parks division and visitors have been marveling at the sculptured chasm and shimmering waterfalls ever since.

Information and Activities

Watkins Glen State Park
P.O. Box 304
Watkins Glen, NY 14891
(607) 535-4511

Directions: In the village of Watkins Glen on Franklin Street. The park office is near the south entrance.

Emergency number: 911 system.

Campground: The 305-site, non-electric campground and large swimming pool are at the south entrance, away from the busy main entrance and gift shop. Immediately upon entering the campground is a lovely stone picnic shelter, with a slate roof and gracefully arched windows and columns. Near the shelter are significant day-use and picnic areas equipped with tables, grills and play apparatus, including a sandbox. The campground is open mid-May to mid-October; the rest of the park is open all year.

Watkins Glen is one of the biggest and most popular state park campgrounds. It's also a mature and well-planned facility. Firewood and a telephone are at the camp office.

Loop 1-105 (Cayuga and Mohawk areas) is a heavily shaded set of loops with mature pencil-straight pines overhead. The plentiful grass and gravel sites are sometimes narrow and dotted with pine trees. The mature woodland camping area is pleasant and gently rolling. Sites 19, 21 and 23 are perched on a ridgeline, while sites 25 and 26 would be terrific sites for two families to share. The brick bathhouse is near site 32. Sites 44, 45 and 48 are notched into the woods and popular. If you have a big RV rig, consider site 48.

This loop is busy, but it doesn't seem overwhelming due to the visual barriers and large trees that frame the views. Site 51, in the Mohawk area, is a pull-through and close to a small playground with a spider-like climber. Site 54 is perfect for a long RV rig. If you need a level site, check the pads in the 60s. Site 68 offers privacy and is near the showerhouse. There's plenty of privacy in the sites in the 70s, which offer an obscured view of the small manmade lake. Sites in the 80s and 90s are in a scenic grove of pines. A blanket of aromatic brown pine needles often covers these sites. Site 99 is one of the finest sites in the campground.

The Oneida Village loop is sites 106-153. The sites are under mature trees and placed on different elevations along the hard-surfaced road. The pads are firm and grassy, and you will find ground-level shrubs

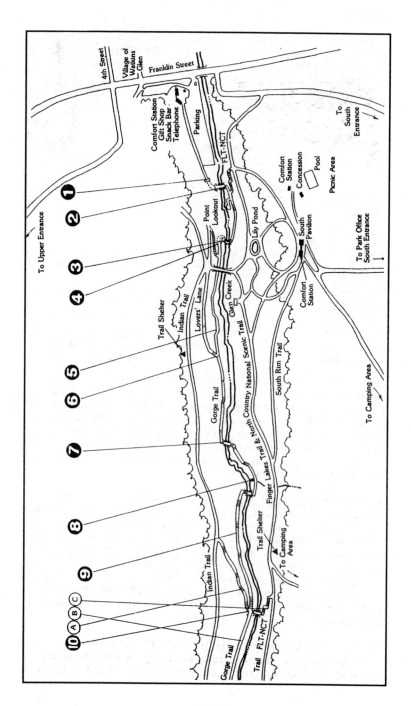

and vegetation separating sites. Site 120 is a good choice if rain threatens, due to its plentiful gravel cover. Many of the sites are notched out of the woods. This loop is a woodsy camping experience. Sites 135-138 receive some midday sunlight. Sites in the 140s are on a higher elevation and have a view of other sites and the surrounding woodlands. There are nine prime sites in this loop.

The Seneca and Onondaga loops are sites 153-203 and 204 -251. Their entrance is across from the day-use area. Again, these loops have plenty of mature trees, but also considerable ground cover and shrubs that offer visual barriers, privacy and shade.

The Seneca loop, sites 153-203, is gently rolling and heavily wooded. The popular loop has sites of different sizes and levelness. Most of the sites are hard-packed gravel and many can easily fit a large RV. For a deep tent site, check out sites 217, 219, 221 and 223. They are down winding paths, about 50 yards off the park road. Site 239 is one of the prettiest sites under an airy canopy of pines. This loop is my favorite.

Sites on the outside of the loop in the Onondaga area are backed up against natural areas. Sites on the inside of the loop are wider and deeper. These loops, with private and rolling sites, tend to attract mostly tent campers. Sites in the 160s are near the showerhouse, while sites in the 170s and 180s are often colonized by colorful tents under towering pine trees. Site 186, which is sunny, is great for a large RV rig. Sites in 190s vary in size; some can accommodate trailers and motor homes.

The Tuscarora loop, sites 252 - 305, is the end loop and quiet and flatter that the others. The farther you go in the loop, the bigger and deeper the sites. Sites on the outside of the loop are backed up against a natural area. All of the sites in the loop are large enough for medium-sized RV rigs. Sites 265 and 266 are open, near the bathhouse and close to a mowed open space. This area also has a well-equipped playground. Family campers who choose sites in the 270s can easily look across the open space and keep an eye on their children playing at the playground. Site 281, under a grove of pines and on a knoll, is a favorite in this section of the campground.

Timespell: Each evening at Watkins Glen from May to October, the outdoor sound and light show called Timespell is presented. The unique theatrical experience is performed in the gorge and allows visitors to sample the sights and sounds of 45 million centuries to the present.

"The time is one million years ago. You're standing on a ledge deep inside an enormous gorge. Suddenly the roar of a prehistoric beast pierces the darkness. The gorge erupts in brilliant color and spectacular sound, as images from the past appear fleetingly on the rock wall

before you."—*from the Timespell brochure.*

You enter the past through a tunnel and 83 steps into the gorge. As you climb a stone stairway, you are surrounded by haunting music. Lights play on the shimmering waterfalls and rocky crags around you. Narrators take you back to the earth's beginnings, 4.5 billion years ago.

You will hear howling wind, the thunder of a volcano, the groan of the land shifting beneath you...it is the dawn of time. The state-of-the-art technology and engaging narration provide a wonder learning and entertainment experience. The show also details the ice age, history of the Seneca Indians and a time-line-like narration that discusses the creation of the beautiful gorge. *For reservations, call (800) 853-7735.*

Day-use areas: A fashionable restaurant, called the Bandstand, has colorful outdoor seating and features a menu of ice cream, grill foods, coffee, curly fries, candy and soft drinks. It's next to the Pavilion Gift Shop just inside the main entrance near the cavernous opening of the glen.

Recreation building: In the campground, a tan wooden building is surrounded by a ball backstop, four-square court, basketball goals, play apparatus and picnic areas. Some recreational programs are offered from the building in the summer and recreational equipment is loaned to campers. A nature trailhead is near the recreational building.

Gift shop: Inside the modern shop are souvenirs, T-shirts, film, hats, jewelry, books, colorful plastic toys for the kids, collectable clowns, name tags, plush animals, wooden post cards and lots more.

Swimming pool: The Olympic-size pool is surrounded by a fence and flanked by redwood bathhouses, rest rooms and concession. The pool is guarded and has a broad sunning deck and small courtyard-like space near the entrance. The pool has three diving boards, two-foot-deep kiddy wading pool and four lifeguard chairs. The pool is surrounded by a sprawling day-use area and connected to the campground by a hard-surfaced road.

Hiking/Nature: Aside from the gorge hike, the park has access to the Finger Lakes Trail and the North Country National Scenic Trail.

You must hike the Gorge Trail to view the glen scenery and learn about the gorge that has been 350,000 years in the making. This trail (and others) is accessible from the main, south and upper entrances. The bulk of park visitors walk uphill from the main entrance (near the gift shop and restaurant) and return. Visitors can also use the shuttle bus to the upper entrance and walk the 1.5 miles back down to the main entrance. Guided hikes are conducted by staff at scheduled times.

Before you start the hike, pick up a park map that has a simple self-guided trail and narrative. Descriptions will match numbers along the trail.

The main entrance and other tunnels in the gorge were hand-cut in the rock through otherwise impassable sections of the gorge in the early part of the 20th century. As you hike the scenic trail, you pass the 52-feet-tall Sentry Bridge where a water wheel once powered a grist mill. At learning station No. 3 is a high waterfall that has eroded rock and formed a deep pool. During this eroding process the waterfall has weathered away the thin shale rock in the cliff wall, allowing visitors to walk behind the gushing—almost mesmerizing-waterfall.

After emerging from the Spiral Tunnel at No. 4, Cliff Path leads under the Suspended Bridge where a three-story house was once perched. During the great flood of 1935, waters rose to within five feet of the 85-foot-tall bridge. As you walk deeper into the gorge, observant visitors will notice the micro-climate that helps interesting moisture-loving ferns, mosses and certain trees flourish.

Also notice the sun-drenched and dry ledges, home of another unique plant community including drought-resistant grasses and wildflowers.

Past station No. 6 there are places where an ocean bottom left ripples in the sand and silt. These rock formations are more than 370 million years old.

There are many places where you can see the evidence of rock form-ing—places where sand turned to sandstone, silt to siltstone and clay became crumbly, weak shale. Look for joints and cracks in the walls that have been caused by the mighty geological pressures.

At the Central Cascade (No. 7), water plunges more than 60 feet into deep pools that are in a constant swirl. Other points of interest include Glen of Pools, Rainbow Falls, Spiral Gorge and a cliff called "Pillar of Beauty."

The scenic Gorge Trail has more than 800 stone steps and they can be slippery from the spray of waterfalls and cascades. Be careful and wear proper footwear along this beautiful walk. From this trail is the best way to view the gorge.

Insider tips: Bring your bike to ride the many park roads, especially at the south end or in the spread-out campground. The village of Watkins Glen is where road racing was reborn after World War II. A $4 million racing facility is a few miles southwest. Two of the world's largest salt-producing plants are in the area. The vein of salt they work is 1,800 feet below the surface. The park has two manmade ponds.

PHONE	PARK	Tent/trailers sites (h = hookups, e = electricity)	Trailer dump	Showers	Camper recreation	Cabins	Food	Store	Picnic tables	Shelters (• reservations)	Swimming beach (• bath house)	Swimming pool (• bath house)	Recreation programs (• performing arts)	Hiking	Biking	Nature trails	Fishing	Playground	Golf (•clubhouse)	Tennis	Pond or lake (• power boats ok)	River or stream (• power boats ok)	Launching site (• hand launch only)	Boat rental	Marina (• anchorage)	Pump out	Ice skating (•rentals)	Cross-country skiing (• rentals)	Snowmobiling	Sled slopes
607 387-7041	**FINGER LAKES REGION**																													
607 955-3482	Bonavista Vista Golf Course	▲	△	▲	△		▲		▲	△	▲		△	△			▲	△	•		△	△	△	△	•	△		△	△	△
607 237-5761	Buttermilk Falls	▲e	▲	▲	▲	▲	▲		▲	△	▲	▲•	△	△			▲	△			△		△					△	△	
315 568-5163	Cayuga Lake								▲	△	▲			△			▲				▲•		△		▲	▲				
315 947-5205	Fair Haven Beach	▲	△	▲		▲			▲	△	▲•		△	△			▲	△			△		▲•		•	△				
315 497-0130	Fillmore Glen	△	△	▲	△				▲•	△	•			△			▲	△			△		△							
315 536-3666	Keuka Lake								▲	•	▲•			△			▲				▲•		△		△	△				
607 582-6246	Lodi Point								▲	△	•			△			▲	△			▲•		△		△	△				
315 364-8884	Long Point								△	△	•		△	△			▲	△			▲•	△	△		△					
607 359-2767	Pinnacle	△							▲	•	▲•			△			▲	△			▲•				•				△	
315 585-6392	Sampson	▲e	△	▲	△		▲		▲	•	▲•		△	△			▲	△			▲•		△		▲	▲		△	△	△
315 789-2331	Seneca Lake								▲	△	•			△			▲				▲•		△		▲	▲				
716 335-8111	Harriet Hollister Spencer								▲				△	△	△		△					△						▲	△	
716 335-8111	Stony Brook	△	△	▲	△	▲	▲		▲	△•	▲•		△	△•		△	▲	△•			△•	△•	△			△			△•	
607 387-6739	Taughannock Falls**	▲e	△	▲	△	▲	▲		▲	△•	▲•		△	△•	△•	△•	▲	△	△•		•	△	△	△	•	△	•	•	△	△
607 739-0034	Soaring Eagles Golf /Mark Twain State Park			▲					△								▲		•		△							△		
607 272-1460	Allan H. Treman								△								▲				△	△	▲		△	△		△		
607 273-3440	Robert H. Treman	△	△	▲					▲				△	△			▲					△						△		△
607 535-4511	Watkins Glen	△	△	▲	△		▲		▲	△•	•	▲•	△	△		△	▲	△			•	△	△				•	△		△
	STATE HISTORIC SITE																													
716 924-5848	Ganondagan												△	△																

△ Availability of service or facility   ▲ Handicapped accessible   * Has ski slopes with tow.

** Walk trails outlining the history and culture of the Seneca who lived in this 17-century Iroquois town.

131

Genesee Region

You'll find the *"Grand Canyon of the East,"* at Letchworth State Park in the heart of the Genesee Region. The 600-foot gorge, three gorgeous waterfalls, history, Glen Iris Inn and 42 miles of trails make it one of the most popular state parks in New York. The Glen Iris Inn has been open since 1914, offering elegant lodging and dining amid a breathtaking natural setting.

Although Letchworth State Park gets much of the attention in this region, there are eight other gems nearby.

Some of the state's best beachfront and camping is at Hamlin Beach, Lakeside Beach and Darien Lakes state parks.

This scenic section of the state offers a wonderful blend of history, beauty, natural wonders and vacation possibilities that will not soon be forgotten.

Genesee Region

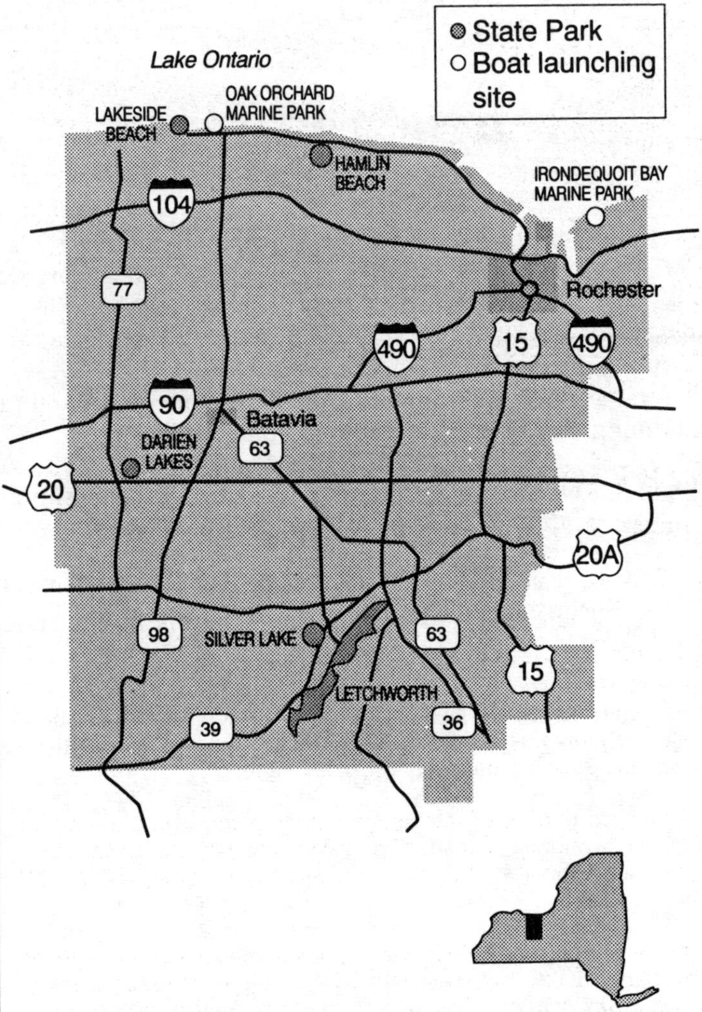

Legend:
- ● State Park
- ○ Boat launching site

Lake Ontario

LAKESIDE BEACH

OAK ORCHARD MARINE PARK

HAMLIN BEACH

IRONDEQUOIT BAY MARINE PARK

104

77

Rochester

490

15

490

90

Batavia

DARIEN LAKES

63

20

20A

98

SILVER LAKE

63

LETCHWORTH

15

39

36

Darien Lake State Park
Land: 1,846 acres   Water: 12-acre lake

Darien Lake State Park was a dream come true for dairy farmer Henry Kohlhagen. In 1963, Kohlhagen dreamed that his rolling land would one day become a state park where all people could come to camp, fish and enjoy the outdoors. He thought his wooded ravines, stream and woods would be a perfect park. So in April 1963, the state arranged a purchase of the land, including the 12-acre lake. Since then, the park has grown to 1,846 acres, 1,500 acres of which are multiple-use areas and open for small and big game hunting.

The developed portion of the park has three picnic areas, a lake for fishing and swimming, a small picnic island and day-use areas. Also, there are two reservable shelters with electricity for groups of 75-150 people.

Campers will enjoy the 150-site campgrounds and the proximity to the nearby Darien Lake Amusement Park. The high-energy amusement park has a Sky coaster, giant wheel, concerts, Adventureland, water rides, Fifties stage, gift shops, Thunder Rapids log flume, The Viper,

The Predator and many other rides and activities.

The park is gently rolling with elevations ranging from 855 feet to 1.030 feet above sea level. Most of the trails are through woodlands and flat grass fields.

Information and Activities

Darien Lake State Park
10289 Harlow Road
Darien Center, NY 14040
(716) 547-9242

Directions: The park is one-quarter mile north of Route 20 on Harlow Road, three miles from the Darien Lake Amusement Park. The brick park office behind the small beach is flanked by two flagpoles.

Emergency number: 911 system.

Campground: Darien Lake State Park has 150 camping sites with 46 having electricity. Pets are allowed in the A camping loop. The campground is open weekends from May to mid-June and seven days from mid-June to September.

In the A loop, site 1 is near an old orchard. Each of the sites has steel fire rings, gravel pads and picnic tables. A basketball goal and small group of play equipment are in the loop. Sites 7-13 are next to the open space day-use area. Site 46 is adjacent to the basketball goal and half court. Sites 47-54 are open and sunny along a two-track gravel road. These sites are good for large RV units if you like the sun.

A mix of beech and maple trees shade most of the other sites. Sites 25, 26 and 28 are shady and pleasant. Site 30 is like a walk-in site. You will park on a small gravel pad and walk down into a large grassy campsite that is 50 feet square. Site 52 is at the edge of an often dry creekbed. Sites 35 and 36 are next to the bathhouse. Sites 38 and 39 are excellent for medium to large RV units.

In camping area B, sites are mostly shady and a small set of play equipment is near the entrance. Site 60 has a view of the small playground, while site 62 is near a water hydrant. In fact, all of the sites in the 60s and 70s are great for popup campers. Sites 74 and 76 are small pull-throughs near an often dry creek. Site 82 is a CAP site. Sites in the high 80s and 90s are very open and rarely are full. Also, watch for sites that are uneven in this area. Sites in the 100s are totally in the open, with no shade nearby. Site 125 allows RV rigs to back in under some

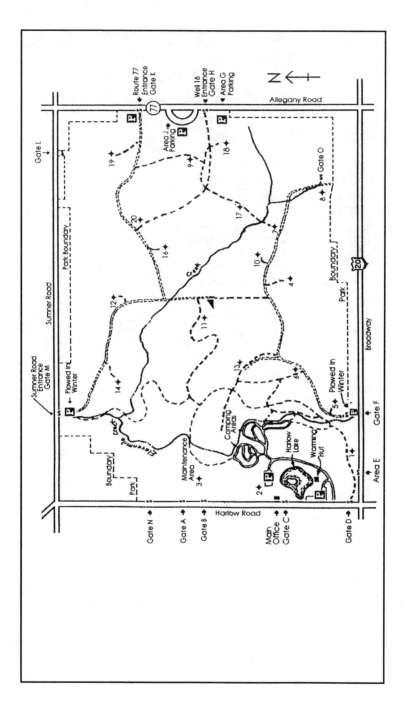

N ←

Allegany Road

Route 77 Entrance Gate K

Well 18 Entrance Gate H

Area G Parking

Area J Parking

Gate L

Summer Road

Park Boundary

Summer Road Entrance Gate M

Plowed In Winter

Park Boundary

Gate O

Broadway

Plowed In Winter

Gate F

Area E

Gate D

Gate C

Main Office

Harlow Road

Gate B

Gate A

Gate N

Boundary

Park

Maintenance Area

Camping Area

Harlow Lake

Warming Hut

Eleven Mile Creek

Creek

SPECIAL FISHING
REGULATIONS
DUE TO BLACK BASS
RESTOCKING PRGM.

trees. It is also next to the bathhouse. Site 130 is attractive with one side heavily vegetated and the other side open and airy.

According to staff, camping sites 60-84 are the most requested, because they are shady. Hydrants are painted white for easy visibility.

Day-use areas: The park has two reservable shelters (shelter No. 1 can accommodate up to 100), horseshoe courts, basketball goals, ball backstop and a picnic area on a small kidney-shaped island that is accessed by a small arched footbridge.

A drinking fountain is near the foot of the bridge where fishermen often are found trying their luck. Also in this area are a small playground and picnic shelter. A few bluebird nesting boxes are scattered throughout the park.

Swimming: The sandy, 175-yard-long beach is open each Memorial Day weekend (full-time in mid-June) and is outfitted with three lifeguard chairs. The water is divided by orange and white buoys. Small children will enjoy the shallow water. The entire shoreline around the 12-acre lake is gentle and safe.

Hiking: The park features 19 miles of trails around the day-use areas and campground. The trails may also be used for cross-country skiing. Most of the trails lie east of the developed area. The park brochure has a small trail map.

Fishing: The lake is stocked with largemouth bass and shoreline access to the small lake is convenient. A popular shoreline fishing site is from the day-use area across from the check-in station. Anglers can fish around the entire lake. Use live bait for panfish, especially from the riprap section of the shoreline.

Hunting: It's allowed in season.

Insider tip: An amusement park is nearby.

Hamlin Beach State Park
Land: 1,100 acres   Water: Lake Ontario

French explorers passed scenic Hamlin Beach en route to the western end of Lake Ontario and beyond in the early 1600s. But it wasn't until late 1687 that Frenchman Marquis de Denonville landed at nearby Irondequoit Bay to capture and destroy Indian villages. Fortunately, most of the Indians saw his advance and escaped, losing villages and crops. Twenty years later, Fort deSables was built to establish friendly trade with the Seneca Indians. In 20 more years the French and Indian War broke out, followed by the American Revolution in 1776 and other hostilities that lasted until 1886, when the British surrendered and peace was declared. The region has a colorful history of fur trading, Indian war and pioneer settlers.

Over the years land speculators came and went until the town of Hamlin was established and Monroe County was settled and organized in the early 1800s. The first recorded development of the lakeshore property was by a man named Billings in 1807. He planted an orchard near Sandy Creek. Just down the road, the Knapp family soon settled on the land that is now a state park. These early settlers quickly learned that the large lake tempered the fertile shoreline and that fruit trees flourished. In fact, the Hamlin area is still one of the finest orchard growing areas in the country.

Originally a county park, Hamlin Beach State Park was dedicated in 1938 after six years of Civilian Conservation Corps construction. Later, work during the postwar years on an extension of the Lake Ontario State Parkway brought more and more visitors to the park to enjoy top-quality camping, swimming, fishing and picnicking. In 1962, the park increased to 1,100 acres, and in 1967 the wonderful 264-site campground was built.

Devil's Nose is a prominent bluff at the west end of the park that has been noted on maps since 1802. No one knows how it got its name, but it has been dangerous over the years. The nose was once 150 feet tall and reached three-quarters of a mile northward into the lake. The jagged and rocky reef that extends beyond the nose is more than 1.5 miles long and has been avoided by sailors for years. Although tales of sunken ships are unsubstantiated, ships have been stuck on the large shoal. According to local legend, the caves and passages near the geologic feature were used by smugglers during the Prohibition. High water and erosion have closed the area to the public, but it is still an easily viewed landmark from anywhere along the park's shoreline.

Information and Activities

Hamlin Beach State Park
Hamlin, NY 14464
(716) 964-2462

Directions: From Rt. 18, take Rt. 19N through the village of Hamlin. The park is 25 miles west of Rochester on the Lake Ontario State Parkway.

Check the bulletin board just past the main contact station for a listing of special events. The park office, which is in a house-like building, has a display of six owl mounts.

Campground: The multi-loop campground has 264 sites that are equipped with fire rings and picnic tables. Each loop has a comfort station and the group camping area is at the end of the camping spur. Some sites have electrical hook-ups. Water hydrants are evenly spaced around the quiet loops. Hamlin Beach has some of the finest campsites in Western New York.

A small laundry, with eight washing machines, is next to the red camp store. The rustic store features ice cream, penny candy, soft drinks, firewood, snack foods and basic grocery items for campers. Also at the store are charcoal starter fluid, insect repellent and some toys.

Next to the campground store is a recreation building that operates during the summer. Games and recreation equipment are available when it is open. Inside are some picnic tables, wall posters and a few game tables. A ball field and yellow basketball goals (there is about 100 yards between each of the goals!) are nearby. A bulletin board is in front of the recreation hall with posting of upcoming special programs and park rules.

Loop A is a wooded and gently rolling loop with most sites of grass and gravel. Most of the sites are separated by a screen of vegetation. Pets are allowed in this loop which is 90 percent shady. Site 15 is a terrific site, while nearby sites 17 and 18 can be wet after rain. The outside sites along this pleasant loop are backed up against a natural area. Sites in the 20s are on higher ground and near the reddish-brown bathhouse that has two shower stalls. Site 32 is open and sunny.

Loop B, sites 40-73, is also a loop for pet owners and shady like Loop A. Site 40, under a solitary pine, is near the entrance and very pleasant. Sites 46 and 48 are excellent for a big rig, offering extra space around them. Site 50 is under a grove of a dozen straight pines that litter the ground with red needles. All of the sites in the loop are pleasant, private and heavily graveled for good drainage. The Genesee District Conservation Project Nature Trailhead is near this loop.

Loop C, sites 74-137, is shaded by many towering pines. Sites 87-91 are in a grove of pine and airy. Some of the sites have hard packed gravel pads, perfect for medium-sized or larger RV rigs. Site 97 is next to the water hydrant and a terrific, private place to spend a long weekend. In many cases, 30 feet of vegetation separates the sites. Many of the sites are also extra deep or oversized. If you like sun, try site 126. Sites in the 130s are under pines spread out upon the bed of needles that coat the forest floor.

Loop D, sites 138-197, are private, shady, dry and gently rolling. Sites in the 150s are under a pine grove that offers shade and a chance for a cooling breeze. There are a few unleveled sites toward the back of the loop, but most are great for medium-sized RV rigs and tents. Site 178 is next to the water hydrant and steps away from the comfort station. Sites in the 180s are in a grove, while some of the sites in the 190s are more open.

Loop E, sites 198-223, are under a canopy of mixed deciduous trees and pines. Again, sites in this small loop are separated by shrubs and some sites are a smaller than in the other loops. Sites 208 and 209 are

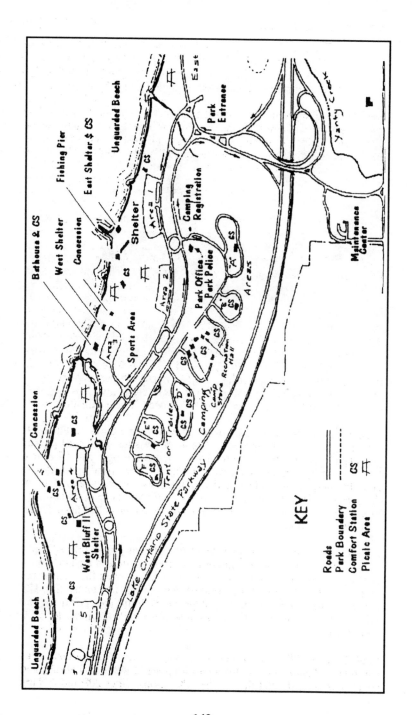

KEY

Roads
Park Boundary
Comfort Station   CS
Picnic Area

perfect for a small camper under a grove of pines. To be near the comfort station choose site 217. Site 220 is wide open, sunny and perfect for big RV rigs.

Loop F, sites 224-264, are toward the end of the spur, near the entrance to the group camping area. Sites in the high 220s and low 230s receive lots of midday sunshine. As you drive farther into the loop, however, it becomes shaded with tall pines. Sites in this loop are medium-sized. Site 245 is a terrific shady site under a small group of pines. A few of the sites in the 250s have a slight incline. These sites are mostly gravel.

Day-use areas: The expansive shoreline is littered with picnic tables and open spaces that have wonderful views of the glistening lake. Each of the day-use areas has parking, rest rooms, grills, picnic tables, play equipment and other amenities. Sometimes Area 5 is closed. The park has four enclosed picnic shelters. Area 4 also has some soccer goals and a playground. Area 5 has a basketball court. Because of the excellent snack bar, Area 4 is always a popular day-use destination.

Swimming: The sandy beach, near Areas 4 and 5, opens in mid-June each year and closes on Labor Day. Visitors can walk along the beach through the entire length of the park.

Hiking: The Tree Trail starts in Area 4 and follows the shoreline. Some of the trees are still labeled. Ask for a self-guided brochure that discusses many species and follow the trail to learn about the natural history of 25 tree species. Tree species include pin oak, sycamore, basswood, hickory, sweet birch, tulip tree, hop hornbeam, black birch, maples, walnut and many others.

The Yanty Creek Nature Trail has a small parking area at its trailhead along the east end of the linear park near the marsh. The trail was built in 1971 and many student groups use it annually. The one-mile-long trail has several natural communities including an old field, marsh, coniferous woods, shrub field, pond and deciduous woodlot. These ecosystems offer visitors an opportunity to observe succession in progress.

The nature trail is divided into roughly six areas. In the old field community, visitors will see a former farm field in secondary growth, filling with large plants and shrubs. Many goldenrod species and lots of Queen Anne's lace thrive near milkweed and fledgling cottonwood trees. The cottonwoods grow best in damp soils with lots of sunlight. The shade they produce allows other trees, such as maple and beech, to establish. Look for horsetails in the field that look like a sapling conifer. Horsetail is also known as scouring rush, because its rough texture was sometimes used to clean pioneers' pots and pans.

Past the field is the marsh, which is fed by Yanty Creek. Here are a mix of oak-hickory near zones where marsh vegetation thrives. Cattails and bulrushes are the major food supply for muskrats and insects. The cattails also provide dense cover and places for the nesting and resting of waterfowl, and lots of noisy red-wing blackbirds. The small pond contains some panfish and pike. Certain areas have water lilies mixed with open water where duckweed sometimes floats. By the way, ducks love duckweed. Rattling kingfishers can sometimes be seen hunting this area, ready to dive in the water for a small fish.

Part of the short hike is in a woodlot of white pine and aspen. These species thrive in the sandy, dry soil that isn't able to support most deciduous varieties. The pine creates a shady forest floor that gets covered by needles, preventing the growth of most herbaceous plants and other pines. Eventually deciduous trees will sprout in this area, but it will take years for the soil conditions to improve. Look for squirrels and chipmunks. Squirrels are often seen busily gathering cones, which they bury in large mounds that may contain 8-10 bushels. When the cones open, the squirrels dine on the exposed seed, and some of the seeds take root.

Also along the walk are shrub fields that have dense thickets of dogwood and viburnum. The manmade pond nearby is slowly filling in due to the action of the plants.

New York State Parks

The small deciduous forest plot is easy to miss. It was planted in the 1930s by the Civilian Conservation Corps and the maple-beech community now thrives. Look at the layers of the climax forest: the canopy, understory, shrub layer and floor. Most of the food in the ecosystem is made in the canopy. The canopy is filled with insects that eat the leaf and their predators. The canopy is productive because it gets the sunlight. One percent of the sunlight that falls on the canopy is trapped for photosynthesis. If the photo energy from one acre was converted to electrical energy, it could power 50 homes.

Fitness Trails: The trails that wind through the day-use areas are called fitness trails and have been set up to benefit everyone visits the park. They are meant to aid guests who are walking, jogging or exercising for physical fitness. There are five trails that are color-coded. Each trail has a sign at the start and finish and at the mid-point.

The Green and White trails start and finish in the southeast corner of the Area 1 parking lot. The Blue Trail (6 miles) starts and finishes in the same parking lot but in the north corner. The Red Trail (8 miles) start and finish is in the northeast corner; and the Yellow Trail (4 miles) start and finish is on the east side of the Area 1 parking lot. All of the trails are marked along the pavement or sidewalk with a bicycle symbol or an arrow. These markers are color-coordinated with the trail color. The fitness trails were built as an Eagle Scout Project in 1991. Boating: Private marinas and sport shops abound in the area.

Fishing: Fishing is allowed in all non-swimming areas. The water off the park has a rocky bottom and lots of excellent structure for small-mouth bass. Spinnerbaits that imitate herring are hot in these waters.

Nature: A bird list is available at the office. The narrow brochure details the natural history of 25 common species including many types of waterfowls (wood duck, mallard, wigeon and coot), bank swallow, common gallinule, Virginia rail, green heron, boblink, song sparrow, great blue heron, black-capped chickadee, marsh wren, wood thrush, belted kingfisher and others.

Special events: Annual events include law enforcement day, hobby cat regatta, arts and crafts festival on Labor Day weekend, triathlon, bike tour and weekly Thursday evening concerts.

Insider tips: In-line skates are allowed in designated areas only. Parking for in-line skating is available in Area 5, a paved road is provided and is 1.25 miles long from start to finish. Check out the brown snack bar in Area 3 that has snacks, ice cream and picnic supplies.

Letchworth State Park
Land: 14,350 acres   Water: Genesee River

The vast region is often called *"The Grand Canyon of the East."* But that phrase barely describes the diverse splendor that awaits visitors. The 17-mile-long gorge carved by the Genesee River has 600-foot cliffs, breathtaking views and dozens of activities, including whitewater rafting, 70 miles of hiking trails, hot air ballooning, cross-country skiing, snowmobiling, camping, history displays and gracious lodging.

The sprawling park has magnificent scenery and dozens of recreational opportunities for all ages. The region's rich history of the Seneca Indians is wonderfully documented in the restored Seneca Council House and museum, and at the grave of legendary Mary Jemison. Cabins and campsites are also popular at the park, and for those who prefer not to "rough it," the Pinewood Lodge with light housekeeping units or the country inn, Glen Iris Inn, offers charming guest rooms and fine dining.

Kids will love the large swimming pools while fishing, biking or lounging can occupy Dad or Mom. Don't forget to check the schedule for a full range of activities that include guided walks, concerts, lectures and arts and crafts sales. Mr. Letchworth is the best-known and largest of the 11 state parks in the Genesee Region.

William P. Letchworth, a businessman, saw the beauty of this land despite recent timbering and set about to buy a large tract and renovated and expanded the house. Letchworth was an ardent conservationist who took up the work of replanting the area with trees and learning about the fascinating history of the Seneca Indians. In fact, Mr. Letchworth was eventually adopted by the Seneca Nation for his wisdom and stewardship of the lands. Visitors should plan to enjoy the splendor of the Middle Falls as Letchworth did. It's easy to see why he called them an iris, which is the greek word for rainbow.

The park hosts more than 900,000 visitors annually.

Information and Activities

Letchworth State Park
1 Letchworth State Park
Castile, NY 14427-1124
(716) 493-3600

Directions: The long state park is 50 miles southeast of Buffalo and 35 miles south of Rochester. Entrances are at Mount Morris, Perry, Castile, Portageville and the Parade Grounds from Rt. 436. The Portageville and Parade Ground entrances are closed in the winter. The visitor center is 15 miles south of the Mount Morris entrance.

Emergency numbers: 911 system or (716) 658-4692.

Campground: All of the 270 camping sites at Letchworth have electric hook-ups. The Highbanks Camping Area is open from May to October and near a 20-station fitness trail. Loops 100 and 200 are designated pet loops. Loops 700 and 800 are more open and often the first choice of RVers. Families like Loop 300 because of the nearby playground, while tent campers often prefer intimate loops 400-600. There is a comfort station/shower building in each loop and each site has a picnic table and fire grill. In a central location are the camp store, laundry and recreation hall.

Loop 300 is fairly open, with little ground vegetation. Medium to large RV rigs can fit in this loop easily. The backside of the 300 loop is shady, high and dry, and in a grove of pines. Site 325 is pleasant and near the recreation building and ball diamond. Site 333 is perfect for a big RV, offering lots of room to maneuver. Site 326 is sunny. Much like the 300 loop, the 400 loop has more pines and fewer sunny sites. Sites 406 and 407 are near the comfort station. Sites 417, 419 and 421 are on high ground. Sites 425 and 435 are private.

The 500 loop has mature trees and a number of sites that have full-day sun. Most sites are level, but check before you park your rig. Water hydrants in this loop are marked to remind campers to not wash clothes or dishes at the spigots. The backside of the loop is against a natural area. Big rigs can fit on site 521.

Loop 700 has plenty of mature trees. If you want to be near the comfort station, check out site 711. The 700 and 800 loops are adjacent to each other. Sites 717 and 721 are deep. Open sites that are big enough for large RV units and with lots of sun in the 700 loop include 718, 720, 735, 737 and 739.

Loop 800 is wooded with the narrow sites separated by low shrubs. Site 825 is deep and grassy. Site 818 has morning sunshine and is near the comfort station. Site 841, between two large pines, also gets some sun during the day. Other sunny sites include 822, 824, 842 and 845. Site 801 is the favorite site in this loop.

Cabins: The park has 82 cabins; some are open year-round, most are open mid-April to mid-December.

All cabins include electric refrigerators, stove, lights, wall outlets, cots with mattresses, table and chairs. Picnic tables and grill are outside. Bring your own bedding, cooking utensils, ice trays, dishes, pail, firewood and garbage bags. There are five cabin areas. *Call (800) 456-CAMP for cabin reservations.*

"A" cabins are in the south end of the park on the west side of the Genesee River in the Lower Falls area. They have a central bathhouse, toilet and laundry building. The cabins accommodate up to six people. These are three-room units with half baths.

"B' cabins also are in the south end of the park on the west side of the Genesee River in the Lower Falls area. There is a central shower, toilet and shower building. Cabins are similar to "A" cabins.

"C" cabins are in the north end on the west side of the Genesee River. Most are three-room models and are open year-round. The log-cabin-style buildings have porches and are heavily wooded. No. 6 and 18 are the most private. Cabin No. 5 is on a lower elevation. Near the bathhouse is a small playground.

"D" cabins are in the south end of the park on the east side of the

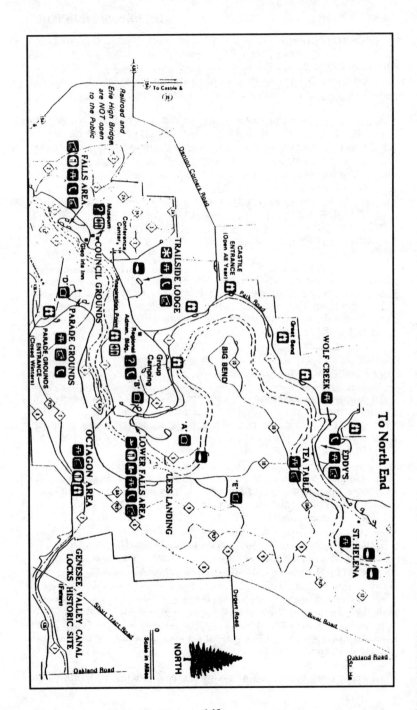

Genesee River and have central toilets and can sleep up to six people.

"E" cabins also are in the south end of the park on the east side of the Genesee River. There are no showers available. Up to four people can stay in the units.

Cabin areas A and C have units accessible to visitors with disabilities.

Glen Iris Inn: The three-story inn with red-brick chimneys is a focal point for many visitors and activities. It was once the personal residence of William Pryor Letchworth. Early in the 1900s efforts were undertaken to restore the inn, room by room. The work uncovered a fireplace in the dining room and other treasures during the painstaking process. Today, the building has been outfitted with reproduction period furniture, a fragrant gift shop, modern kitchen and sprinkler system. The inn has lovely sleeping rooms.

The neatly tended ground, towering pines and nearby museum offer visitors a wonderful place to learn. The inn's dining room is beautiful, appointed with rose-colored dining chairs and carefully set white tableware.

Inside the elegant gift shop with floral carpeting are many fine items including candles, glassware, spices, cards, frilly dolls, tea cups, jams and jellies, T-shirts, wind chimes, wreaths, key chains, Victorian hoop games and many other ornate gift ideas. The shop is next to a sitting room with fine furniture, globe lamps and oil paintings. Also in the sitting room is a large oil portrait of William Pryor Letchworth.

The Pinewood Lodge, which has efficiency units, is a short distance from the inn.

Day-use areas: Overlooks, a wildlife area, four snack bars, camp store, laundry, picnic shelters and day-use areas are scattered through the park. The park has 12 picnic shelters, 10 of which can be reserved for group outings.

Museum: A beautiful white entrance flanked by columns guides you into the impressive stone building that houses lots of information on local history, especially Mary Jemison and Mr. Letchworth. Items on display include bullet molds, letters and photographs, books, period Native American Indian tools, early American firearms, beads, a mastodon skull, organ, high-wheel bicycle, shoes, piano, sewing machines, diorama about how the gorge was formed, geology information, pioneer tools, Mr. Letchworth's personal library, park photographs, meeting room with a VCR and much more. The museum opened in 1913.

The impressive mastodon skull, which is in a large glass case under the beam ceiling, was from a huge mammal that roamed this area as the last ice sheets retreated 10,000 years ago. This skull was found by local farmers near the village of Pike, about seven miles west of the museum. The remains were purchased by Letchworth and mounted in a natural history collection established by Prof. Henry Ward in Rochester. The mastodon was displayed at Pike Seminary until 1898. It was then moved to the Genesee Museum, located on the Indian Council Grounds. In 1914 it was moved by wagon to the present museum.

Letchworth purchased the original 197 acres in 1859 for $37 per acre. These lands stretched along the west side of the Genesee from the Upper Falls to just beyond the Middle Falls. Shortly after purchasing the property, Letchworth added the name "Glen Iris" to his letters, a romantic reference to the rugged landscape and the classical goddess of rainbows often seen at the Middle Falls.

On a ridge behind the museum is a restored Seneca Indian Council House and the grave of Mary Jemison, a reminder of the region's turbulent history. The small log structure with interpretive signs was preserved by Mr. Letchworth as part of his ongoing interest in preserving history and the Seneca culture.

Mary Jemison: *"The White Woman of the Genesee,"* as Mary Jemison was called, is a fascinating figure in the region's history. She was born on a ship as her family came to the New World and spent her early life as a pioneer in Pennsylvania. During the vicious struggle between England and France over control of North America, Mary was taken captive with her family in 1758 at the age of 15 years. Although her family was killed, she was adopted as Deh-ge-wa-nus, meaning "The Two Falling Voices," and spend the rest of her life with the Indians whom she grew to love and respect. Jemison came to own an 18,000-acre reservation of fertile land, lost her three sons and husband to other Indians and eventually had her life story written by James E. Seaver in a book that was first printed in 1824. The popular book is available at the park.

Also available from the Visitor Center is a small booklet entitled the *"Historical Highlights of Letchworth State Park."* The booklet details the early treaties, incredible canal development, nearby villages, pioneer history of the region, and the life of social reformer Letchworth. Serious researchers can also access many other resources at this world-class state park.

The Falls: There are three waterfalls where the Genesee River cascades, including a 107-foot drop at the Middle Falls.

The Upper Falls can be reached by hiking .3-mile southwest on the Gorge Trail. The falls is 70 feet tall and has a horseshoe-shaped crest

that is more than 300 feet wide. A large part of the crest is overhung or nearly vertical, allowing the rushing water to crash over the break.

The 107-foot Middle Falls is also about 300 feet wide and has a vertical crest. It is considered by some to be the third most impressive waterfall in the western half of New York, preceded by the Horseshoe Falls and American Falls at Niagara. Lights illuminate the spectacular Middle Falls after dark from May through October.

The Lower Falls is a short hike from the Octagon Parking lot down a stairway into the gorge. The falls are very different than they were in the 1950s. Over the past generation, large sections have dropped off more than 40 feet. Today, the 300-foot-wide falls has eroded into two smaller falls and the waters are deeper beneath them.

The park has 21 other falls that are detailed in a book entitled, "Waterfall Guide to Letchworth State Park," by Scott Ensminger and Douglas Bassett. The handy guide is available in the gift shop and details how to view the many lesser known falls in the park including Wee Water Willy, Inspiration Falls, Three Sisters Falls, Stepmother Cascade, Crucifix Cascade, Wriggling Waters and others. The book includes maps to each of the described waterfalls.

Swimming: Swimming in is two large pools in the north end of the park in the Highbanks Recreation Area, and the south end of the park in the Lower Falls Area (near cabin colonies A and B). The pools are open during the summer when the lifeguards are on duty, generally from 11 a.m. - 6 p.m. weekdays and 11 a.m. 7 p.m. on weekends and holidays. Day-use areas, parking, ball backstops, shelters and modern playgrounds are nearby.

The Harvey Pool buildings are striking, featuring lounge areas, flag-poles, bleachers, nearby sun decks, benches and snack bar.

Mount Morris Dam: The Mount Morris Dam was built to provide flood protection for the farmlands, residential areas and industrial development of the Genesee Valley, from the dam site north to the metro area of Rochester to Lake Ontario. Before its completion in 1952, a major flood ravaged this picturesque valley about once every seven years. The dam was built at a cost of $25 million, but the dam has already prevented more than $250 million in flood damage and proved its value during tropical storm Agnes in 1972. There is a small snack bar at the dramatic dam overlook. The small concession sells grill goods and souvenirs and is a tourist information center.

Hiking: Letchworth State Park is for serious hikers. From the 21-mile-long spur of the Finger Lakes Trail which travels the entire length of the park from Portageville to Mount Morris, to shorter but scenic trails like Smokey Hollow, Dishmill Creek or Bear Hollow, the park has 26 trails of various lengths. Most of the trails range from easy to moderate in difficulty.

One of the most popular—and beautiful—trails at the park is the Gorge Trail, a seven-mile trail that tracks along the western rim of the gorge past the three main falls. The trail is marked with a white double-diamond on a red square. The trail also passes Table Rock, Cathedral Rock, over stairs, under a railroad trestle, along the edge of the gorge and river, and up to the 107-foot Middle Falls.

Boating: A permit from the park office is required to paddle the gorge stretch of the river. The trip can start at Lee's Landing below the Middle Falls for the fun, whitewater run (class II & III). During the summer, channels are obvious and the trip is good for intermediate paddlers. Above and below the gorge, the Genesee becomes a big quiet river, great for family canoe trips.

Whitewater rafting and canoe trips are available. Call Adventure Calls rafting at (716) 343-4710.

Fishing: The Genesee River from the town of Mount Morris up to Rochester is cool and can be a very good walleye fishery. A few small-mouth bass are also taken in the early season. Locals use nightcrawler rigs for walleye, and small crankbaits will work on smallies. Access to the river for fishing is limited. The upper Genesee can be fly fished from a canoe with excellent results. Fishing is also available in the Trout Pond in the southern part of the park.

Nature: The 22 square miles of diverse habitats of Letchworth are the home to 200 species of birds, three dozen species of mammals, 12 types of snakes and turtles, 100 species of trees and dozens of wonderful butterflies and insects. In all, more than 10,000 species of plants and animals live within Letchworth State Park. The park publishes a birding list that is available from the Visitor Center. The handy list details the unique location of the park on the minor flyways and details more than 200 birds, including 140 nesting species identified in the park. The park has 25 species of nesting wood warblers, 21 types of waterfowl, seven species of thrushes, 10 types of flycatchers, five owls, seven types of woodpeckers and many others.

From tiny shrews and moles to deer, woodchucks, beavers, foxes, raccoons and rabbits, the park is a terrific place to view wildlife. Letchworth has one of the finest interpretive programs in the state, offering an array of programs including interpretive hikes, natural history tours, outdoor workshops, guided activities, evening nature presentations, handouts and the publication of "The Genesee Naturalist." Natural history programs might include butterfly walks, wildflower hikes, bird identification, tree hikes, all-day adventure hikes and discussions with guest speakers. The programs include canyon sunset, Fiddler's Elbow hike, Big Bend Gorge trek, geology walk, edible plants walk, mushroom walk, Smokey Hollow hikes, Native American heritage day, life and the times of the CCC and more.

For a copy of *"The Genesee Naturalist,"* a quarterly publication dedicated to local natural history, contact the park office or ask to be put on the mailing list (small fee).

Winter: Winter sports at the park include cross-country skiing, snowshoeing, skating, snowtubing, snowmobiling in designated areas, and hiking.

Insider tips: The annual arts and crafts show held Columbus Day weekend in October is a major event featuring quality juried vendors. There is lots to do at Letchworth, including a wonderful gift shop at the Visitor Center that feature nature books, T-shirts, mugs, candles, small souvenirs, postcards and park information. Take a walk by the old schoolhouse and pioneer cemetery where the Jones brothers, who were the first settlers to the area, are laid to rest. To balloon over Letchworth, call (716) 237-2660. Other points of interest include the Seneca Council Grounds, nearby Genesee Valley canal locks, Portage Bridge and the "ghost" towns of St. Helena and Gibsonville.

GENESEE REGION

PHONE	PARK
716 493-3600	**GENESEE REGION**
716 493-3600	Conesus Lake Boat Launch Site
716 547-9242	Darien Lake *
716 964-2462	Hamlin Beach *
716 964-2462	Irondequoit Bay Marine Park
716 682-5246	Lakeside Beach
716 493-3600	Letchworth *
716 964-2462	Lock 32 Canal Park
716 682-5246	Oak Orchard Marine Park *
716 493-3600	Silver Lake

Facility	Conesus Lake Boat Launch Site	Darien Lake *	Hamlin Beach *	Irondequoit Bay Marine Park	Lakeside Beach	Letchworth *	Lock 32 Canal Park	Oak Orchard Marine Park *	Silver Lake
Tent/trailers sites (h = hookups, e = electricity)		• e	e			▷			
Trailer dump		▷	▷		▷				
Showers		▶	▶		▶	▶			
Camper recreation		▶	▷		▷	▷			
Cabins		▶							
Food		▶	▷		▷				
Store		▶	▷		▷				
Picnic tables	▷	▶	▷	▷	▷	▷	▷	▷	
Shelters (• reservations)		▶ •	▶		• ▷				
Swimming beach (• bath house)					• ▷	▷			
Swimming pool (• bath house)		▶ •							
Recreation programs (• performing arts)		▶ •	▷		▷	▷			
Hiking	▷	▶	▷		▷	▷			
Biking	▷	▷	▷		▷	▷			
Nature trails		▷			▷	▷			
Fishing	▷	▷	▷	▷	▷	▷			
Playground		▷	▷		▷	▷			
Golf (•clubhouse)									
Tennis									
Pond or lake (• power boats ok)	•	▷	•	• •	• ▷	▷	•		
River or stream (• power boats ok)	▷	• •	▷						
Launching site (• hand launch only)	• ▷			▷	•	▷			
Boat rental									
Marina (• anchorage)									
Pump out									
Ice skating (•rentals)		▷				▷			
Cross-country skiing (• rentals)		▷	▷		▷	▷			
Snowmobiling	▷	▷	▷		▷	▷			
Tubing slopes		▷							

▷ Availability of service or facility   ▶ Handicapped accessible   • Bridle paths

Long Island Region

Our tour of Long Island begins with a glimpse of some of its 19 state parks, which attracts 21 million visitors annually.

If you love big beaches, plan a visit to Jones Beach, which has the reputation of being one of the finest beaches in the country. More than 8 million visitors annually swim, sun or attend a world-class concert at Jones Beach Theatre.

Beach freaks will also love Robert Moses State Park which offers a huge open ocean beach, boat basin, fishing and pitch-and-putt golf.

Speaking of golf, Bethpage State Park has five golf courses, tennis courts, bicycling, hiking and a scenic polo field.

Bring your surf casting rod—or boogie board—and visit Montauk Point or Hither Hills state parks. Or bring your fly rod only to Connetquot River State Park Preserve for some of the finest trout fishing in the country.

The Long Island Region also has many other beach fronts, golf courses, arboretum, camping and day-use areas.

Long Island Region

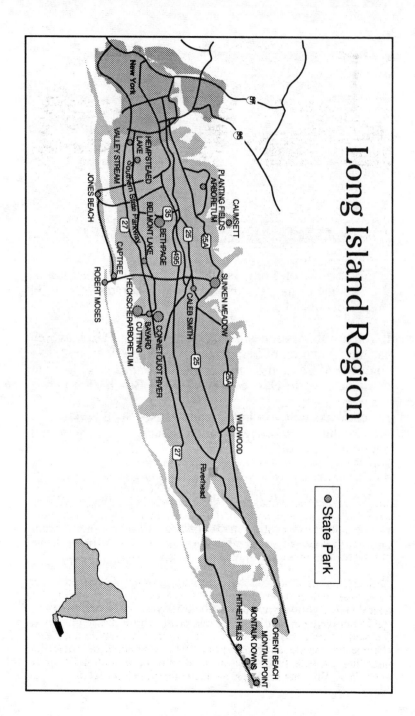

New York

HEMPSTEAD LAKE

VALLEY STREAM

JONES BEACH

Southern State Parkway

PLANTING FIELDS ARBORETUM

BELMONT LAKE

35

27

CAPTREE

BETHPAGE

495

25

25A

CAUMSETT

SUNKEN MEADOW

ROBERT MOSES

HECKSCHER

BAYARD CUTTING ARBORETUM

CONNETQUOT RIVER

CALEB SMITH

25

25A

WILDWOOD

27

Riverhead

HITHER HILLS

MONTAUK DOWNS

MONTAUK POINT

ORIENT BEACH

◎ State Park

Bethpage State Park
Land: 1,475 acres

Bethpage State Park has five regulation 18-hole golf courses that are on par with any set of courses in the country. The lush courses are known as the Blue, Red, Black, Green and Yellow courses. All five are hilly, expertly manicured and feature a complete irrigation system. Best known is the narrow and hilly Black Course, which is a championship caliber course, also referred to as the Championship Tourney Course. This tough course is the longest and most difficult—sometimes known to make grown men cry.

Although the park doesn't have camping, boating, fishing and other traditional outdoor recreation activities, it does have a polo field, clay tennis courts, a driving range, clubhouse and restaurant, nearby private stables, bridle path, ballfields and one picnic area in the north part of the park. Polo is played every Sunday from mid-May through mid-October by the Meadowbrook Polo Club. Champion polo matches including the U.S. Polo Open have recently been held at Bethpage State Park. Bleacher seating is available for all polo matches.

New York State Parks

The park can be busy with horseback riders and casual hikers during the spring when the pink and white blooms of dogwoods are on display. Park users will also enjoy the carefully-tended landscape and flowerbed planted in front of curving red-brick walls and around many buildings.

When not golfing, try some winter activities at Bethpage. The park offers cross-country skiing and sledding.

Information and Activities

Bethpage State Park
Farmingdale, Long Island
New York
(516) 249-0701

Directions: Near Farmingdale, on Long Island, 37 miles from New York City. The state park has direct access from the Bethpage State Parkway. The park closes at sunset.

Emergency number: Park police, (516) 669-2500.

Golf courses: All of the courses are rolling and the fairways are lined with mature trees that are said to occasionally eat golf balls. The turf is tightly mowed, meeting shaggy roughs and sand traps that dot the courses.

Most courses have cart paths, blue, red and white tees, cart rentals and a starter's shack that keeps things organized. Golf starter booths are located at the first tee of all courses. Here golfers sign-up by presenting their valid greens fee ticket to the starter at least 20 minutes prior to their tee time. Scorecards are available at all starter booths and signage explains park rules and golf etiquette.

Gas golf carts are available for rent on the Blue, Red and Yellow courses only. The Black and Green courses are for walkers only. Pull carts are also available for rent on all courses at the Clubhouse. Carts are rented not more than twenty minutes prior to tee time. All carts must be kept at least twenty feet from greens and are not permitted on tees.

The huge practice green in front of the clubhouse is outlined by a hedgerow that curves toward the parking area and joins various planting pockets and flowerbeds. There are also two practice putting greens in the back of the Clubhouse allowing golfers ample space to practice before teeing-off.

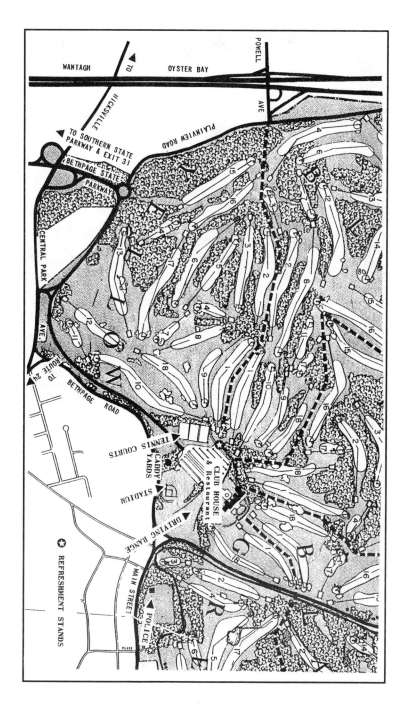

Bethpage offers golfers the ability to make golf reservations twenty-four hours a day by using our automated reservation system. New York residents can purchase a New York State Golfer Identification for twenty dollars which is valid for three years. Holders of this card can make reservations up to seven days in advance. For those who do not have a Golfer ID Card, reservations for tee-times can be made up to four days in advance. The phone number for Golf Reservations is (516) 249-0707.

Driving range: Outlined by a white rail fence and on a low ridge, the tidy range is a place to practice or take lessons from PGA professionals. Also at the driving range is a small sign that says, "Practice Makes Perfect." A special teaching area at the end of the range is used by the pros and students. Yellow benches and soft drink machines are near the elevated tees. The driving range is next to the stately clubhouse and includes 28 tees.

Clubhouse: The beautiful clubhouse is of Long Island colonial design and serves all five courses. The red-brick building has a circle drive and contains lockers and showers for men and women, a golf pro shop, cocktail lounge, dining porch and grill. The cafeteria, outdoor restaurant overlooking the golf courses and 91st Hole lounge, serves hungry golfers light breakfasts, sandwiches, salads, juice and soft drinks. The lounge features vaulted beam ceilings, wood fixtures, brass lamps and golfers planted around small tables dreaming about their next round. The Clubhouse is open year-round.

On the walls of the bar are photographs of professional golfers including Jerry Pate, seniors player Orville Moody, Andy North and others, all of whom have provided golf exhibitions at Bethpage State Park. A large fireplace and constant laughter in the air helps create a warm environment to relax and tell golf stories (lies?). Behind the highly polished wood bar is a large graphic that depicts the course layout. Also nearby in the Club Room is a trophy case and private meeting or dining area. A rich history of local golf can be found in the clubhouse.

The colonial dining rooms are available for group use and is often the site of wedding receptions. The carefully varnished doors and polished brass make the clubhouse an elegant site for many types of events and meetings.

The large pro shop inside the clubhouse sells quality golf bags, balls, gloves, towels, brand name clubs, racks full of putters and many other accessories.

The clubhouse is also the site of the annual Winter Arts Festival sponsored by the Long Island State Park and Recreation Commission.

Day-use areas: Near the upscale polo field is an equally nice picnic area. The expanse contains two arching ballfield backstops, clusters of tables shaded by breezy groves of trees, ground-mounted grills, cream-colored rest room building and playground with colorful climbers, swings and slides. The small playground is fenced and has several spring animals, teeter-totter, sand and benches for weary parents.

The park also has 12 tennis courts that are surrounded by a green fence. Eight courts have a clay surface, and four have all-weather surfaces. The courts are rented by the hour and tickets may be purchased from the cashier in the clubhouse.

Hiking: The multi-use hiking/biking trail is a two-way trail that connects day-use park amenities. Bike riders are asked to yield and stay on the right side. Multi-use sections run from the north part of the park to the Bethpage Picnic Area. The Long Island Greenbelt Trail comes through the undeveloped areas of the picnic area as does cross-country trails and a nature walk.

Mountain bikers are also asked to ride or walk bikes on the right side of the multi-use path. Maximum bike speed is 15 mph, on the paved bicycle trail only. Wear your helmet; it's the law. The bike path is open during daylight hours only.

Insider tips: Runners, walkers and bikers will love the well-maintained path. A 5K run is conducted annually on the multi-use path. Bethpage is a high-class state park. From clay tennis courts to championship golf. Carts can be rented from a shack near the tennis courts. Ask about golfing discounts offered after 4 p.m.

A number of events are held including the Long Island Golf Classic, New York State Open and others. A nearby private stable rents horses; call (516) 531-9467.

Connetquot River State Park Preserve

Land: 3,473 acres
Water: Connetquot River

Connetquot River State Park Preserve is a special place. Forget your beachball, baseball, golf clubs and the usual recreational stuff, because there are no picnic areas, bicycling, playgrounds or sprawling day-use areas at this natural unit. The park is a preserve, with special rules, dedicated to passive outdoor recreation like walking, top-quality fly fishing and horseback riding. The park is highly regulated; even walkers must obtain a permit to use the beautiful area.

How can a nearly 3,500-acre natural oasis remain on Long Island? The answer is in the deed which was held by a syndicate of wealthy sportsmen who owned the private trout stream and hunting preserve for more than 100 years. When the property came to the state, the deed restricted commercial development, preserving the tract for future generations. Before the elite sportsmen's group owned the land, its patent dates to pre-Revolutionary times.

During the 100 years that the sportsmen's club operated, some famous people visited to hunt and fish. Those who once walked these fields include Daniel Webster, Ulysses S. Grant, General Sherman, Lorenzo Delmonico and Charles L. Tiffany.

In 1963, the state acquired the tract, but didn't open it to the public until 1973. The emphasis is on maintaining the natural character of the land and outdoor education. Activities today include guided nature walks featuring the grist mill, trout hatchery, cross-country skiing, hiking, photography and birding.

To enter the preserve you must have a permit. You must send a letter of request to the preserve. This letter should include the following: Your name, address, activity and number in the group. Your letter and a legal-size, self-addressed stamped envelope should be sent to the address below. Be patient, the permitting process ensures a quality park and outdoor recreation experience.

Information and Activities

Connetquot River State Park Preserve
P. O. Box 505
Sunrise Highway
Oakdale, NY 11769
(516) 581-1005

Directions: This is probably the most difficult park to find in the entire state. The tree-lined entrance is off the Sunrise Highway, Route 27. The highway is double lanes headed in opposite directions. Visitors must be in the westbound lane looking for the park sign and white pavement markings of a short exit lane. Look for the heavily wooded area and a small park sign along Rt. 27W. The entrance is a half mile from Connetquot Avenue.

The park is open year-round 8 a.m. to 4:30 p.m. Wednesday through Sunday and on Tuesday from April through Labor Day.

Hatchery: The natural hatchery, built in the 1800s, is a one-mile walk from the check-in station. The front part of the old-style hatchery is open and anglers can view fish from fry size to adults in the 11 concrete raceways. Park naturalists often have weekend educational programs at the hatchery. The hatchery has netting to prevent raptors from feeding on the trout.

The hatchery raises 40,000-60,000 trout annually. Fishing sites 17-32 are near the hatchery; 9-16 are south of the hatchery. Fish are stocked regularly almost year-round (except late-October thru February).

After reading a large sign at the entrance, you will learn that the trout have many natural predators including great blue heron, raccoon, black-crowned night heron, great egret, osprey and man. The hatchery uses low-tech, manual hatchery techniques. Even with old methods, the facility produces excellent stock.

Grist mill: Connetquot's mill was built between 1702 and 1751 by William Nichols, the owner of Islip Grange. Islip Grange included most of what is now the town of Islip. Nichols received the land in two grants from Governor Dongon in 1684 and 1697. The first part of the grant concerned acquisition of the land on the west side of the Connetquot River and the second part gave him the land on the east side of the river.

The shingled mill, which stands on the southwest corner of the park, served the many needs of local farmers and other residents. It ground grain, pulled woven cloth and probably sawed wood. Farmers grew wheat, rye, buckwheat, oats and corn. The mill has six-over-six windows and rough wood floors that contain various tools and the machinery that once ground grain. A turbine water pump is still next to the restored mill house. The mill is near fishing sites nos. 2 and 3 and next to a tree-lined pond. The resident population of Canada geese are often seen around the mill and pond.

The millers always had grain because Nichol's fee was usually eight or 10 percent of the weight of the raw grain. Residents who were not farmers could buy grain and have it ground by the miller. Customers who did not want to pay in grain or currency could barter other goods or services. The items or services bartered were equal to the cost of 10 percent of the unprocessed grain. The miller may have desired or needed his horse shoed or carpentry done, and accepted these services in exchange for payment.

The people of the 1700s and 1800s depended on grain-based foods. They made Johnny cake (corn bread), cornmeal mush (samp) and a large variety of breads, pies and pastries. They used the bran (the coarse outer husk of the wheat kernel) to feed animals. The hardy pioneers also used corn, barley and oats. Recipes using grains are available from the education staff.

A farmer would have to harvest his corn, separate the ears from the stalks, shuck the corn, dry it out, shell the kernels from the cob, pound the dried kernels into flour and separate the flour from the bran. This took a long time. A grist mill provided a way for farmers to grind their grain into flour and meal in a rapid and efficient way. It separated the

flour from the bran and gave the farmer choices of types of grinds.

The mill was accepted by the National Registry of Historic places in 1972 and was restored by the New York State Office of Parks, Recreation and Historical Preservation.

Club House: The huge wood building was once a hotel, called Snedecors Tavern. Old South Country Road passed at its doorstep. It was built in 1820 and many travelers once stayed here. Later in 1866 to 1973, it was used as a clubhouse by the Southside Sportsmen Club of Long Island.

Today, the impressive shingled building is used for offices, including the regional environmental education staff. Other wonderful buildings house the park manager's residence and administrative offices. There is a handicapped accessible comfort station in the administrative building. Look for the ornate weathervane on the main house.

Boating: Small rowboats are rented to anglers near the clubhouse, mill and dam.

Fishing: Some premier trout fishing is offered at the preserve by permit only. All fishing must be done with conventional fly fishing equip-

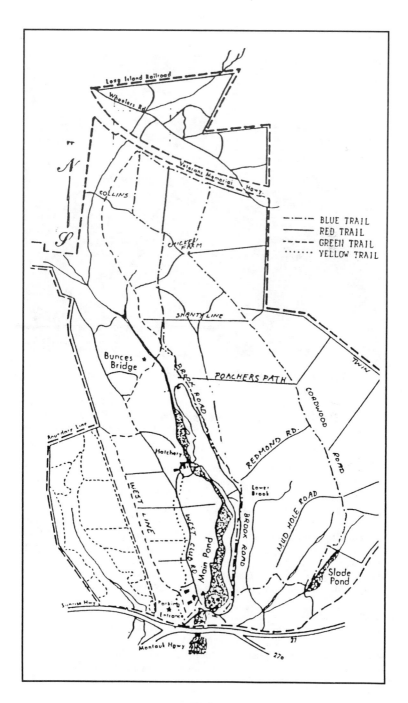

ment. You are not allowed to use a weighted leader, but a weighted sinking line is permissible. Any other type of fishing tackle is prohibited. Artificial flies and streamers are defined as being constructed of natural or synthetic materials, so long as the flies are constructed in the normal fashion on a single barbless hook with components wound on or about the hook.

Prohibited are molded facsimiles or replicas of insects, earthworms, fish eggs, fish or any invertebrate or vertebrate either singly or in combination with other materials. Also prohibited are other lures commonly described as spinners, spoons or plugs made of metal, plastic, wood, rubber or similar substances or combinations. To protect the environment, no lead weight, split shot or other lead items may be used.

April through October, anglers must stop fishing when they catch two trout. During February and March, you must catch and release.

Anglers must walk to their site along trails. Your site includes your wooden platform and another halfway to the next site. Fishing from the platforms protects the stream banks and fragile vegetation. Use stream courtesy and respect other anglers' sites. Only one rod may be actively fished per site. At fishing sites 8-15, you may wade.

The river is heavily stocked by the on-site hatchery from February to October. Brooks, browns and rainbows are stocked and anglers must register and fish from one of the 30 designated sites along the river. Many native fish are also in the river.

Reservations are due by 8 a.m. Sunday one week in advance of fishing. Specific sites cannot be reserved in advance, but are issued first-come, first-served.

Hiking: The bird sanctuary is closed to hikers and horseback riders, but all of the other mowed and hard-packed trails are open to use by permit. Much of the area is a young oak forest. There are miles and miles of trails at the park, including a section of the Greenbelt Trail and glimpses of the Connetquot River.

Nature: The preserve's natural area is typical of the glacial outwash plain of Long Island. Its varied habitats support many species of interesting plants and animals. In fact, the trout hatchery produces opportunities to see herons, egrets, kingfishers and osprey.

Many species of duck winter on the main pond. The mixed hardwoods and pitch pine woodlands provide nesting opportunities for many songbirds. Warblers and raptors can be seen during the spring and fall migrations. Ask for a bird list that details sightings by season and gives information on abundance of particular species.

The checklist details songbirds, raptors, shorebirds and others. The park has eight species of bitterns and herons, 25 types of waterfowl, nine kinds of hawks and eagles, seven species of sandpipers and phalaropes, five gull species, 26 types of wood warblers, vireos, mockingbirds, sparrows, 10 types of finches, blackbirds, tanagers, brown creeper, wrens, kinglets, six species of woodpeckers and many more.

Insider tips: There are few places in the world where trout fishing is this good. There are wild turkeys and deer on the property. There is no longer hunting at the preserve (the last hunting was for waterfowl in 1972). A good population of red fox are in the park.

On some Mondays, New York-area sportsmen's clubs book the entire park, especially Trout Unlimited clubs. There is no whirling disease at the park. Try to get a tour of the natural hatchery; you'll see some huge trout. Remember to use the rod holders that are attached to the fence near the parking lot.

Heckscher State Park
Land: 1,679 acres   Water: Great South and Nicoll bays

Heckscher State Park is on the south shore of Long Island near the mouth of the Connetquot River. It borders three miles of Great South Bay. The waterside park is mostly flat and includes freshwater, wetlands, salt marshes, woodlands and grassy open fields. The mixed deciduous forest and shrub habitats offer park users a terrific chance to see native Long Island wildlife.

The park was once the sprawling estate of George C. Taylor. The 1,500-acre tract was a self-sufficient farm that included a large manor house built in 1886, 30 outbuildings, stables, greenhouses, carriage and dairy barns, as well as employee housing. Taylor was known to stock the fields and woods with game birds and deer, including peacocks and a herd of elk.

After Taylor's death in 1908, the huge property laid fallow for 16 years. In 1924, the newly created Long Island State Park Commission offered to manage the tract as a public park. This notion set off a firestorm of opposition from local estate owners who feared the park would hurt the area. The local landowners used every legal device they could over the next five years to block the development of the state park. However, on June 29, 1929, after lots of wrangling, the commission officially named the park Heckscher State Park in gratitude to August Heckscher for his gift which assisted in purchasing the scenic land.

Over the years the park commission has improved the unit to include huge parking fields, full-equipped picnic areas, a beach, modern swimming pool complex, game fields and a campground that was built in the 1930s.

The Heckscher Parkway loop was completed in 1960, opening all parts of the park with a scenic drive. The boat basin and popular launching ramp were completed in 1969, and in 1971 the South Beach Pool Complex opened. Over the years additional land has also been acquired.

About 1.2 million visitors annually come to Heckscher State Park to enjoy the outdoor recreation opportunities. The park is about 50 miles from New York City.

Information and Activities

Heckscher State Park
East Islip, NY 11730
(516) 581-2100

Directions: 50 miles from Manhattan on the south shore of Long Island, with the East Islip/Great River area in Suffolk County at the end of Heckscher State Parkway.

In a colonial-style building, the park police and park offices offer information and a small brochure rack. The office is near a ballfield in play field No. 1. Unlike many parks, Heckscher has some good information readily available.

Emergency number: Park police, (516) 669-2500.

Camping: The 69-site campground is surrounded by woodlands. Five sites are accessible to persons with disabilities. The campground features 13 water hydrants, 14 water fountains and a centrally located brick comfort station. The oversized sinks in the comfort station are handy for filling coolers and buckets with water. The campground is about 50 percent shady, provided by mature mix deciduous and some pine trees. A soft drink machine is at the campground check-in station. A horseshoe court, bocce courts and informational boards are also near the tan-colored office. The campground is often full on summer weekends.

Sites are mostly grassy and have cement pads where a picnic table can be conveniently set. Each site has a picnic table and pedestal grill. Site 45 is one of the most shady. All of the sites are flat and can accommodate medium to large RV rigs. Sites on the outside perimeter, toward the back of the area (sites 60-69), are backed up against natural vegetation.

Children's movies are often shown on Saturday and Sunday during the summer in the campground. The television is at the back of the check-in building. A bulletin board details upcoming events and programs.

Day-use areas: Many play fields are equipped with picnic tables, game fields, playgrounds and an occasional volleyball court. Play field No. 2 & 3 can be used by permit only and a fee is charged. Make reservations by calling the permit office. The park maintains some huge day-use areas that have shady areas and hundreds of picnic tables scattered around.

Try a game of bocce (lawn bowling) at the timber-framed court. Bocce is played with eight balls, 4.5 inches in size, and a small Jack ball which is 2 3/8 inches. The Jack is always the target ball. Bocce may be played with one to four players on each team and the toss of a coin usually determines which team begins the play. The captain decides which player will start. The winning team of each frame starts the next frame.

The object of the game is to place the bocce ball closer to the Jack ball than your opponent. The teams alternately bowl the balls. After the initial toss of the Jack, the opposing team bowls until their balls are placed closer to the Jack than the opponent's ball. When the ball is placed closer to the Jack than the opponents', play is passed to the other team, which proceeds to place the ball still closer, if possible. Play continues in this manner until all the balls are played. Alternating each time, the ball is placed closer to the Jacks. At the end of each frame, the team with the closest ball to the Jack scores one point. Thus it is possible to score from one to four points each frame. Only one team can score in each frame. The game is usually 21 points.

Bocce balls and a copy of the rules are available from the office.

Beaches: The west beach has huge day-use areas along the bay where boats and ships can be seen in the distance. The beach is surrounded by wide expanses of parking and open spaces. Lifeguard stands are white, equipped with telephones and are evenly spaced along the sandy

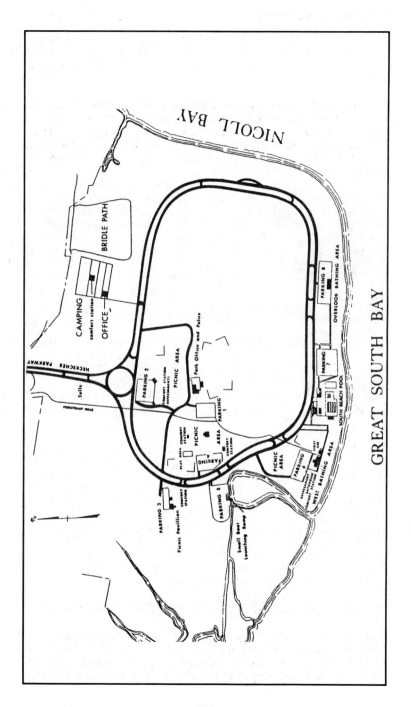

NICOLL BAY

GREAT SOUTH BAY

CAMPING
comfort station
OFFICE

BRIDLE PATH

HECKSCHER PARKWAY

Tolls

PEDESTRIAN WALK

PARKING 2

Comfort Station
Refreshments

PICNIC AREA

Park Office and Police

PARKING 3

Picnic Pavilion

COMFORT STATION

PLAY AREA COMFORT STATION

PICNIC AREA

PARKING 4

COMFORT STATION

PARKING 5

Small Boat Launching Ramp

PICNIC AREA

PARKING 6

REFRESHMENT COMFORT STATION

FIRST AID

WEST BATHING AREA

PARKING 1

SOUTH BEACH POOL

PARKING 7

PARKING 8

OVERLOOK BATHING AREA

beach. The water in front of the lifeguard stands is sectioned off by floating buoys to concentrate swimmers in the supervised areas. Ball fields and timber-style play apparatus are nearby.

Outdoor showers and rest rooms are along the windswept beach and wide day-use areas. The coarse sand beach is packed on hot summer weekends.

Swimming pool: The T-shaped pool, at field No. 7, features a concession stand and popular sunning deck. A scattering of tables are near the food stand and have a view of the pool that is sectioned off by blue and white buoys. No food, drinks or coolers are allowed in the pool area. Green and white lounge chairs are scattered around the wide cement pool deck, and a small shallow kiddy's pool is within the complex. A diving area supervised by lifeguards is the source of lots of hooting and hollering.

Several wooden structures that offer comforting shade are near the pool, along the wide deck. The pool is surrounded by black wrought iron fencing, containing planting pockets and a nearby bike rack. The pool complex is open 10 a.m. - 5:30 p.m. Wednesday - Sunday. There is a small admission fee. Men and women's locker rooms are inside the bathhouse. The pool is accessible for swimmers with disabilities.

Hiking: The mostly shady, hard-surfaced pedestrian trail runs north and south, connecting the west bathing area to picnic areas, parking and the main entrance. The trail can be used for walking or biking and connects most park amenities.

The Southern Section of the Long Island Greenbelt Trail can be accessed from the state park. The 34-mile-long trail is a designated National Recreation Trail that opened in 1978. It passes through some 12,000 acres of open land, including four state parks and many municipal holdings. Between sandy beaches on the Great South Bay and the bluffs overlooking the Sound, hikers will find unspoiled pine barrens, upland hardwood forests and the hills of Ronkonkoma Moraine.

Roughly following the courses of the Connetquot and Nissequogue rivers, the trail offers views of ponds, marshes and clear streams. Among the wildlife found along the trail are deer, fox, osprey, heron and wild turkey.

The Greenbelt Trail is easy to follow. Look for the white blazes, about two by four inches, on trees, rocks and fenceposts; a double blaze warns of a sudden turn in the direction indicated by the upper of the two marks.

Hikers don't need special gear to enjoy the trail. Sneakers or sturdy shoes with non-skid soles are all you need. Bring a light day pack, lunch and water.

Primitive camping is permitted at Lakeland and Blydenburgh county parks. Call (516) 854-4949 for details and reservations. The most popular hike from Heckscher is up 11 miles to Lakeland. For more information about the trail, contact the Greenbelt Trail Conference, Inc., 23 Deer Path Road, Central Islip, NY 11722. Call (516) 360-0753.

Boating: The four-lane, hard-surfaced launching ramp is at Parking Field No. 5. The basin has a courtesy dock and nearby red-brick rest room building with a pay phone and soft drink machine. Three black metal benches look out on the cove, and often on the resident flock of Canada geese. There is no overnight mooring at the launch or along the improved shoreline and wooden boardwalk.

The protected cove-side ramp has a two-lane boat washing area. The park also operates a small area that is designed for windsurfers that is open from April to the end of October. This designated sandy area is in parking field No. 7. The offshore winds make this area a wind-surfers' paradise.

Fishing: Anglers often try for the following species: summer flounder, white flounder, blackfish, bluefish, Atlantic cod, pollock, striped bass, red drum, Spanish mackerel, Atlantic sturgeon, black sea bass and porgies.

Snapper, also called bluefish, has sharp teeth 6-13 inches long. The best season in these waters is late July to early October. Snappers like shallow bays, estuaries, harbors and rivermouths. Try light tackle and a single snapper hook suspended 12-36 inches below a small float, or tie directly to the line. For bait, local anglers often choose spearing, sand eel, fish fillets and squid. Small silver spoons, small jigs, tube lures and minnow imitations also work.

Summer flounder, also known as fluke or flatfish, are brown and white ranging from 6-20 pounds. Summer flounder are taken April to October from the sandy bottom. Standard single hooks work on 6-20 pound test bottom rigs with 2-6 sinkers and tipped with sand eel, smelt, snapper or other fish strips. For artificials, try white jigs or plastic body jigs like Salty Dogs or Sassy. Some shad-style lures also work. The technique is to bottom fish with a back-drop style.

Nature: The park is comprised of a variety of natural resources including a bay beach, tidal marshes, fields and secondary growth woodlands. The various habitats are host to more than 280 species of resident and migrating birds. Parking field No. 4 provides access to beach, marsh and woodland habitats, while fields 6, 7 and 8 provide direct access to the shore.

A birding checklist is available from the park office. The handy list details bird activity by season and abundance. Species listed include two types of loons, three species of grebes, 11 species of bitterns and herons, 28 types of waterfowl, eight types of kites, eagles and hawks, two dozen species of shorebirds, a barn owl, many types of gulls and wood warblers, kinglets, finches, pipits and many other interesting avians. Bald eagles are seen about once every five years.

Insider tips: About 15 deer each year are killed by cars in the park. Notice the Burma Shave-like signs along the park road that offer information about wildlife and safety. The New York Philharmonic has summer concerts at the park in a huge mowed field near the campground. Remote control model airplanes are often flown by enthusiasts in parking field No. 9. Look for red fox; they are often seen in the grassy fields looking for mice.

A livery stable is nearby. Large herds of deer are often seen at dusk. Look for the obvious browse line along woodland edges. Other summer programs include a cultural arts concert series, summer children's theater, spring festival and summer run series.

Hither Hills State Park
Land: 1,755 acres Water: Atlantic Ocean

The coastal park is at the east tip of Long Island, near scenic Montauk Point, on a long finger of land that connects prehistoric Montauk Island with South Fork at Amagansett. The linear park includes a sandy triangle that is the eastern shore of Napeaque Harbor, the western half of the morainal upland, and about 1.3 miles of ocean and campground to the south. The shingle-sided park buildings are carefully designed to perfectly fit into the sandy, oceanside environs. They offer information about the interesting area.

Hither Hills offers an unparalleled chance to experience life on the beach. The steady breeze, low dunes and lapping waters make this an excellent park to beach comb, camp at or day-use.

Hikers will also enjoy trails that skirt the shoreline, beach and wooded uplands on the east. One of the best walking areas is at the nearby Walking Dunes, where a fascinating group of dunes is slowly creeping across flat land due to steady northwest winds. As these dunes move, they cover trees in their path that must strain to grow taller. Ask the park staff for directions to the dunes.

Other places to explore in and around the park are Goff Point along the harbor shore and the Fresh Pond, where children can catch lots of pan-fish at dusk.

Park campers may also want to day-trip to the many fine restaurants, shopping and other scenic places at the tip of Long Island. If you visit at the right time of year, you might see the annual shark fishing tournament or big surf if a tropical storm is spinning in the Atlantic. The montauk area also has great nightlife including the Blue Marlin, Caswells, Dooleys, Gurney's Inn, Tipperary and many others. For family fun, try the Deep Hollow Ranch for pony rides, petting zoo, wagon rides and special events.

Information and Activities

Hither Hills State Park
RR2, P.O. Box 206A, S. Fairview Ave.
Montauk, NY 11954
(516) 668-7600

Directions: Four miles west of Montauk, off State Route 27 (Montauk Highway).

Emergency number: 911 system.

Campground: Camping is ocean-side on grass and gravel pads along long narrow loops. The campground is open, offering almost no shade and little privacy. Each of the camping sites has 12-foot-square cement pads where a picnic tables can be placed. Blue drinking fountains are scattered throughout the flat campground that is only steps from the ocean's edge. The busy, quality campground is well-maintained and clean. Bathhouses in the campground have showers, soft drink machines, skylights and pay telephones that seem to attract guilty businessmen. All sizes of RV rigs use the multi-loop campground. Big rigs will find the maneuvering easy.

Sites in the A loop are on sand and against a grainy dune that is sprouting increased plant growth. Sites A4 and A5 are next to the dune and near the dune crosswalk. Don't walk on the fragile dunes!

Sites B19 and B20 face a shrubby dune made of white sand held together by various grasses. A horseshoe court is near site B10. A few

sites in this loop are separated by some sparse clusters of low shrubs. If you want to be near the neatly maintained ballfield, choose site B1 or A1.

Sites along row F are near a shrubby natural area. Sites F25 and F26 are near a sand dune. Camping sites in the G row are slightly smaller than others and face the low dunes. Access to the beach is near G7. If the wind is right, you can hear the surf from this loop. These rows tend to fill up with pop up campers and lots of families with small children. G18 and G19 are two of the most private sites in the campground. Sites along the I row are up against some natural vegetation and grassy spaces. Site 16 has some shade.

Day-use areas: The small bathhouse is surrounded by a gray stockade fence, and white columns hold up the roof. Nearby, the park's newer playground is on sandy ground and features many colorful climbers, slides and swings. The baseball field, which often has chalked lines and a game going on, is centrally located near the playground, store and bathhouse. A tether ball, bike rack and benches are also at the playground.

The bathhouse has a deck that is sometimes used for youth programs like story hours and arts and crafts. In the front section of the bath-

house is a small library filled with popular novels and trashy romances. A nearby information board about fishing and park activities helps orient new visitors. The back side of the bathhouse has a small room from which crayons, puzzles and games can be borrowed. Staff is also nearby and busy with lots of youth programs during the summer.

A dune-top picnic area above the campground affords a terrific park and ocean view.

Beach: The sandy beach and crashing waves are spectacular. Boogie boards are allowed in designated areas. A section of the beach is open and guarded for swimming. A sand volleyball court is on the beach. The windswept beach is great for sunbathing, swimming or walking in the foaming surf. Some outside showers are near the lifeguard stand and bathhouse.

General Store: In a brown shingle-sided building with white shutters, the small store has bike parking in front and a handful of weathered picnic tables scattered next to it. The General Store has a 32-inch television mounted in the front window that points outside, providing evening movies for campers. A film is shown each night at 8:45 p.m. during the summer. Bring your blanket and chair.

Inside the cafe are coolers, toys. small boogie boards, candy, grill foods (try the basket of fries!), soft drinks, cold beer, pizza, ice cream, canned goods, toiletries, sunscreen, lighter fluid, tea and coffee. Other items include simple camping, cleaning and cooking supplies. Notice the doorway into the store; it demonstrates marvelous craftsmanship.

Hiking: Bring your in-line skates or bike; the hard-surfaced areas are smooth. Goal-oriented hikers should obtain a Hither Hills map from the town clerk at East Hampton on 159 Pantigo Road (Rt. 27). Serious walkers might also want a copy of the South Fork-Shelter Island Preserve Guide, available from the Nature Conservancy, P.O. Box 5125, East Hampton, NY 11937. The 75-page booklet details 28 near-by preserves and offers trail directions.

Fishing: Surf fishing is popular along the beach, while boat anglers do well offshore. Species commonly taken include winter flounder, summer flounder, blackfish, weakfish, pollock, Atlantic cod, striper bass, red drum, Atlantic and Spanish mackerel, Atlantic sturgeon, black sea bass and porgy. Try for bluefish and striped bass before dawn.

Freshwater anglers can try the 40-acre pond that contains panfish and largemouth bass.

Nature: The park is working hard to reconstruct and protect the scenic but delicate dunes that roll through the tract next to the shoreline. The dunes that protect the campground are a product of learning, foresight and cooperation. In the past unrestricted access across the dunes resulted in trampling of the dune vegetation. These plants tolerate some very harsh growing conditions including nutrient poor and extremely dry soil, salt-laden winds and blazing heat. One thing they cannot tolerate, however, is human traffic trampling their leaves and compacting the sand around their roots.

In 1970, no plants were growing on the dunes and they were quickly eroding and blowing away. The state park staff had to clear out drifting sand from the campground. In some years, road scrapers and other heavy equipment moved more than 1,000 cubic yards of sand off the campsites.

In the early 1980s, park staff developed a long-term strategy of dune stabilization. Their plan was to stabilize the dune by planting hardy American beachgrass. Beachgrass protects itself from wind-driven sand by secreting a tough silica layer to the outer surface of the blade. To conserve water, the inside of each grass blade has vertical ridges that can be tightly compressed, closing the openings through which water is released during photosynthesis. The plant's wandering roots absorb minerals from the salt spray that washes through the sand. This is the perfect plant to help hold together the sand dunes.

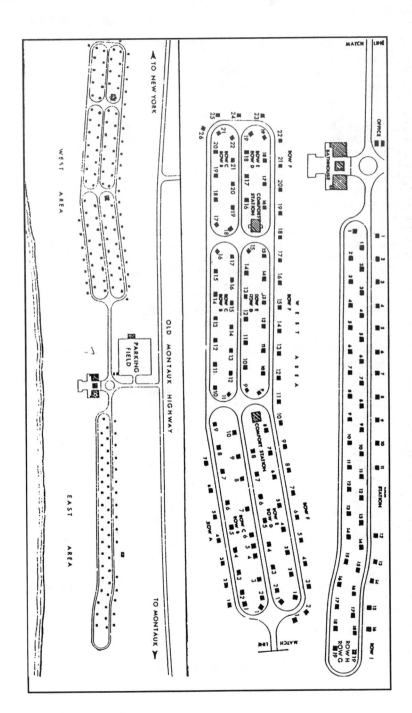

183

The beachgrass's root network stabilizes an otherwise fragile hill of sand. American beachgrass not only survives well in the dune environment, its growth is actually stimulated by blowing sand. In fact, the translation for the botanical name of beachgrass is "ammorphila," which means "sand-loving." Wind-driven sand is intercepted by the leaves. As sand collects around its stems, the plant sends out horizontal underground runners called rhizomes from which new leaves sprout.

In addition, the plant is able to grow upward fast enough to escape complete burial. Thus the beachgrass rises and helps create a growing hill of sand. The end result is a root system that penetrates deep into the sand and also spreads out under its surface forming the dune's internal framework. During a storm this root framework absorbs wave energy and protects the dunes from being washed away.

More than 400 Boy Scouts have gathered 20,000 beachgrass plants, wrapping them in burlap bundles of 100 and carefully replanting then on disappearing dunes around the park.

Park programs include dune ecology, walking near the dunes, a camping jamboree, campfire singalongs, softball and volleyball games, story hour, crafts and more.

Insider tips: Kite flying and surf fishing are popular along the breezy beach. Protect the dunes, use the designated crosswalks. When camping at Hither, bring an umbrella or other shade device. Remember the nightly movies at the cafe/store. Beach walking is excellent at the park. Park amenities (playground, store, office, bathhouse, etc.) are clustered together.

Considerable tracts of land around the park are owned by the Nature Conservancy, including beachfront and mixed pine-oak forests. Stop at the overlook on Rt. 27. This is a high moraine. Nearby a 1986 forest fire decimated the area. September is a wonderful time to visit—the crowds are gone and the water is still warm.

Jones Beach State Park
Land: 2,413 acres   Water: 6.5 miles on the Atlantic Ocean

Famous Jones Beach gets it name from a colorful Irish soldier of fortune, Major Thomas Jones, not to be confused with Tom Jones. Jones built the first brick house on Long Island in the middle 1690s and acquired more than 6,000 acres as a wedding present—including most of what is now Jones Beach State Park—when he wed Freelove Townsend. Also at the time, he was the sheriff of Queens County and Ranger General of Nassau. By 1700, the ambitious Jones also established a whaling station near the site of the state park.

The ocean side of the barrier island is windswept and has rolling dunes and salt marshes that stretched to the bay near where Jones' whale station stood. It's uncertain how long the whaling operation was in business, but for the last 200 years this area has been known as Jones Beach, including sections called Hemlock Beach, High Hill Beach, Short Beach, Gilgo Beach, Cedar Beach and Oak Beach.

About five years before the tract became a state park in the 1920s, author Birdsall Jackson described the region: "In a sailboat with a fair wind, the trip to Jones Beach took about one hour, and with a head wind, three hours. If you were not familiar with the many shoals and crooked channels you would not get there at all. An excursion to Jones Beach was always planned as a full day's outing and the day chosen so the voyager went out with the ebb tide and came back with the flood. All night sojourns on the sand flats were not uncommon."

The area opened as a state park in August 1929 amid a howling sandstorm that provided a field day for critics of the project. Undaunted, Governor Franklin D. Roosevelt and former Governor Alfred E. Smith were principal speakers on this fateful opening day. In the first year of operation, the park hosted more than 500,000 visitors. Today, more than 7 million visitors trek to the park to swim, sunbathe and enjoy the many amenities.

Since the windy opening day nearly 70 years ago, millions of clumps of beachgrass and other vegetation have been planted to prevent sandstorms. The popularity of the park has soared. Now the park has sprawling sandy beaches, a two-mile-long boardwalk, 3,000 lockers in two bathhouses, nine beach shops, bait & tackle shop, ice cream shop, pitch putt golf, more than a dozen places to eat, boat basin, softball diamonds, surfing and surf fishing, four fishing piers, flower gardens, 6.5 miles of beach frontage, picnic areas and a huge, well-known theater that hosts top acts each summer.

Information and Activities

Jones Beach State Park
P.O. Box 1000, Ocean Drive
Wantagh, NY 11793
(516) 785-1600

Directions: The famous beach is 33 miles from Manhattan via the Meadowbrook Parkway South or Wantagh Parkway South to the park.

Many huge parking fields are connected to the beach area via tunnel under Ocean Drive. The pleasant courtyard-like walk to the beach is lined with flower beds and other landscaping.

Emergency number: (516) 669-2500.

Day-use areas: Most of the amenities at Jones Beach are along the beach. Features include a bandshell and bleacher seating, first aid stations, pedestrian walkways, exercise routes, mini-golf course with a nautical theme and fairways that are separated by vegetation (open 10 a.m. - 11 p.m. seasonally), 22 heavily-used shuffleboard courts, picnic areas, 15 lighted paddle tennis courts and a large timber-frame play structure. The beach-side bandshell is often the site of square dancing, line dancing and children's theater productions.

The colorful play structure has a triple purple slide, crossbars, stair steps, climbers, climbing ropes, tubes that connect the various pieces of apparatus, beams and bench seating for parents. The complex-looking sandy play area is surrounded by a black fence and was donated by area Saturn car dealers in 1995.

The feature that causes the most squeals from children is the saddle-like balance beam. Plan a visit to the active playground with your 5-12 year-olds.

Close to thecentral mall beach are the pitch-putt golf course, four basketball goals, bathing area, sun shelters and fishing areas. All this is near Parking Field No. 4.

For group outings (picnics or day camp), call (516) 669-1000, Ext. 223.

Theater: On Zach's Bay, north of the beach at Parking Field No. 5, the huge theater was reconstructed in 1991 and 1992. The outstanding facility seats 11,200 and features top-rate acts, upgraded seating, rest rooms, service stations and sparkling concession stands. The Jones Beach ticket office is open 10 a.m. - 6 p.m. daily and noon - 6 p.m. Sunday. The box office takes cash only. Tickets are also available through Ticketmasters and various retailers. For weather and additional ticket information, call (516) 221-1000.

The huge brown brick theater has giant light towers, bright white flagpoles, nearby police office, box office and sprawling parking and day-use areas near the lapping beach. Typical summer acts include the Beach Boys, Jackson Brown, Michael Bolton, Moody Blues, Hootie and the Blowfish, Boston, Linda Ronstadt, Sting and many others top-quality entertainers.

A concession stand with outdoor tables is at the Zachs Bay beach near the theater. This beach, complete with comfort station and outdoor showers, is popular with families. An umbrella rental is also operated here. Children will enjoy the enclosed playground near the beach that has a yellow and red slide, climber and benches for mom and dad.

The Tower: The Jones Beach Tower is a familiar landmark at the park and is modeled from the campanile of St. Mark's Cathedral in Venice. It is 231 feet tall, made of brick and stone and contains a steel tank holding 315,000 gallons of water pumped from four deep wells. Each well is more than 1,000 feet deep.

Swimming pool: The park has two Olympic-size swimming pools and huge bathhouses. The fieldstone bathhouses recently were renovated and the big pools can get busy. Concession stands serve bottled water, pretzels, soft drinks, grill items, draft beer and ice cream. You can even get a breakfast roll at the concessions; or try a barbecue sandwich, they are great! The east pool is open 9 a.m. - 7 p.m. on the weekends. The west pool is open 9 a.m. - 7 p.m. everyday. Outdoor seating is near the concession and the view of the beach and ocean is terrific. The buildings have buttressed corners and an Empire State Building theme and visual elements.

Beaches: The west bathhouse has a game area, bathhouse and a playground. Also here in a red brick building are a busy soft serve ice cream window and nearby large concession stand that features grill items, cold beer, pizza by the slice, meatball and hero sandwiches, grilled chicken breast sandwiches, bottled water, cheeseburgers, French fries and lots more.

Next to the full-service concession is the large Boardwalk Restaurant, surrounded by a wide wooden boardwalk and an ocean view. The appealing restaurant has glass walls and seating with a view of the beach. It serves a children's menu and full lunch and dinner. Try the beer batter cheese sticks. On the walls of the restaurant are many historic black and white photos.

Outside the restaurant that has tall vaulted ceilings is a breezy patio area with pleasant eating tables. Also near the restaurant are a lifeguard shack, coin-operated viewers, park information office, umbrella rental and the start of a .6-mile health walk with several fitness stations. The park information office has an interesting display of sea shells, seating, customer service counter and a wall mural depicting lifeguards from the 1930s to the present day.

Next to the park office, along the boardwalk, is a beach shop shaded by a blue awning. The shop sells sunglasses, sunscreen, chairs, post cards, T-shirts, colorful plastic toys, hats, sand toys, small boogie boards, games, souvenirs, candy, windchimes and more.

Golf: Aside from the mini-golf course at the west beach, the 18-hole pitch-putt course is near the beach and behind the boardwalk. Equipment can be rented at the small gray starter's shack. The longest hole on the gently rolling course is 79 yards, with many holes 50-60 yards long. The course is a par 54. Children under 10 years are not permitted to play, and kids 10-15 must be accompanied by an adult. The small course has designated tees, red flags marking the holes in the medium-sized greens and a senior citizen discount program. Parts of the course are outlined by split-rail fences and many of the holes are protected by sand traps. Hole No. 2 has a bunker guarding its left side.

Boating: Near the West End Beach, on the State Boat Channel, is a boat basin with 76 slips that are available for day visitors. A fish cleaning station and plenty of parking are at the modern basin. Anglers will find good surf fishing at the park.

Surfing: The designated surfing area at Jones Beach State Park is at the far west end, where the ocean and Jones Inlet meet. Surfing is open Dec. 1 to Labor Day. Surfers must respect protected shorebird nesting areas. No body boards are allowed. Parking is available at the west end II.

When surfing, wear a leash, don't surf alone, beginners should stay away from crowds, be courteous and pick a landmark and stay in front of it.

Nature: The park consists of a mixture of developed and undeveloped areas encompassing more than 2,400 acres. Jones Beach provides a delicate balance among the recreational demands of the public, preservation of an environmentally fragile landscape and the protection of wildlife indigenous to the region.

A birding list for the park encompasses the length of Jones Beach Barrier Island from Jones Inlet on the west to Captree State Park on the east. The list details bird sightings by season and abundance. As expected, the list details many types of shorebirds and gulls. In fact, 21 gulls, terns and skimmers are counted. The park also has 28 types of waterfowl, 10 species of bitterns and herons, 31 kinds of sandpipers and phalaropes, 35 species of wood warblers, creepers, vireos, 21 kinds of sparrows and many other songbirds, hawks and eagles.

The Long Island Chapter of The Nature Conservancy is working to save two rare birds, the piping plover and the least tern. Once abundant on the shores, the birds nearly disappeared in the late 1800s as they were hunted for sport and for their feathers. Protected from hunting in 1918, the population slowly recovered, reaching a peak in the 1940s.

Today the population of both species are lower then they've ever been. The development and recreational use of the species' essential habitat, Long Island's beaches, is the cause of the decline.

Piping plover are small, sand-colored birds with plump, short, black-tipped orange beaks. Because their color matches that of the pale dry sand, they blend remarkably into the background of open beach environments. Even if you don't see one right away, you may hear one. Piping plovers are named for their clear, bell-like whistles. Long Island beaches are home to about 200 nesting pairs of the rare shorebirds.

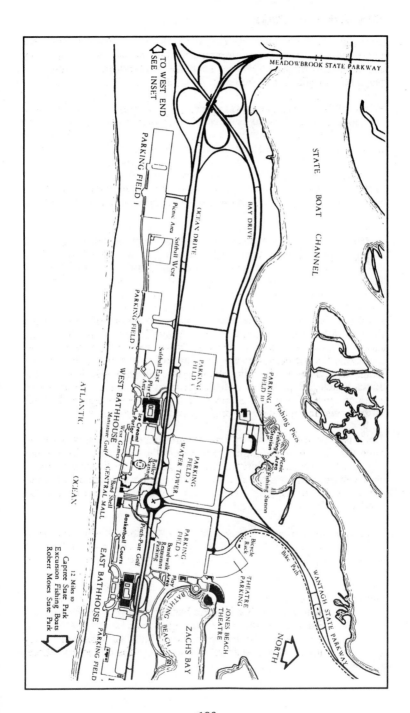

TO WEST END
SEE INSET

MEADOWBROOK STATE PARKWAY

STATE

BOAT

CHANNEL

PARKING FIELD 1

Picnic Area

OCEAN DRIVE

BAY DRIVE

Softball West

PARKING FIELD 2

PARKING
FIELD 3

PARKING
FIELD 10

Picnic
Area

Fishing Piers

Softball East

Play
Area

WEST BATHHOUSE

Ice Cream
Parlor

West Games
Miniature Golf

CENTRAL MALL

PARKING
FIELD 4

WATER TOWER

Fishing
Station

Fishing
Area

Fishing Station

ATLANTIC

OCEAN

Roller
Skating

Band Shell

Basketball Courts

Pitch-Put Golf

PARKING
FIELD 5

Boardwalk
Restaurant
Parking

Play
Area

Bicycle
Rack

Bike Path

WANTAGH STATE PARKWAY

EAST BATHHOUSE
PARKING FIELD

BATHING BEACH

ZACHS BAY

THEATRE
PARKING

JONES BEACH
THEATRE

NORTH

12 Miles to
Captree State Park
Excursion Fishing Boats
Robert Moses State Park

190

Least terns are gray and white birds, smaller and trimmer than sea gulls, with white foreheads topped with a striking black crown and long black-tipped yellow beak. Their call is a high-pitched, threatening screech. There are 1,500-2,000 pairs on Long Island.

Today, hundreds of volunteers are fencing in and posting nesting areas, educating landowners and beachgoers and keeping tabs on the birds. If you would like to know more or help, call The Nature Conservancy at (516) 367-3225 or (516) 329-7689.

Dunes protect the low shoreline along Jones Beach. Dunes are born as an object, such as a piece of driftwood or plant, slows the wind, causing it to drop its sand. This small mound blocks more wind-blown sand. The roots of beachgrass and other vegetation help hold the sand in place and gradually the small pile of sand develops as a dune. Hardy American beachgrass is being planted in places to help protect the rolling dunes. The grass protects the dunes by sending out roots that eventually sprout new shoots, which further protect and stabilize the dune.

Insider tips: Check out the drinking fountain in front of the Boardwalk Restaurant (it's made from an old ship's wheel!). The 14 parking fields can hold 23,000 cars. The west end beach is high energy and the least developed. The east beach area is more for families, especially the beach area near the theater. The boardwalk links all beach areas. The boardwalk is lighted for evening oceanside walking. Jones Beach has the feel of a giant day-use park.

Bring your surf board. Notice the beautiful flowerbeds that line the walkways and dot the park. The well-known theater is alcohol-free. Look for interesting birds in the salt marshes and wetlands along the shoreline.

Robert Moses State Park
Land: 875 acres   Water: Atlantic Ocean/Fire Island Inlet

Fire Island, a string-bean-shaped barrier island, has one of the world's greatest beaches. The narrow island stretches 32 miles from Democrat Point on the west to Moriches Inlet on the east. It includes 17 small communities, a county park, much of the Fire Island National Seashore and the popular Robert Moses State Park. The U.S. Park Service also has terrific visitor centers at Sailor's Haven, Watch Hill and Smith Point. The centers offer a wonderful opportunity to learn about the unique beach, area history, lighthouses and nearby natural areas. In places the interesting island is only a few hundred feet wide.

The park is on the western end of the island. You can reach the island by crossing the causeway and bridge over Great South Bay and Fire Island Inlet to several huge parking fields that can accommodate more than 8,000 cars.

The broad, flat beach draws an assortment of visitors. Some come to walk the ocean beach and survey the spacious sky, while others fry in the sun or splash in the surf. Some even come to ride the surf on a colorful boogie board. Some of the most interesting visitors, however, are fast-footed shorebirds, especially the scurrying sandpipers that dart to the surf's edge, probe the sand and always fly ahead, keeping their distance from wandering human visitors.

The beach was once known as the Great South Beach and the lighthouse in the distance was built in 1856, replacing the first one built in 1825, five miles away. The U.S. Army Corps of Engineers is almost constantly dredging the shipping channel that separates Fire Island from the next island so that the island doesn't wander westward. Learn more about the force and impact of blowing sand at nearby Sunken Forest.

Robert Moses was the president of the Long Island State Park Commission from 1924 to 1963.

The Captree State Park faces Robert Moses directly across the bay.

Information and Activities

Robert Moses State Park
Robert Moses Causeway
Fire Island, NY
(516) 669-0470

Directions: The park is on southern Long Island, 49 miles from New York City. It is at the end of the Robert Moses Causeway.

The park office is near the water in a gray shingle-sided building with white trim. Park police are stationed at the office.

Emergency number: Park police, (516) 669-2500.

Day-use areas: The sprawling park serves huge, well-equipped picnic areas and wide beaches. The park is crowded on hot summer weekends with swimmers, picnickers and sunbathers. Beach volleyball is popular. Each of the large parking fields has concession stands, swimming beaches and picnic areas. If you would like a close-up view of the lighthouse, park in field No. 5, at the east end of the park. You can walk from there.

Pitch-putt golf: Accessed from parking field No. 2, the lush 18-hole, par 55 course is open daily during the season. The last tee-off is at 6

p.m. daily. Golfers tee-off from a small wooden platform that is covered with artificial grass. The entrance to the small executive-style
course is along the ocean and near rows of sandy dunes. Along the
walkway to the course are picnic tables sitting in the sand a short distance from the surf's edge. It's great fun to hear the surf breaking while
lining up a putt on the tightly cropped course.

The small brick golf course building operates a cafe that serves rolls,
donuts, bagels, juice, milk, cookies and soft drinks. A pay phone and
club rental are also at the tricky little course.

The longest hole on the course is the 110-yard, par four 13th. Most of
the holes are 70-80 yards long and are par three. Bring your pitching
wedge(s) and a putter.

Beaches: The sand is as much like sugar as you will find along the
East Coast. Along the wide, flat beach is a large brick concession stand
that has glass walls extending up to the A-frame roof. Around the concession are hard-surface patio-like areas with hunter green metal-leg
picnic tables and a nearby first aid station.

The tasteful concession features draft beer, soft drinks, bagged ice, bottled water, pretzels, ice cream, vegetarian burger, ham on a roll, turkey
burgers, pizza, French fries and many other snacks. The concession is
open 8 a.m. - 6 p.m. daily during the season and 8 a.m. 6:30 p.m. weekends.

The gray and white lifeguard shack is outlined by a thick marina rope
and bits and pieces of lifesaving gear. Behind the concession are full-
service bathhouses and a nearby umbrella rental, outdoor shower, foot
bath and coin viewers.

Swimmers are to stay between the green flags and in front of the lifeguards. The view from the beach includes low dunes, far-off lighthouses, surf and ships.

Another guarded swimming beach is at day-use area No. 3 near the
Robert Mosses water tower. The small beach has a concession stand
with outdoor seating and an open-air bathhouse. Boogie boarders are
kept in restricted areas on all beaches. This smaller swimming beach
also has an umbrella rental and some scenic vistas. The older,
Colonial-like bathhouse has an interesting weathervane and roof line.

Other beaches are at the various day-use areas. Each of the swimming
beaches has small concession stands, pay phones and bathhouses. One
of the nicest swimming beaches is at area No. 5.

Hiking: You can walk the firm beach for an hour in either direction.
If you are seeking solitude, try visiting after a storm, on rainy days or

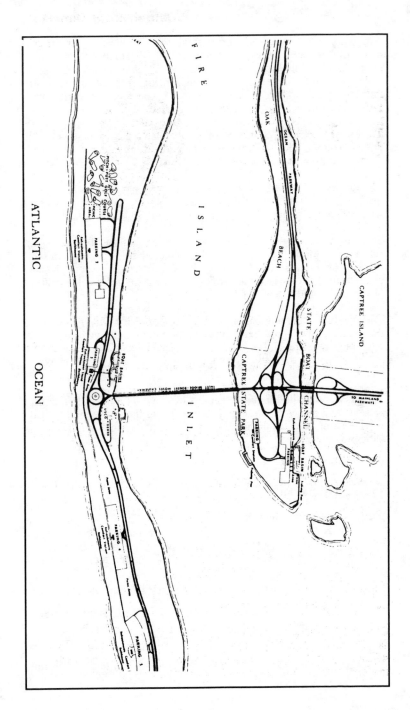

ATLANTIC OCEAN

FIRE ISLAND INLET

during the off-season. The crowds thin out if you hike east.

Boating: Temporary mooring is available at the boat basin.

Fishing: Many charter fishing boats offer an excellent chance to catch fish from their sometimes crowded decks. Many anglers also fish from piers and shorelines near the causeway. Most of these anglers use spreader rigs and live bait.

Species taken from these waters may include summer and winter flounder, snappers, bluefish, weakfish, pollock, striped bass, red drum, Spanish mackerel, American eel, crabs, fluke, black sea bass and others.

Near the park office, along the protected cove and boat basin, is wooden walkway with shoreline fishing access. The modern pier has an aluminum rail and allows anglers a good opportunity to get their lures and bait into some deeper water. From this vantage point, you can see Captree State Park across the bay.

Captree State Park has many charter boats that operate from its marina. The boats are of different sizes and offer ocean fishing, moonlight sails and sport diving. The Captree Boatmen's Association provides a free charter boat booking service. The office can provide information on sailing schedules, carrying capacities and various features. For more information call (516) 669-6464.

Nature: In many places around the park are gently rolling dunes sparsely covered with grasses and shrubs. Some dune restoration is underway at the park, especially at the east end. Fire Island exists because of grains of sand have been captured by beach grass. These grasses, sometimes called "lovers of sand," helped to form and shape the island.

This land formation has also caused its share of shipwrecks, the first recorded in 1657. More and more wrecks over the centuries caused the first lighthouse to be built in 1825, becoming operational in 1826.

Some of the most interesting walking is near the lighthouse or over the boardwalk near cranberry bogs and along the Great South Bay. Notice the trees with a bald south side. This is a result of salty winds and abrasive sand blowing steadily against them many months of each year. Watch out for poison ivy if you get off the trail or near clumps of natural vegetation.

Fire Island is on the Atlantic Flyway, a migration corridor that is heavily used by passing waterfowl, raptors and songbirds. Spring and fall bird watching is excellent. Shorebird watching is good in late spring, summer and early fall.

Surfing: Most of the boogie boarders wear colorful baggy shorts and their hats on backwards. It's your pleasure on appropriate surfing apparel—but do try the surf. Depending on conditions, surfers sometimes congregate near the older swimming beach near the lighthouse.

Surfing areas are designated at all field areas, beyond the lifeguard areas. During the off-season only field Nos. 2 and 5 are open to the public, fishermen and surfers. Surfers are allowed to use the entire west side of each of these large fields.

Surfers are reminded to wear a tether, don't surf alone, beginners should stay away from crowds, pick a landmark and stay in front of it, be courteous and help keep the beach clean.

Off-road fishing area: Before entering the four-wheel drive-only fishing area, you must have your permit and equipment checked. An attendant at the check-in station has a map and regulations governing the use of beach vehicles. All vehicles must have a shovel, tow rope and chain, jack and jack board, tire gauge capable of measuring a minimum of 5 PSI and tires that do not exceed 33 inches in diameter nor 12.5 inches in width. Access to this area is from the western end of the park road.

Vehicle permits are issued to bonafide sport fishermen only. Permits are valid for four-wheel drive vehicles only and you must stay on designated access roads and not exceed 10 mph. Fishing is in designated areas. You may enter between 5 p.m. and 7 a.m. A night fishing permit is also available.

Insider tips: Try the tidy, waterfront golf course. Surf anglers who have a four-wheel drive vehicle and permit should try some night fishing. As the sign says in the modern concession, "No ID, No Beer."

Be kind to the dunes; use the access routes to the beach. Bring your boogie board or surf board; the waves can build. The park is scenic, mixing the sights of causeways and large charter boats with dainty shorebirds, oily sunbathers and sometimes roaring surf. Try a charter boat fishing trip from neighboring Captree State Park.

Some years, more than 25 deer are killed by cars on the park roads. Drive carefully, especially at dusk. Notice the silver-colored trash barrels. Plan a visit to Sunken Forest (the harsh climate and bitter winds have stunted an entire forest's growth) and the Lighthouse Visitor's Center. The island can be reached by ferry. A 26-site family campground on the island, accessible by boat or ferry, is at Watch Hill.

Gov. Alfred E. Smith/Sunken Meadow State Park

Land: 1,200 acres
Water: Long Island Sound

The Long Island park takes its name from the low meadowland that separates the narrow sandy beach from the uplands. For many years, access to the area was by a quarter-mile-long boardwalk erected on thin stilts across the lush meadow and creek. Today, huge parking lots, a modern bridge and roadway for cars provides access for the hundreds of thousands who annually enjoy the beach, golf courses, long boardwalk, hiking and special events.

Sunken Meadow is well organized and adapted to serving huge crowds. The public recreation spaces are oversized, well-designed and properly identified. Most visitors head for the big beach and walk the three-quarter-mile boardwalk that features a concession stand and plenty of places to people-watch.

The park also has some wonderful and diverse natural areas including 200 acres of sandy bluffs, a brackish creek, salt marshes and densely wooded uplands that offer habitat for 84 species of birds. Another 60 or so avian species are seen seasonally in the woodlands and along wetlands.

The northern terminus of the Nissequogue River flows into the Sound at the park's east edge not far from large tracts of undeveloped lands that offer nesting and resting for migratory birds. The park has a bird checklist available from the park office.

Sunken Meadow has one of the best beaches on the north shore of Long Island. It has been open since the 1920s when legendary Robert Moses bought an abandoned estate in the area. Moses saw the potential for public recreation on the Sound directly north of the park that bears his name. Today, the park is so popular that many people visit during the off-seasons. Early September can be a great time to use the beach as the water and sun are still warm, while the crowds are gone. Hikers and walkers will enjoy the colorful fall or early spring in the diverse park.

Information and Activities

Gov. Alfred E. Smith/Sunken Meadow State Park
P.O. Box 716
Kings Park, NY 11754
(516) 269-4333

Directions: Off Rt. 25A on the north shore of Long Island, 43 miles east of Manhattan.

Beach: Some massive sycamore trees with their mottled bark shade the walk to the sprawling beach. A wide boardwalk is three-quarters of a mile long with a concession stand offering grilled foods, soft drinks and ice cream snacks. The concession has a cafeteria-style setup and a small sales counter that features children's sand toys, water bottles, beach balls, sunglasses and sunscreen. The view of the Long Island Sound is wonderful.

Outdoors, in front of the concession, are umbrella tables and coin-operated binocular viewers that allow you to scan the surf or bathing beauties. Along the giant elevated boardwalk are a stainless handrail and a great view of children splashing in the water and all types of people relaxing on the sand and fine-gravel beach.

Swimmers must stay between the flags in front of the lifeguards. A handicapped accessible ramp is available for beach-goers with physical limitations. A sand operated wheelchair is available at the park office.

Golf: The park operates three nine-hole courses, driving range and a practice putting green. The Blue Course is 3,060 yards, Red Course is 3,040 yards and the Green Course is a healthy 3,125 yards long. The courses are rolling, and plenty of mature trees line the watered fairways and medium-sized greens.

The tidy elevated practice tees at the driving range are separated by a brown, triangular, knee-high wall. A few benches and the pro shop are nearby. Yardage markers on stop-sign like signs tease golfers into hitting the ball farther. Soft drink machines are at the tree-lined driving range, they are busy after golfers plaster a bucket of balls into the field.

The park's pro shop sells golf shoes, many types of clubs, clothing, bags, umbrellas, hats and balls. Next to the sales floor is a sparkling clean cafeteria that features egg salad, turkey and ham sandwiches, assorted drinks, cookies, fruit cups, a breakfast menu and ice cream. Try a candy bar kept in a cooler near the food bar.

All golfers must register for a tee time. The course can be busy seven days a week. The last tee-off time each day is approximately 1.5 hours before sunset. A computer operated telephone call in reservation system can be accessed by calling: (516) 269-5351. Reservation cards can be purchased at the clubhouse and allows seven-day reservations. Non-card holders may make four-day reservations.

The Blue Course is the most difficult with narrow wooded fairways and multiple doglegs. The Green Course is the easiest, offering flat, wide fairways and simple pin placement. The Red Course is medium difficulty and popular.

Near the cafeteria is a small bar that features outdoor seating overlooking the busy starter's shack. Inside the bar are blue chairs on gray floors and many choices of cold beer. Split-rail fences outline various parts of the course, staging area and walkways.

Day-use areas: No skateboards or rollerblades are allowed on the pedestrian walkways near the beach. Thick stands of wood are mixed with open and rolling day-use areas. The park has hundreds of picnic tables scattered throughout the day-use areas.

Parking field No. 1 has the park office and bathhouse. The red-brick pavilion-like bathhouse has bulletin boards and is the gateway to the

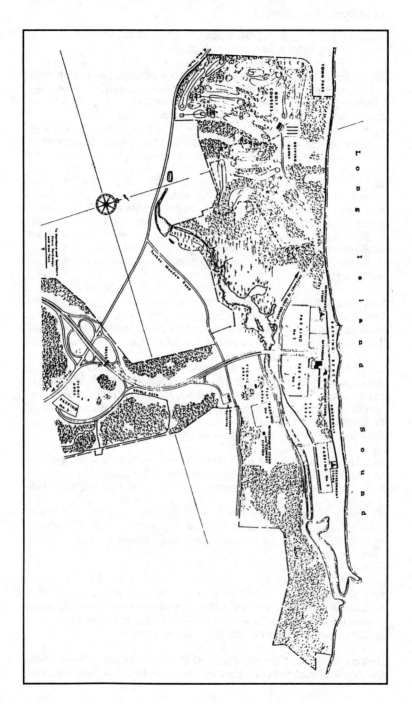

huge beach. This area also offers several soccer fields, basketball courts, baseball fields and children's playground.

Field No. 3 has expansive parking lots, baseball fields and access to the beach and boardwalk. Field No. 4 features three baseball backstops, colorful playground area with a tube slide and tiny steam shovel-like apparatus, hundreds of picnic tables and a pedestrian walkway.

Field No. 5 accesses the bridle trails and a children's environmental learning lab operated by Boces.

Hiking: Sunken Meadows has some wonderful places to walk, especially during the off-season when the park is quiet. A favorite walk is the Greenbelt Trail, which begins at the footbridge near the southwest corner of parking field No. 3. The walk wanders along the high bluff to Old Dock Road where you can drop down to the beach and return along the shoreline back to the parking field. The 2.5-mile loop offers views of the Nissequogue inlet and estuary, salt marshes and a long tract of firm beach.

No in-line skates are allowed on the boardwalk.

Fishing: Tautog, also known as the blackfish or bullfish, is identified by black and gray modeled white splotches and two or three large canine teeth. They range in size up to 15 pounds. They can be taken in the spring and fall and over offshore wrecks throughout the year. They prefer rocky bottoms, wrecks, bridge abutments and shellfish beds. Use medium-sized tackle, 15-30 pound line and a single tandem-tied bottom rig with a No. 2 or 4 Virginia-style hook. For bait try skimmer, crab or mussels.

Snappers, sometimes called baby blue or snapper bluefish, are thin streamlined bodies with a blue back, silver sides and small sharp teeth. Snappers can be 6-13 inches long, occasionally larger. They are best caught from late June to October in shallow bays, estuaries, harbors, rivermouths and other protected areas. Use a simple snapper hook, suspended 12-36 inches below a small float tied directly to the line. Try small segments of sand eel, fish fillets or squid as bait. Sometimes artificals like silver spoons, small jigs, tube lures and minnow imitations can work.

Summer flounder are often called flatfish or doormat fish. They are brown on top and white on bottom with a single triangular spot on the tail. These fish are usually less than six pounds, but a few 20 pound individuals are taken annually. The best fishing is from late-April to October. Summer flounder prefer sandy bottoms and will respond to a standard single-hook bottom rig with two-or three-ounce bank sinker. Try various cutbaits like squid, fish strips, sand eels, snappers or smelt. Also try lead-head jigs with a plastic jig body like a Salty Dog or Sassy

Shad-style.

Anglers pursuing weakfish, also known as sea trout, should try Long Island waters from late April to October, with peak activity occurring in the May-June spawning season. Weakfish prefer sandy shallow bottoms and shellfish beds during the summer and migrate to deeper water during the winter. Most anglers use 8-20 pound line, whippy rods, and slip-sinker or bottom rigs. For baits try clam, bloodworm, fish or squid strips, shrimp, liver or chunks of bunker, plastic worms, plastic body lead-head jigs, bucktails, minnow imitations and Salty Dogs. Present the lure, let it drift and work around shorelines, jetties, docks and other structure.

Winter flounder, a member of the flatfish family, are brown to reddish-brown and can be up to six pounds. These denizens are taken from early spring to fall and often relate to mud bottoms and shell flats. Use 8-20 pound line with single or tandem hooks and sinkers tipped with strips of clam, blue mussel, bloodworm or other cutbaits.

Scup, better known as porgies or silver dollar fish, have a small spiny mouth and silver sides. The best fishing is from June to October along gravel bottoms and mussel beds. Try a tandem-hook bottom rig tipped with a clam, bloodworm, squid, eels or mussels. Small jigs, plastic grubs and spoons can also produce scup if you fish on the bottom.

Other species in these waters are red drum, stripped bass, Atlantic cod, sea bass and crabs.

Nature: Bulletin boards at the bathhouse and park office feature nature history information. They list a variety of flora and fauna native to the area including great egrets, Canada geese, fiddler crab, jungle shell, oysters and others.

The park has three distinct environments: beach, salt marsh and wooded upland.

One of the more interesting aquatic critters native to the region is the blue mussel. At low tide blue mussel are sometimes exposed and easily seen. They are attached to jetties, rocks and pilings where they must hold their shell tightly closed until they are covered by the next high tide, when they can open up and begin to filter the water for the microscopic plants they eat.

Herring gulls is one of the most commonly seen of all gulls along the beach (and in parking lots). The immature bird is a dull brown. By the third year of its life it gains the snow white adult coloration. Gulls eat a variety of plants, animals and marine life and are important as natural scavengers. Some people call them "garbage cans with wings."

As you walk the shore, look for piping plovers. These tiny shorebirds forage and make their nest on sandy beaches. Unfortunately, their number have declined and are now a threatened species.

Also along the beach are hard-shelled clams. This bi-valve species is the chief commercial clam along the East Coast. It was a favorite food of Indians, early settlers and epicureans today, but it is sensitive to pollution and many of the hard beds of offshore Long Island have been closed.

Hikers may pass some cordgrass which is vitally important to the salt marsh community where it grows densely between the high and low tidal zones. It filters sediment and pollution from the water, aerates the muddy bottom and forms the beginning of a complex food web.

Along the edge of cordgrass flats you might see some snowy egrets that were once hunted almost to the point of extinction for their brilliant plumage. These birds have made a great comeback. Look for them along the marsh during the warmer months chasing after small fish in the shallows.

Occasionally horseshoe crabs are spotted along the beachfront. Horseshoe crabs aren't crabs at all—they are actually more closely related to spiders. This living fossil has not changed in 200 million years. In the late spring they come into the shallow waters and lay their eggs on the sand. The crab's pointed tail is used for steering, not defense. Fiddler crabs are also seen at the beach—or at least their small holes in the intertidal zone of the salt marsh are seen. Fiddlers are known as an indicator species due to its sensitivity to pollution. One of the male claws is much large than the other.

Along the dunes and uplands, shrub oak, a member of the black oak family, can tolerate poor soils. Its acorns are food for many species of birds and mammals. Often salt spray rose, a species introduced from Japan in 1872, is also seen along the marsh. The plant produces rose hips which are eagerly eaten by wildlife.

Bayberry can also be observed in this the park's diverse habitat. The shrub produces clusters of small round nuts covered with a grayish-white wax. Early settlers melted the wax to make sweet-smelling candles.

About 135 species of birds have been recorded at Sunken Meadows. The park has an active osprey nest at the west end of the creek. The fish-eating birds have been here since 1991 when two chicks were born. There are an estimated 30,000 pairs of osprey left in North America. The birds weigh three to four pounds and are 20-24 inches in length. They can have a wingspan of four to five feet and females can be slightly larger than males, having a darker necklace-like marking. Osprey are identified in flight by their continuos, heavy and labored wing beats. They are often seen soaring high or hovering over water before diving for a fish.

The osprey's foot has a reversible outer toe so that it can dive with its feet outward to grab fish that are close to the surface. Sometimes the birds become submerged before blasting out of the surf, shaking their wings free of water and rearranging the captured fish to be carried head-first. Osprey often carry small fish with one foot back to their nest or feeding station.

Special events: Golf tournaments, children's theater, runs and other youth activities are offered.

Insider tips: If you see a sea turtle, report it by calling the 24-hour hotline, (516) 728-8013. Call ahead; the golf course can be very busy. While walking around the park, observe wildlife in the many wetland and marsh zones. Bring your own grill; the ground-mounted grills can be hard to use. The regional state park office is at nearby Belmont Lake State Park. Plan a visit to watch the summer youth theater at Sunken Meadow. Model airplane shows and cross-country skiing are also popular at the park.

PHONE	PARK	Tent/trailers sites (h = hookups, e = electricity)	Trailer dump	Showers	Camper recreation	Cabins	Food	Store	Picnic tables	Shelters (• reservations)	Swimming beach (• bath house)	Swimming pool (• bath house)	Recreation programs (• performing arts)	Hiking	Biking	Nature trails	Fishing	Playground	Golf (•clubhouse)	Tennis	Pond or lake (• power boats ok)	River or stream (• power boats ok)	Launching site (• hand launch only)	Boat rental	Marina (• anchorage)	Pump out	Ice skating (•rentals)	Cross-country skiing (• rentals)	Sled slopes	Bridle paths
516 669-1000	LONG ISLAND REGION						▲		▲		▲•		▲	▷	▷	▷	▷	▲	▲•	▷	▲			▲			▲	▷	▷	▲
516 269-4333	Gov. Alfred E. Smith/Sunken Meadow						▲		▲		▲•		▲	▷		▷	▷	▲	▲•									▷		
516 581-1002	Bayard Cutting Arboretum						▲		▲				▲	▷		▷	▷	▲												
516 667-5055	Belmont Lake						▲		▲				▲	▷		▷	▲	▲			▷			▲				▷		▲
516 249-0700	Bethpage						▲		▲				▲	▷	▷	▷		▲	▲•	▲					•			▷		▲
516 265-1054	Caleb Smith State Park Preserve													▷		▷	▷													
516 669-0449	Captree						▲		▲				▲				▲	▲							•	▲				
516 423-1770	Caumsett												▲	▷	▷	▷	▲											▷		▲
516 581-2100	Heckscher	▲	▲	▲	▲		▲	▲	▲		▲•		▲	▷		▷	▲	▲			▷									
516 581-1005	Connetquot River St. Park Preserve													▷			▲													▲
516 766-1029	Hempstead Lake						▲		▲	▷			▲			▷	▲	▲			▷									▲
516 785-1600	Hither Hills	h,e	▲	▲	▲		▲	▲	▲		▲•		▲	▷			▲	▲												
516 669-2461	Jones Beach			▲			▲		▲		▲•		▲				▲	▲	▲•	▲•										
516 668-5000	Montauk Downs			▲			▲		▲			▲•	▲			▷		▲	▲•	▲•										
516 668-3781	Montauk Point						▲		▲								▲													
516 669-0449	Robert Moses						▲		▲		▲•		▲				▲													
516 323-2440	Orient Beach						▲		▲		▲		▲	▷		▷	▲	▲												
516 825-4128	Valley Stream								▲				▲					▲												
516 929-4314	Wildwood		▲								▷		▲	▷		▷	▷											▷	▷	
STATE HISTORIC SITE																														
516 922-9200	Planting Fields Arbtm. State Historic Prk.																													
516 427-5240	Walt Whitman Birthplace																													

▷ Availability of service or facility   ▲ Handicapped accessible   * Administered in conjunction with the Walt Whitman Birthplace Association

Tour the "Gold Coast" Coe estate and enjoy its historic mansion, gardens and greenhouses.

Here at this 19th-century Long Island farmhouse Walt Whitman, "poet of democracy," spent his earliest years.

207

Niagara Frontier Region

A merica's oldest state park is next to the roar of the mighty Falls. The park is complete with a wonderful high-tech visitors center and formal gardens where 4 million people annually come to see the Falls.

You can also view the Falls from the Observation Tower or take an exciting cruise on the famous Maid of the Mist. Don't miss a chance to walk right into a rainbow at the Cave of the Winds and over the footbridge into the breathtaking and thundering Niagara rapids.

The region has 13 wonderful parks that offer unlimited recreation.

You can sport fish, swim, attend a top-notch concert or play, learn from talented artists at the Artpark, cross-country ski, camp along Lake Ontario, visit the Schoellkopf Geological Museum, view the Niagara gorge, take a fall color drive or relax in a clean, quiet day-use area.

Old Fort Niagara State Historic Site is also nearby offering one of the finest living history and educational opportunities in the state.

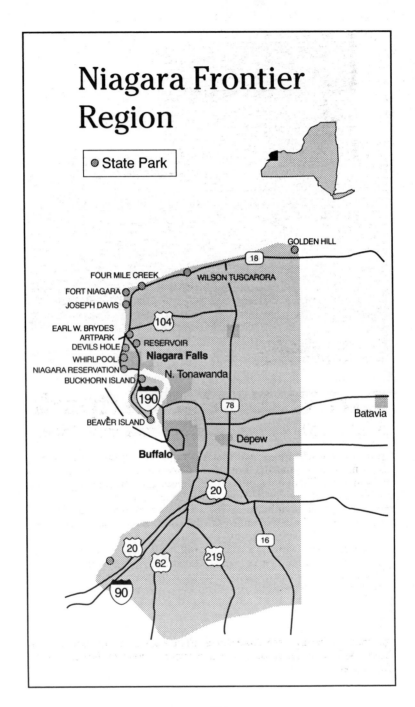

Niagara Frontier Region

◉ State Park

GOLDEN HILL

18

FOUR MILE CREEK
WILSON TUSCARORA

FORT NIAGARA
JOSEPH DAVIS

104

EARL W. BRYDES
ARTPARK
DEVILS HOLE
RESERVOIR
WHIRLPOOL
Niagara Falls
NIAGARA RESERVATION
BUCKHORN ISLAND
N. Tonawanda

190

78

Batavia

BEAVER ISLAND

Depew

Buffalo

20

20

16

62

219

90

Earl W. Brydges Artpark
Land: 200 acres Water: Niagara River

The wonderful Artpark is dedicated to preserving the finest in performing and visual arts programs. These days, the busy park relies on admission fees, donations and corporate sponsorships to continue quality art programs for this part of the state. Artpark & Company, a non-profit group of volunteers, operates the programming and productions, while the state park maintains the grounds and many buildings.

Performing arts events can include Buffalo Philharmonic Orchestra, Broadway musicals, internationally acclaimed dance companies, concerts, opera and top names in jazz, blues, folk and pop music. The park also conducts a variety of visual arts classes, workshops and demonstrations.

The Artpark is near many Niagara County attractions and campgrounds, including Four Mile Creek State Park in Youngstown, New York. Ask about group discounts and transportation to the park's performances.

Earl W. Brydges Artpark
P. O. Box 302
Lewiston, NY 14092-0028
(716) 754-9000 ext. 221

Directions: Just 10 minutes from Niagara Falls. Take the 104, 18F Lewiston Road exit off Robert Moses Parkway.

Theater: The stage has red steel supporting beams that carry the load of the steel doors and vaulting roof. Seating in front of the outdoor stage is notched out of the hill and outlined with wood landscape timbers. The theater can seat 2,324 and can accommodate 1,500 on the viewing lawn.

The ArtEl: Up on the broad wooden boardwalk which contains a number of Visual Arts and performing spaces, where various art activities take place. Performances are also held on the huge elevated, covered deck.

Self-guided tour: The park has an easy and interesting self-guided tour that winds through the park, stopping at nine learning stations (relating to the park's local and natural history). A four-panel brochure is available from the park office.

Visitors will learn that Lewiston was at the head of navigation of the lower Niagara River in the 17th, 18th and 19th centuries in a place where the Seneca Indians used to portage goods for the French to sites above the falls. They had to struggle up the steep terraces with their heavy loads. This difficult escarpment path became known as "crawl-on-all-fours." Along this route you will also see the fishing docks and walk along the edge of the Niagara River on red Queenston shale. This rock layer is about 435 million years old. This escarpment is where Niagara Falls began about 12,000 years ago.

The British engineer, Montressor, in 1764 built a wooden railway to expedite the carrying of goods up the escarpment portage. On the front lawn of the park, visitors will pass a 2,000-year-old Indian burial ground that contains the remains of Seneca and Neuter Indians. Many artifacts from the archaeological site are displayed at the Buffalo Museum of Science.

Buried by modern development and a painted parking lot is the site of the first trading post on the Niagara frontier. It was built by a Frenchman, Joncaire, in 1720 after he won the approval of the Seneca Indians, whose village was near the trading post. The bold paint-

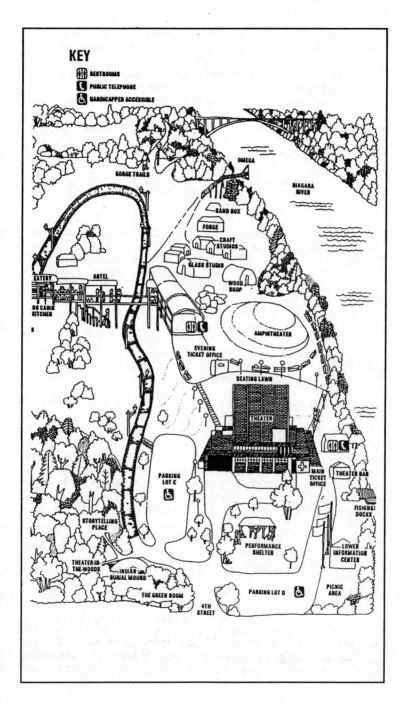

KEY

RESTROOMS
PUBLIC TELEPHONE
HANDICAPPED ACCESSIBLE

GORGE TRAILS

OMEGA

NIAGARA RIVER

SAND BOX

FORGE

CRAFT STUDIOS

GLASS STUDIO

WOOD SHOP

EATERY

ARTEL

LOG CABIN KITCHEN

N

AMPHITHEATER

EVENING TICKET OFFICE

SEATING LAWN

THEATER

PARKING LOT C

MAIN TICKET OFFICE

THEATER BAR

FISHING DOCKS

STORYTELLING PLACE

PERFORMANCE SHELTER

LOWER INFORMATION CENTER

THEATER-IN-THE-WOODS

INDIAN BURIAL MOUND

THE GREEN ROOM

4TH STREET

PARKING LOT D

PICNIC AREA

striped parking lot was the work of Gene Davis and a crew of eight. They used 600 colorful gallons of paint on the hard surface.

One of the most interesting art projects along the self-guided walk is the Omega Project at the foot of a former suspension bridge built in 1899. The unusual 30-ton structure jutting out over the Niagara River was designed by Owen Morrel, and built with mirrors reflecting the sky below and the water above. Presently the Omega is closed for repairs.

In the distance is General Brock's monument. The 130-feet-high monument is directly across the river in Queenston, Ontario. The British commander and administrator of Canada was killed near the site by American troops who scaled the steep cliffs in a surprise attack. The British eventually regrouped and won the battle.

Finally, along the pleasant trail is the old haul road which was used to haul thousands of tons of rock for the building of the Robert Moses Generating Plant upstream. Thirty-two dump trucks removed debris 24 hours a day to build up the fill the Artpark is constructed on.

Day-use area: The information center is in a brown brick building with a white canopy not far from the main entrance. Near the front entrance are many shady picnicking sites.

Other interesting outdoor spaces include the Green Room, Storytelling Place, Theater in the Woods and small performance stage with four tiers of seats and the Indian Burial Mound.

The park is also the location of Fort Jauntier, the second building in Lewiston, constructed in 1720. A palisade trading post was the first French fort on the Niagara River.

Red Road: Along the red brick walkway are a number of small gray workshops. Also along the walk are the forge, Quonset-type work spaces, Omega sculpture, picnic tables and grills, day-use shelter and rest room, clay studio, gas kiln and raku kiln. Inside the small studios are simple tables and supplies. Along a ridge line above the park are portable offices and 10 gable-roofed cabins that house artists. The resident artists interact with the public as they use the various workshops scattered around the Artpark. Some of the smaller studios in the park are on skids and can be moved to suit artists and programming needs.

Programming: The park is programmed for several weeks during July and August. Activities and events are open to the public on Tuesday through Sunday from 10 a.m. to 4 p.m. A reasonable park user fee is charged for workshop participation. The park is open year round for picnicking, walking and fishing. Patrons should call the Artpark Administrative Offices for a listing of events, dates and times. A variety of visual arts workshops for youth and adults are offered in the

upper park. Artist workshops and classes are also scheduled for the public. The park also hosts Elder hostel programming for 55-year-olds and over, children's day camps and young writers camp.

Public programs include a summer children's series and Camp Artpark, a day camp for youth. Pre-registration is required for some programs.

Special events: Varies each season.

Insider tips: Nearby Lewiston is clean and green. Walk the elevated boardwalk that connects the performance areas to the back end of the park. Fishermen also visit the park to shoreline fish the Niagara River. I saw a red fox near the cabin colony during my first early spring visit to this unique park.

The Joseph Davis State Park is between the Artpark and Fort Niagara.

Beaver Island State Park
Land: 952 acres   Water: Niagara River

Beaver Island State Park is on Grand Island between Buffalo and the city of Niagara where the first visitors to the area camped more than 3,500 years ago. Grand Island was called *"Owanungah"* by the Neuter Indians, *"Ga-We-Not"* by the Senecas who conquered them, and *"LaGrande Isle"* by the first French explorers.

After fur trading in the great oak forests of the island came rapid commercialization and the sawmill town of Whitehaven, a center for wood barrel stave making. In 1833, the East Boston Company of Massachusetts bought the 16,000-acre tract and timbered the island, using the quality wood for clipper ship construction. After stripping the island of its forest and cattle grazing, a grand hotel and expensive homes were developed.

Aside from the busy beach, boardwalk and 18-hole golf course, the most impressive building in the park is the River Lea, home of cattle rancher and farmer Lewis F. Allen, uncle of Grover Cleveland, the

22nd and 24th President of the United States. Built in 1849, the building is now the home of the Grand Island Historic Society. The museum is open occasionally.

Allen's sprawling farm was the major portion of the land that became the Beaver Island State Park in 1935. During the early years, the Civilian Conservation Corps built many of the facilities including the prominent and popular Casino-Bathhouse, which was leveled by fire in 1992.

Information and Activities

Beaver Island State Park
2136 W. Oakfield Road
Grand Island, NY 14072
(716) 773-3271

Directions: Grand Island is between Buffalo and the city of Niagara. The park is on the southern tip of the island. Toll bridges take you on and off the large island. The office building was built more than 100 years ago.

Emergency number: Park police, 278-1777.

Golf: The U.S. Golf Association-recognized golf course is a 6,779-yard, par 72 course that offers wide tree-lined fairways leading to large greens. A state-of-the-art sprinkler system keeps the course in excellent shape throughout the summer.

Golf lessons, a junior golf program and small concession with a few indoor tables are part of the 18-hole golf course operation. The food concession sells foot-long hot dogs, soft drinks, burgers, tuna sandwiches, ice cream and light breakfast items. A large practice green is near the first tee. The small pro shop features limited golf items.

A practice driving range is near the small brick concession stand and pro shop.

Day-use areas: Five picnic areas with nine shelters, a sandy and guarded beach, transient marina, boardwalk and golf course offer visitors variety at a quality state park near major metropolitan areas. Two of the shelters are in the marina area.

Swimming: The 600-yard-long sandy beach is flanked by a volleyball court, day-use shelter, performance stage, play equipment and wooden walking deck. The beach opens full-time in mid-June of each year from

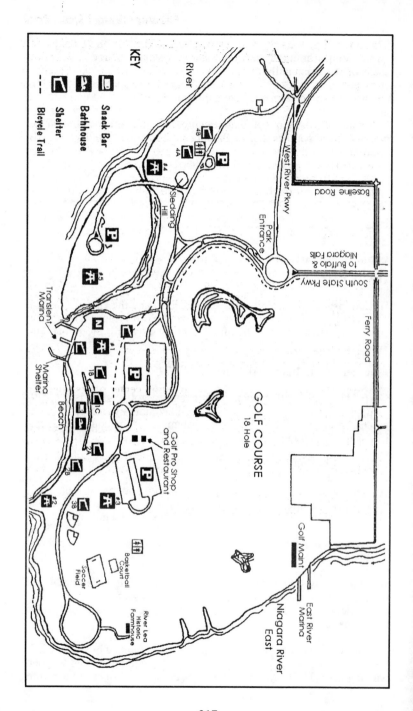

KEY

Snack Bar

Bathhouse

Shelter

Bicycle Trail

River

West River Pkwy

Baseline Road

Park Entrance

to Buffalo & Niagara Falls

South State Pkwy

Sledding Hill

Transient Marina

Marina Shelter

Beach

Golf Pro Shop and Restaurant

GOLF COURSE
18 Hole

Ferry Road

Golf Maint

East River Marina

Niagara River East

Basketball Court

Soccer Field

River Lea Historic Farmhouse

217

11 a.m. to 7 p.m. daily. The beach is next to the marina and open only when lifeguards are on duty. A water temperature gauge is on the outside of the lifeguard's office. The rest rooms behind the beach are attached to the park police headquarters and was once part of the large bathhouse and park office before burning in 1992.

Marina: An 88-slip (20 amp electrical service and water) transient marina is in the state park. Just six miles west is the Big Six Mile Marina which has nine docks, launching ramp and 134 slips. Boaters are urged to not pick up mil foil, watercress or zebra mussels and transport them from lake to lake. The tiny harbormaster's office has some local boating information, and nearby picnic tables makes this a pleasant spot to watch the boat traffic.

Boaters can stay at the Transient Marina up to two weeks.

Fishing: Shoreline access is gentle and excellent at Beaver Island, especially along the small bays in Picnic Area No. 5. As a whole, the Niagara River is a terrific year-round fishery. In places, it can be 160 feet deep and 200 yards wide filled with smallmouth, yellow perch, trout (lake, rainbow and browns), walleye, carp, catfish, smelt, coho and Chinook.

Winter: The park operates a sledding hill, snowmobile trails. Cross-country skiing and ice fishing are popular.

Nature: The seasonal colonial-looking nature center offers youth and some adult programs each summer. The picnic shelter is surrounded by plenty of day-use areas and amenities. A huge sycamore tree towers over the nature center that contains some free-standing glass-front display cases. The humble displays exhibit shells from the Niagara River, wasp nests, insects, a plant collection, seed pods and other natural history information. There are also nature activities available here.

Insider tips: The sandy beach is one of the largest in the region. Hard-surfaced bike paths connect park facilities.

Golden Hill State Park
Land: 378 land acres (133 acres are under water) Water: Lake Ontario

The state acquired the park in 1962, only four years after the Thirty Mile Point Lighthouse was decommissioned by the U.S. Coast Guard. A replacement light on a tall steel tower is now located near the boat launch about one mile from the original kerosene-powered lighthouse.

Golden Hill State Park is a wonderful getaway spot for those who want a quiet camping experience along the sometimes blustery Lake Ontario shoreline. Visitors will enjoy the rocky banks of exposed Queenston Shale that was deposited here 450 million years ago during the Ordovician Period. The rock was formed from sand, silt and clay eroded from Taconic Mountains on the East Coast. This shale, which is completely devoid of fossils, has small amounts of iron oxide which color it rusty red. Today, a thin layer of glacier till composed of silt, gravel overlies the shale.

The park along the lake has lots of recreation opportunities including hiking, camping, cross-county skiing, fishing, hunting, historic programs and wildlife viewing. The park has eight types of goldenrod, 50 species of wildflowers, stands of red cedar, white pines, and dogwoods that flower along the high banks.

Information and Activities

Golden Hill State Park
Lower Lake Road
Barker, NY 14012
(716) 795-3117
(716) 795-3885 - campsite office

Directions: The park is off Route 18, along the Lake Ontario shoreline. The small park office has an ice machine, pay phone and newspaper machine in front of it.

Emergency number: Park police, (716) 278-1778.

Campground: The on-the-water camping sites are excellent at Golden Hill. These sites have a glorious lake view with easily seen Canada in the distance on clear days. The campground has 22 electric/water/pull-through and 28 non-electric sites. You can see the water from every site in the park.

Loop A campsites are wide open and sunny. The campground is only filled on holidays and a few prime summer weekends.

Loop B sites are gravel and grass with many pull-through sites. If you would like to be near the lighthouse choose sites 29 or 30. These sites are about 40 feet above the lake surface and you can hear the waters washing against the rock shoreline. One of the nicest sites is 33, which allows you to pull your rig under a small grove of pine trees. This site has a panoramic view of the sparkling lake.

Loop C is west of the lighthouse and open. A few small trees are scattered throughout this section. Under a few shade trees are sites 39 and 40. Both of these sites are on a slight rise and offer an excellent water view. Moving westward in the loop, campers will find top-quality, shadier sites like 44, 45, 48 and 49. All of these sites can accommodate large RV rigs.

Lighthouse: The stone lighthouse has a slate roof and a red top and a tan clapboard building joining it. In the summer the lighthouse is open 2 p.m. - 4 p.m. Friday-Sunday from July 1st to Labor Day. A park interpreter offers programs. A self-guided brochure is available for the lighthouse grounds.

The Thirty Mile Point Lighthouse was built in 1875 near the mouth of Golden Hill Creek to warn approaching vessels of a shifting sandbar and dangerous rocky shoals extending out into Lake Ontario. Before the construction of the powerful light, five large vessels were wrecked. The unfortunate ships include the French LaSalle (1678); unnamed French vessel (1688); Ontario, an English naval ship (1780); Mary (1817) and an unknown steamer (1873).

A schooner brought hand-carved stone from Chaumont Bay near the source of the St. Lawrence River to be used in the construction of the handsome lighthouse. These heavy blocks of stone were hauled ashore and up a steep bank by sturdy horses driven by George B. Hood and William Atwater.

The tubular building is more than 60 feet high and has a light cranberry-colored slate roof. Access up the tower is by a circular steel stairway that leads visitors to a wonderful panoramic view. A huge six-sided fresnel lens, brought from France for $15,000, looks like a "giant cut glass bowl," according to Somerset town historian Lorraine Wayner. The one-ton, precision cut optical piece magnified the light from a kerosene brass lamp to 600,000 candlepower. The focused light could be seen for up to 18 miles, and it guided ships safely for many years before electronic navigation aids. Originally, the light turned on a precision clockwork mechanism, but later it was hooked up to an electric motor. The light had a distinctive flash-pattern that helped ships' captains identify the exact shoreline location. Today, the modern beacon is on top of a steel tower next to the fog horn building. This automatic light is maintained by the U.S. Coast Guard.

As shipping increased, the structure was altered to accommodate two families, one on the ground level and one upstairs. The pair of caretakers worked 24-hour shifts checking the light every three hours and logging the weather every four. It is reported they also scrubbed the engine room and polished the brass daily. The lighthouse is in fairly good condition for a building that has remained unheated for many years.

The U.S. Coast Guard bought the lighthouse in 1935 and operated it until 1958. It was closed because the sandbar eroded and newer lighting and navigational devices were developed. The lighthouse was closed and dismantled when purchased by the state in 1984. The Friends of Thirty Mile Point, a volunteer group, assist with restoration, preservation, interpretation and promotion of the lighthouse.

A barn stands behind the lighthouse that previously served as a carriage house.

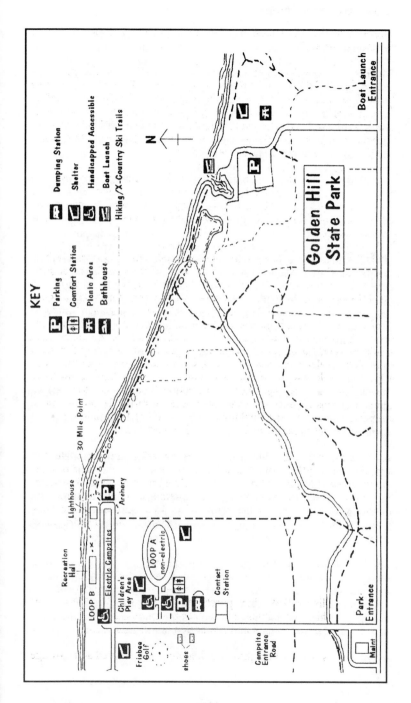

KEY

Parking

Comfort Station

Picnic Area

Bathhouse

Dumping Station

Shelter

Handicapped Accessible

Boat Launch

Hiking/X-Country Ski Trails

Golden Hill State Park

N

30 Mile Point

Lighthouse

Recreation Hall

LOOP B

Electric Campsites

Archery

LOOP A non-electric

Children's Play Area

Frisbee Golf

shoes

Contact Station

Campsite Entrance Road

Park Entrance

Maint.

Boat Launch Entrance

Day-use areas: A volleyball court is near the check-in booth and several small picnic shelters are scattered around the open day-use areas. A small play area with swings and benches is near the camping sites. A baseball backstop and one basketball goal are near Loop C in the campground. Access to the day-use area at the boat launch is free. This area has a small shelter and picnic tables scattered near the water.

Recreation hall: This tan brick building is about 50 yards from the lighthouse and contain a foosball game, ping pong and air hockey tables, and place for indoor recreation programming. A red handrail leads along the shoreline from the recreation hall. The recreation hall building once housed a foghorn and compressed air tanks that made it honk.

Boat launch: Located about a half-mile east of the main park, the launch was built in 1988. In the launch area are trailheads, portable toilets and day-use areas. The two-lane ramp is on a protected cove. There is also some good fishing from along the shore at the ramp. There is a fee to launch.

Fishing: You may fish off the small pier beneath the lighthouse or carefully dock a small boat there. Anglers may catch white perch year-round from the small pier using a minnow. Panfish, a few walleye, salmon, trout and some bass are also taken from the park access, especially in the spring and evening. Most shoreline anglers use jigs and minnows or twister tails.

If you catch an Atlantic salmon, help with the restoration by sending in the date and location of each catch, method of capture, color of tag and number, and length of fish. Call (716) 691-5456 for more information about the Atlantic salmon program.

Hiking: The park maintains 5.5 miles of mowed hiking trails that are open year-round.

Request a copy of the yellow covered self-guided trail brochure. The educational hiking trail is less than a mile long and starts at the lighthouse following the lake to the boat ramp. Cross-country skiing is popular at the park when conditions are right.

Visitors hiking the self-guided nature trail will learn about local geology, cliff swallows, trees (including hawthorns, spruce, mountain ash and juniper), gulls, a grove of red oak and their usefulness to man, Golden Hill Creek, willow trees that love the moisture and sunlight, and facts about the huge lake. The current in the lake is one-third mile per hour and the average depth is 283 feet, with some places up to 800 feet deep. A stick thrown into the lake at the park would take 18 days to reach the St. Lawrence River.

Nearby state park: The 390-acre Wilson-Tuscarora State Park offers a boat launching ramp, handicapped accessible fishing pier, hiking trails and wetland area. The park also has scenic views of Lake Ontario.

Also, a 823-acre Lakeside Beach State Park has 274 campsites, three playfields, a picnic shelter and picnicking areas. The park has scenic views of Lake Ontario.

Insider tips: The waterside camping sites are some of the finest in the state. From these sites you can watch the azure blue water and the occasional ship slowly pass by. This is a peaceful, low energy park, ideal for history buffs, fishermen and folks who want to camp near the sometimes windy lake. Bring your boat; there's plenty of room to park your craft at the campsite. A great ice cream shop is near the entrance to the boat ramp. By the way, that curious round red building next to the lighthouse is a well and pump used for drinking water.

Fort Niagara State Park and Old Fort Niagara Historic Site

Land: 284 acres   Water: Niagara River and Lake Ontario

No other American historic site has experienced such a lengthy military occupation as this point of land at the mouth of the Niagara River. The history of the fascinating site spans 300 years. During these three centuries garrisons were maintained on this flat, slightly elevated peninsula that is a strategic gateway to the Great Lakes.

Because Fort Niagara was on the westward route to the heartland of the continent, it has undergone numerous transformations. After the opening of the Erie Canal in 1825, however, the strategic value of the fort diminished. Yet it remained an active military post into the 20th century.

The site proved to be adaptable. From its beginnings as a small stockade, the fort grew and changed with the military technology of the times. The buildings within the walls of the large complex are preserved and represent the different phases of development and military use.

Three nations' flags are flown daily above the parade ground symbolizing the countries that have held the fort. Each competed for the support of the fourth nation, the powerful Iroquois Confederacy. The French established the first post, Fort Conti, in 1679. It's successor, Fort Denonville (1687-88), was equally short-lived. In 1726 the French erected a permanent fortification with the construction of the impressive "French Castle."

Britain gained control of Fort Niagara in 1759 during the French and Indian War, after a 19-day siege. The British held the post throughout the American Revolution but were forced, by treaty, to yield it to the United States in 1796. Fort Niagara was recaptured by the British in 1813. It was ceded to the U. S. a second time in 1815 at the end of the War of 1812.

That was the old forts' last combat, and since has been a peaceful border post. During both World Wars, the fort was a training center and barracks for American soldiers. The last units were drawn out of the complex in 1963. The old fort was restored between 1926 and 1934 and it is operated by the Old Fort Niagara Association Inc., a nonprofit organization, in cooperation with the New York State Office of Parks, Recreation and Historic Preservation, which operates the adjacent Fort Niagara State Park.

Information and Activities

Old Fort Niagara
P. O. Box 169
Youngstown, NY 14174
(716) 745-7611

Fort Niagara State Park
1 Maintenance Avenue
Youngstown, NY 14174
(716) 745-7273

Directions: The historic park is 17 miles north of Niagara Falls. Reach the fort from the Robert Moses Parkway or by Route 18F from the village of Youngstown.

The fort: The fort is open 9 a.m. until late afternoon, year-round. There is a fee and many special events are conducted at the fort. Events include encampments, artillery school, King's birthday and 1812 French and Indian War re-enactments, century field days and many other history-based activities.

The long and complex history of Fort Niagara is best understood by taking the self-guided walking tour of the site. A detailed brochure is given to all visitors upon entering the fort. Today the fort contains some of the finest collections of 18th century military architecture, and it all begins at building No. 1, the provisions storehouse.

Provision storehouse (1762): Built by the British, the stone building was used as a depot for military supplies for much of the Great Lakes. Basic rations of rice, salted meat (usually pork), dried peas and butter were transported in barrels for trips to Michigan and beyond. The foods had to be salted or dried to withstand up to two years of storage and slow land travel. Today the building houses historic oil paintings, displays and dioramas about the Campaign for the Colors, samples of French uniforms, a birch bark canoe, historic flags, a cannon and written historical information.

Powder magazine (1757): This massive building is one of two surviving French-built structures. The thick building was designed to hold huge quantities of explosives needed to support the French military in the Ohio Valley. Notice how the magazine was carefully designed to withstand hostile bombardment. The four-foot-thick walls and heavy stone arches were reinforced with layers of earth and rubble between the arch and roof. At one time, hundreds of kegs of gunpowder were held on wooden racks along the walls. Today, inside the cool building are exhibits detailing archeological digs at the fort, examples of long guns, various ornate military uniforms, fur trading information, musket balls and more.

South Redoubt (1770): Today, this stone structure near the entrance to the park is where the ticket booth is located. About 200 years ago, it was the first guard post. It was also one of the first imposing structures that could withstand enemies with more military might more than Indians. From this time on, earthen fortification was not totally relied upon.

18-pounder battery (1843): During the vicious War of 1812, Fort Niagara had many artillery volleys with Fort George. During mid-1800s modernization, the 18-pound cannons were added. From their position, you can see the Niagara River toward the village of Youngstown.

Casements (1872): The casement and other land defenses are important features of fortification. The subterranean galleries once housed cannons, 24-pound howitzers and muskets. Near station No. 7 you can learn about the land defenses that included thick earthen walls, slopes and dry ditches. Sometimes the earthen features were sided with wooden planks. Imagine the smoke and deafening noise of each report.

The Three Historical Flags: In the middle of the fort are three flag-

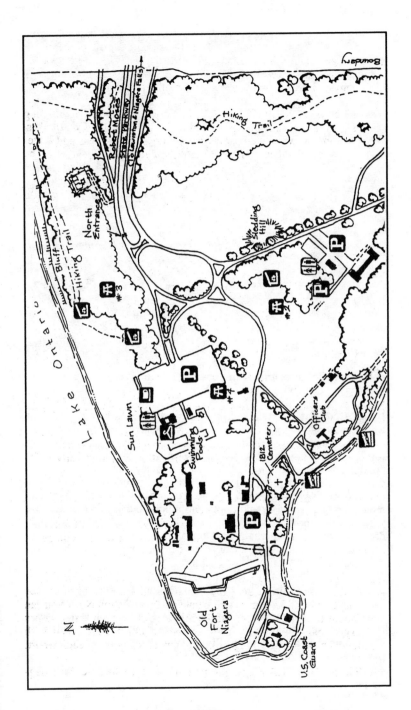

Boundary

Hiking Trail

Robert Moses
State Parkway
(To Lewiston & Niagara Falls)

North
Entrance

Sledding Hill

Bluff
Hiking Trail

#3

#1

Lake Ontario

#2

Sun Lawn

Swimming Pools

1812 Cemetery

Officers Club

Old Fort Niagara

U.S. Coast Guard

N

poles that fly the colors of the countries that have occupied it. The flags have been flying since the 1930s.

North Redoubt (1771): Like the south redoubt, this stone building was designed to support light artillery on its second floor, while a guard of 20 men could be sheltered on the first floor for long periods. The fort's pair of stone redoubts are unique in North America. The back-breaking labor need to build these solid structures came from the soldiers. Their labor produced these functional buildings that had elements of classical Greek and Roman architecture: temple fronts, pediments, arched windows and doors and a belt course of stone near the parapet. The roofs, however, have the flaring eves of a Chinese pagoda. As you walk up the steps, notice how the thick timbers have cupped from years of foot traffic. The cannons are also polished from being touched by thousands of visitors.

French Castle (1726): The largest and most interesting building in the fort is the "French Castle." The wonderful structure has guarded the entrance to the Niagara River for more than 250 years. It is considered to be the oldest building in North America between the Appalachian Mountains and the Mississippi River. With thick stone walls and dark passages, the building truly is castle-like.

The castle was the center of the fort established by the French, and was initially referred to as the "house of peace," after six years of negotiations with the Indians. It was enclosed by a simple stockade, but was more than a mere trading house. Its stone walls were proof against muskets and arrows and was strong enough to withstand an all-out attack by the British while housing and feeding a garrison. The building could meet all the needs of 60 men, including quarters, storehouse, a powder magazine and even a well was located within its walls.

Visitors can enter the castle through one of three doors on the ground floor. The middle door was the main entrance during the 18th century. It opened on a main vestibule that connected to all other parts of the main floor. Barracks and storerooms are clustered around the vestibules, much like buildings that were situated around the parade ground of the fortress. Here the soldiers reported for duty and protected their source of drinking water in the event of an attack. Near the well is a wonderful wall display that detail the grounds.

The centrally located well is one of the best known features of the fort. One of the intriguing stories about the fort is of a headless ghost of a French officer who is said to inhabit the building and has supposedly been seen sitting on the curb of the well. Notice the huge hand-hewn supporting beams that were used to carry the tremendous weight of the fortified stone building.

Other rooms on the ground floor include a trade room (which had an inventory of cider, furs, food and other products), soldier barracks a guardhouse, powder magazine, a small room that was occasionally used as a solitary confinement cell called the "black hole," a general storeroom and bakery. Notice the thick shutters on the outside of the windows and the method of how the massive front door is locked. Also, try opening and closing this mighty door—you'll be surprised!

The first floor of the castle was used as living quarters, with the officers in the rear of the building and the enlisted men in long, tray-like bunks with thin stuffed mattresses. The first permanent place of worship is Western New York, where priests were occasionally stationed. The chapel was probably used until 1757, at which point it was replaced by a separate building, which was eventually converted into offices. Seven officers apartments of the French period are here with stone floors, which greatly reduced the chance of fires. Most of these floors were eventually replaced. In fact, the small powder magazine is the only room remaining with stone floors. Also on the floor are the commander's quarters and a small room that historians are still uncertain of its use. Some think the room was used to house important prisoners like Major Robert Rogers, the famous British ranger who arrived in chains from Michigan's Fort Michilimackinac.

The last three rooms on the floor include two officers apartments and a

large kitchen where meals were prepared. Above this floor is the attic that comprises a large single room. The day-to-day use of the large room is still unknown, but it was probably used for storage, a place for heavy gun positions and possibly an entertainment space. If possible, join one of the many guided tours to the castle. The interpreters have wonderful stories of the lives behind the walls of Fort Niagara.

Gift shop: A small gift shop is in a lighthouse at the edge of the parking lot. The bigger, well-stocked gift shop is inside the fort walls in a log building. The Trading Post gift shop has lots of books, maps, quilts, Christmas tree ornaments, Indian toys, hard candy, jaw harps, wood toys, photographs, jewelry, an old forge, leather goods, refreshment counter (soft drinks, ice cream treats and snack foods), candles, small flags, arts and crafts. Other items include bead work, porcupine quill earrings and local and native American artwork.

History books include Ghost of the Haunted Well, A History and Guide to Fort Niagara, Memories of the Wars in North America, War Along the Niagara, War of Independence, British Firearms and Indian Guide to the Great Lakes. Several videos also are available. The log cabin-style gift shop has a stone fireplace, beam ceilings and wood floors.

Conference center: Inside the red brick building are offices and the park police headquarters. This area is outside the fort complex.

Day-use areas: Shady picnicking areas are along the shore and throughout the heavily used park. Other facilities include a windsurfing area, cross-country ski trails, soccer goals, old lighthouse gift shop, basketball goals, tennis court and several large brick buildings. Small groups of play apparatus are scatters around the expansive day-use areas. One of the most attractive places to picnic is under the wide canopy of the double row of maple trees that bisects the park. The pool, nature center, fishing, boat ramp and day-use areas are outside of the fort complex.

Swimming pool: The pool has a beautiful view of the lake, food concession with three walk-up windows and bathhouse. Inside the pool are picnic tables near the deck, a diving pool and a large sunning lawn. The pool is outlined by a green chain-link fence and Lake Ontario. The adjoining park and day-use areas are huge.

Nature center: Near the swimming pool and lake is the small brown nature center that is open seasonally. Inside the center are polished hardwood floors that have many showcase-type displays positioned around the room. Themes of the displays include the geology of the Niagara, mammal and raptor mounts, creatures of the night and others. There is a small space for classroom work and programs. The walls are covered with posters about the wind, winter season, birds, Niagara frontier, New York state and plenty of other natural history information. About half of the building is used as an equipment storage shed.

Fishing: Try the Niagara River or Lake Ontario where game and panfish are plentiful. Many species are present including coho and chinook salmon, brown, rainbow and lake trout, pike, walleye, perch, catfish and many types of rough fish.

Boat launch: Two ramps are next to each other and charge a small fee. A fish cleaning station is at the northern set of ramps. The pair of ramps have twin hard-surface lanes and 50-foot-long wooden courtesy docks. A small marina with mooring slips is nearby.

Nearby parks: Four Mile Creek State Park has 266 campsites, 100 outfitted with electrical service. The park has hot showers, swimming, 200-year-old oaks, fishing, day-use areas and trails. This park is a great place to camp and then visit the many attractions in the area. Call (716) 745-3802. The park is four miles from Fort Niagara.

Insider tips: Take a guided tour of the fort, if possible. Plan a half day or more to wander around the fort complex. A terrific long weekend could be planned around visiting the fort and nearby related attractions including the Fort Niagara Light, Fort Niagara Military Reserve, Salt Battery, Youngstown, River Road, learn about the Battle of La Belle Famille, Portage Road, Devil's Hole and, of course, Niagara Falls. Use your imagination for what it was like to build and live in a wilderness fort like this one 200 years ago or more. The famed French explorer, LaSalle once occupied the fort. Try to see the CN Tower in Toronto through the coin viewers along Lake Ontario. The archeology building, at the fort entrance, is open to the public on a limited basis, i.e., during archeology week each fall.

Niagara Reservation State Park
Water: Niagara River and Falls

Early on the tremendous power of Niagara Falls was harnessed to drive huge water wheels used to grind grain, salt and tan hides. It wasn't until the turn of the century that we discovered a whole new way of using water power. Diversion of the fast-flowing river spun turbine wheels that generated electric power which could be sent far from the river. In 1958, excavation began for what would become the Western world's largest hydroelectric plant, the Niagara Project, built by the New York Power Authority. Today, one-third of the state's electricity is generated by the New York Power Authority. Be sure to visit the power plant, just north of the Robert Moses Parkway. To feel the power of the Falls, visit Terrapin Point at the Cave of the Winds on nearby Goat Island.

"There is an incredible cataract that has no equal," said Father Louis

Hennepin, the first to chronicle the Falls. He riveted the eyes of Europe on this key to the new world. For whoever controlled the Niagara River controlled the trade of the entire Great Lakes region. In the centuries that followed, Niagara became the ultimate destination for manufacturers, entrepreneurs, adventurers, honeymooners and tourists. Today, three million people visit the Niagara Reservation each year.

The Falls are a living story of geologic forces in action. At the end of the last ice age a river was formed by melting glaciers. It flowed from Lake Erie and poured over the Niagara escarpment seven miles north of where the Falls are today. That was 12,000 years ago. Since then the Falls have cut into the cliffs, moving their position upstream and carving the sheer-faced Niagara gorge as they went. The powerful Falls also created an unusual misty environment that allows rare plants and flowers to grow, creating surroundings of exquisite beauty. If you want to learn more about the ecology and geology of the falls, be sure to visit the Schoellkoph Museum (call 716-278-1780) and nearby aquarium just north of the visitors center. Take the trail; it's a scenic walk.

Niagara Reservation, the crown jewel of the New York state park system, was established in 1885. But it wasn't always that way. A little over 100 years ago there were no state parks and the area around Niagara Falls was a mixture of trampled woods and rampant commercialism. Naturalists and landscape architects decided that something had to be done to preserve and restore Niagara. A 16-year struggle to make that dream a reality culminated in the reservation landscape plan. The first superintendent, Thomas Welch, initiated the ambitious construction effort. Today, New York state is working to further preserve the natural wonder. From the state park you will have the closest and best view of the falls.

Information and Activities

Niagara Reservation
P.O. Box 1132
Niagara, NY 14303-0132
(716) 278-1770

Directions: North of Lake Erie on the Niagara River at the America Falls. From Buffalo area North on Rt. I-190 to the Robert Moses Parkway. If coming from the points East, take Routes 18 or 104 to the Robert Moses Parkway. If arriving from Canada, best bridges to cross are the Lewiston-Queenston Bridge or the Rainbow Bridge.

Orin Rehman Visitor Center: This beautiful granite building with an arched glass roofline houses a wonderful series of exhibits that detail the history of the Falls and offers lots of interesting facts about the area. From the building you can hear the thunder of the Falls in the distance. The lower level of the visitors center has a small snack bar, rest rooms and professionally prepared exhibits.

Some of the most interesting artifacts are the old black and white photos of the earliest tourist efforts. Other colorful and educational exhibits highlight the inspiration, technology, history and science of the Falls. A giant screen theater (small admission) and a heavily-stocked gift shop are also in the lower level. Here are photos and the exciting stories of the devils and stunt men who risked their lives climbing over cataracts for a chance of fortune and fame.

Great Lakes Garden: The turf is like that found on the finest golf course and flowers from a lush nursery. In the spring, under flapping flags, tulips blossom and splashes of color surround the hundreds of thousands of visitors who annually stroll the winding walkways through the formal garden. The 85th longitude cuts through the garden where round ground-mounted placards detail historic facts and several statues stand guard over the manicured flower beds. Tasteful green street lights illuminate the gardens at night and line the walkways to the Falls, where an aluminum hand rail is next to the river and winds toward the deafening Falls. There are a number of benches and coin viewers along the rushing river.

Observation area and tower: The wide hard-surfaced observation platform is dotted with coin viewers and visitors pressed against the rail looking down at the seemingly small Maid of the Mist tour boats below, the Skylon Tower, Minolta Tower, American Falls, Horseshoe Falls, Victoria Restaurant and the sheer gorge walls. Also from the observation area visitors will see birds flying along the cliffs, rainbows and mist over the gushing Falls.

There is no greater bargain than the 50-cent fee to ride the elevators to the top of the observation tower for a panoramic view of the Falls, city scape, the base of the American Falls, colored foaming waters, rainbows and gulls flying along the river looking for stunted fish that were flung over the watery edge. Coin viewers are on the top deck that is outlined by a green safety railing. One of the most interesting views is of the people below, pressed against the railing gawking at the thundering water as it plunges over the huge ledge. On a busy summer day, as many as 10,000 people daily ride the elevator to this spectacular view of one of North America's greatest natural wonders.

The Falls: The Falls, one of the modern wonders of the world, are a thundering wall of water that visitors will feel vibrating the ground as they approach the area of the cataract which produces the world's

largest waterfall by volume.

The Falls began 12,000 years ago when the meltwaters of the Wisconsin glacier created the Niagara River. The reason for such a dramatic vertical wall of water, and also the shape of the canyon downstream for the falls, is due to the hard Niagara dolomite overlying soft under layers that can be easily worn away. Every so often support of the uppers layer is eroded causing it to break off and move the falls a little further upstream. The falls were originally near the town of Queenston, about seven miles downstream from the present location.

The falls are eating their way upstream at a rate of about one inch per foot per year. The erosion was faster before hydroelectricity began and took one-half to three-quarters of the river flow.

There are three falls. The largest is apply named the Horseshoe Falls on the Canadian side of the border, separated by the straight-crested American Falls by Goat Island and the relatively small but beautiful Bridal Veil Falls. The Horseshoe Falls accounts for 90 percent of the total flow and has crest more than 2,200 feet long. Some 155 million liters of water hurdle every minute down the 50-meter drop. The river below the Falls is deeper than the Falls are tall. The American Falls are a little higher, but rubble at the foot of the cliffs reduces the free fall to less than 25 meters in places.

Evidence of human activity around the Falls dates back at least 7,000 years. Military struggles over the years were also common. The French built Fort Niagara near Youngstown to protect their interest in the area, but lost to British and Colonial interest in 1759. Later the during American Revolution and the War of 1812, the area saw considerable military activity.

Fun facts:

• The surface area of Lake Ontario is 7,340 square miles and the average depth is 283 feet, with the greatest depth of 802 feet. The lake cycles every eight years.

• Niagara means "neck." Some say it means "split in the flatland."

•The American Falls was probably never straight across.

• The average flow over Bridal Veil and the American Falls is 8,000 to 10,000 cubic feet (60,000 to 75,000 gallons) per second. Horseshoe Falls varies from 42,000 to 90,000 cubic feet (315,000 to 675,000 gallons) per second.

• The water rushing over the falls is falling at 32 feet per second.

• In 1954, an 185,000-ton chunk of rock broke off at the American Falls.
• The Niagara River is 36 miles long and it flows north.

• After water flows over the Falls, it flows 14 miles north to Lake Ontario. The St. Lawrence River then takes the water from Lake Ontario to the Atlantic Ocean.

• The speed of the river rapids can reach 30 mph.

• The water at the Falls looks green because of algae on the rocks and the high percentage of oxygen.

• The foam at the base of the Falls is a natural phenomenon, a mixture of decay products composed of mostly lignins and tannins.

• There has never been an accident on the Maid of the Mist tour boats. They have been operating since the 1846.

• Only the American and Bridal Veil falls have totally frozen (in 1909, 1936 and 1938) in this century.

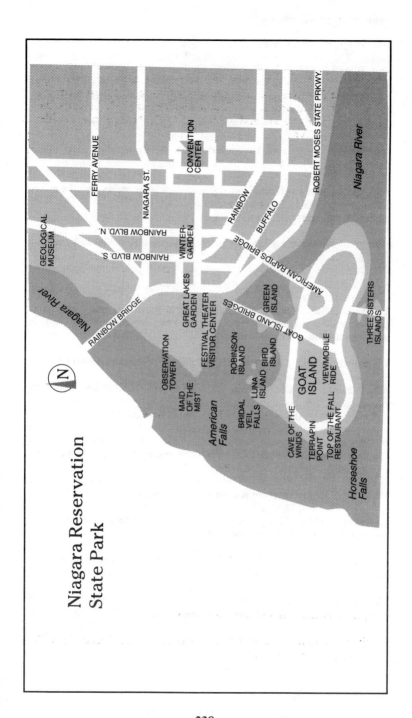

Niagara Reservation State Park

• Goat Island got its name from the goat that survived a harsh winter there. The goat was put on the island with other animals to escape wolves prowling around the mainland.

• Accidents and suicides average about one or two weekly during the summer, May to October.

• Steve Trotter went over the Horseshoe Falls in a pickle barrel and survived. Many survivors have used oak barrels over the years; others have used large rubber balls, inner tubes and converted tanks.

• At it again Steve Trotter and Lori Martin went over the Horseshoe Falls in two water heaters welded together in 1995—and survived. Jessie Sharp went over in a kayak in 1990 and didn't survive.

• Most fish survive the stunning drop over the falls. Those that don't are food for the many gulls that skillfully patrol the frothing waters.

• The falls are illuminated at night year-round.

Fishing: Many types of fish are taken in the lower and upper river including salmon, rainbow trout, brown trout, smallmouth bass, smelt, walleye, northern pike and muskie.

Insider tips: Plan a visit to the Schoellkopf Geological Museum (open 9:30 a.m. to 7 p.m. daily). The museum is only a half-mile from the observation tower and visitors center. The museum has a triple screen presentation on how the Falls came into existence, area geology exhibits, fossil and mineral interpretive displays, rock garden and nature walk. Don't forget to visit Terrapin Point on Goat Island where thundering water comes over a wide expanse and sweeping curve of Horseshoe Falls.

Fort Niagara State Park is 18 miles north on the Robert Moses Parkway. Near Niagara Reservation is a pedestrian walkway to Canada, hotels and shopping. The beautiful formal garden is one of the finest in the state. Take a ride on the Viewmobile that circles the Falls area and attractions; call (716) 278-1730. The nearby Whirlpool State Park has an interpretive trail along the river. The Aquarium on Niagara is great; call (716) 285-3575. The Top of the Falls Restaurant is on Goat Island. Call ahead for a reservation, (716) 278-0340.

Cave of the Winds: On Goat Island. Take an elevator down, walk through a tunnel, take a path along the river's edge. Then walk on wooden decks over the rocks, through the mist, right up to the Bridal Veil Falls. Raincoats and special non-slip footwear are provided.

NIAGARA FRONTIER REGION

PHONE	PARK
NIAGARA FRONTIER REGION	
716 278-1770	Earl W. Brydges Artpark
716 754-9000	Beaver Island
716 773-3271	Big Six Marina
716 773-3271	Buckhorn Island
716 754-8781	Joseph Davis*
716 278-1762	Devil's Hole
716 549-1802	Evangola
716 745-7273	Fort Niagara
716 745-3802	Four Mile Campsite
716 795-3885	Golden Hill
716 278-1770	Niagara Reservation
716 278-1762	Reservoir
716 278-1762	Whirlpool
716 273-6361	Wilson-Tuscarora
716 745-7611	**STATE HISTORIC SITE**

Facility columns (left to right):

Tent/trailers sites (h = hookups, e = electricity); Trailer dump; Showers; Camper recreation; Cabins; Food; Store; Picnic tables; Shelters (• reservations); Swimming beach (• bath house); Swimming pool (• bath house); Recreation programs (• performing arts); Hiking; Biking; Nature trails; Fishing; Playground; Golf (•clubhouse); Tennis; Pond or lake (• power boats ok); River or stream (• power boats ok); Launching site (• hand launch only); Boat rental; Marina (• anchorage); Pump out; Ice skating (•rentals); Cross-country skiing (• rentals); Snowmobiling; Sled slopes

▷ Availability of service or facility ▶ Handicapped accessible *Disc golf only

Exciting, colorful events take place throughout the year at this fortification.

240

New York City Region

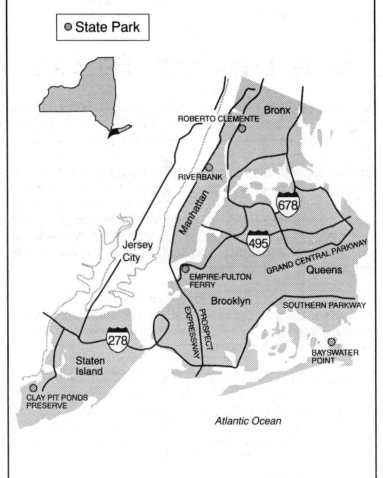

State Park

ROBERTO CLEMENTE

Bronx

RIVERBANK

Manhattan

678

495

Jersey City

GRAND CENTRAL PARKWAY

EMPIRE-FULTON FERRY

Queens

Brooklyn

SOUTHERN PARKWAY

PROSPECT EXPRESSWAY

278

BAYSWATER POINT

Staten Island

CLAY PIT PONDS PRESERVE

Atlantic Ocean

New York City Region

You can go to some terrific state parks in New York City. The region encompasses five boroughs and includes five state parks that are busy year-round.

Visitors can go hiking or horseback riding in a wilderness of distinct ecological habitats at the 250-acre Clay Pit Ponds State Park Preserve. Year-round environmental education programs are also offered. The state's newest park, Riverbank, features full-service, year-round recreational opportunities including swimming, skating, cultural activities and athletic/field games.

Roberto Clemente State Park, the region's first, is an intensely used urban park that offers a swimming complex with Olympic-size pool, ballfields, an entertainment pavilion and waterfront promenade.

Empire-Fulton State Park is at the foot of the Brooklyn Bridge, overlooking the East River. The park has a spectacular view of the Manhattan skyline. Baywater Point State Park, on Jamaica Bay, is an 11 acre park which forms part of the "Buffer the Bay" project. A variety of recreational outreach programs, including Operation Explore, a youth outdoor education program.

NEW YORK CITY REGION

PHONE	PARK	Food	Picnic tables	Swimming pool (• bath house)	Recreation programs (• performing arts)	Hiking	Biking	Nature trails	Playground	Track and field	Carousel	Ice skating	Tennis
212 387-0271	NEW YORK CITY REGION												
212 387-0271	Bayswater Point		△		△								
718 967-1976	Clay Pit Ponds State Park Preserve*	▶	▶		▶	△	△	▶					
718 299-8750	Roberto Clemente	▶	▶	▶	▶	▶		△	▶				
717 858-4708	Empire-Fulton Ferry				•								
212 694-3600	Riverbank	▶	▶	▶	▶	▶	▶	▶	▶	▶	▶	▶	▶

△ Availability of service or facility   ▶ Handicapped accessible   • Bridle paths

Palisades Region

Along the west side of the Hudson River, south of the Catskill Mountains, there are 16 state parks that encompass nearly 80,000 acres.

The region has 300 miles of trails, wilderness solitude and a segment of the famed Appalachian Trail. The region includes the 46,000-acre Harriman State Park, the state's second largest park.

Harriman State Park has several individual areas that include campgrounds, cabins, beaches, playfields, cross-country ski trails and a children's camp; all surrounded by a scenic forest.

Nearby is the renowned Bear Mountain Inn, Trailside Museum, Zoo and overnight accommodations. Swimming is popular at many of the Palisades Region parks.

Minnewaska State Park was designated by the *Nature Conservancy* as one of the "75 great places in the Western Hemisphere." A 50-mile network of carriageways are used year-round.

The region also boasts the nation's first historic site, Washington's Headquarters, in Newburgh.

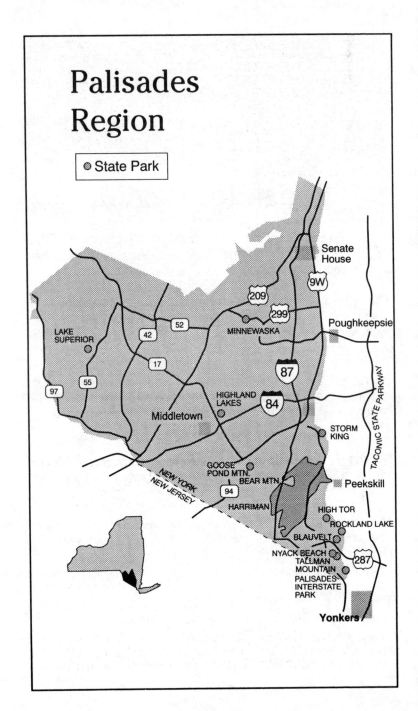

Palisades
Region

◉ State Park

Senate House

9W

209

299

Poughkeepsie

52

42

LAKE SUPERIOR

MINNEWASKA

17

55

87

97

HIGHLAND LAKES

84

Middletown

STORM KING

TACONIC STATE PARKWAY

GOOSE POND MTN.

NEW YORK
NEW JERSEY

BEAR MTN.

Peekskill

94

HARRIMAN

HIGH TOR

ROCKLAND LAKE

BLAUVELT

NYACK BEACH
TALLMAN
MOUNTAIN

287

PALISADES
INTERSTATE
PARK

Yonkers

Bear Mountain State Park

Land: 51,000 acres (Harriman and Bear Mountain) Water: Several lakes

Bear Mountain and adjacent Harriman State Park are a pair of the oldest and biggest parks in the Palisades Region. Together they equal more than 50,000 acres, offering miles of streams, mountains and hiking trails. The area also has 28 lakes and thick forests to explore. On a clear day from Bear Mountain, you can see the Manhattan skyline, wander through the trailside zoo, hike an extensive trail system, access the Appalachian Trail, visit museums, fish, swim, ski or stay in the massive stone Bear Mountain Inn. Bear Mountain is the most developed day-use park in the system.

These Palisades Interstate parks are big and busy. The interstate park system is a corridor of nearly three dozen recreational destinations totaling more than 81,000 acres of land in two states and five counties.

Bear Mountain is the headquarters and featured park in the sprawling system.

The Palisades Interstate Park Commission started in 1900 as an effort to save the towering palisades cliffs that line the Hudson River. These cliffs, on the west bank, were first seen by Europeans when Verranzano sailed the Hudson in 1524. The tops of the cliffs were rich with expansive forests that seemed to provide an inexhaustible supply of firewood for New York City. In the mid-19th century, talus rock at the cliffs' base was found to be remarkably suitable as ship ballast, for the construction of brownstone buildings and in concrete aggregate. For a time, this region of the state fueled explosive development throughout the state.

The decimation of the scenic cliffs appalled local services groups and residents who took up the fight to save the pristine area. By the spring of 1900, their efforts culminated in the establishment of the Interstate Park Commission that has since preserved, developed and operated the significant park and natural region.

Information and Activities

Bear Mountain State Park
Bear Mountain, NY 10911
(914) 786-2701
(914) 786-2731 - Inn
(914) 947-3654 - Fax

Directions: Forty-five minutes from New York City. Take U.S. 9W or exit 14 off the Palisades Interstate Parkway.

Emergency number: 911 system.

Bear Mountain Inn: The inn is a grand stone and wood structure that dates to 1914. It is the host of meetings, banquets, conferences, seminars and overnight guests. The lovely inn has an attractive slate roof and huge stone pillars and can accommodate up to 600 banquet guests. A well-stocked gift shop inside the huge inn sells T-shirts, hats, pennants, flags, plush animals, toys, flying discs, charcoal and lighter fluid, paper plates, mugs, glasses, candy, post cards other souvenirs and picnic supplies.

Across from the tidy gift shop is the front desk. Up the floral carpeted steps to the second floor is the Wildflower Restaurant (try the Sunday buffet), bar, and meeting and large banquet rooms with window walls. The upstairs spaces have polished wooden floors, huge fireplaces

(more than 12 feet wide with a tree trunk mantle!), vaulted bare log ceilings and large hanging light fixtures made of birch wood and brass. The tiny panes of glass, polished wood floors and expansive views of the mountains make Bear Mountain Inn a popular destination for business meetings or vacations.

A total of 11 guest rooms are on the third floor. Also at the lodge are a video entertainment room, first-floor cafeteria, wall-size map of the region and vending machines. The cafeteria serves pizza, hot dogs, chips, cookies, soft drinks and assorted grill items. A few outdoor tables are off the cafeteria.

The Tudor timber and stone regional headquarters across a large open field from the inn has a brochure rack and information about the district's facilities, especially the trail system.

Day-use areas: Bear Mountain has extensively developed day-use areas including sprawling picnic areas, a lighted ice rink, zoo, lake and museums.

In-line skating hockey leagues are popular at the park. During the summer in-line hockey teams use the rink at the foot of the mountain The rink has lockers, vending machines, rubber floors and excellent bleacher seating for cheering dads and other spectators. The view from the high-energy rink is of mountains and day-use areas. In the winter, the rink is used for ice skating.

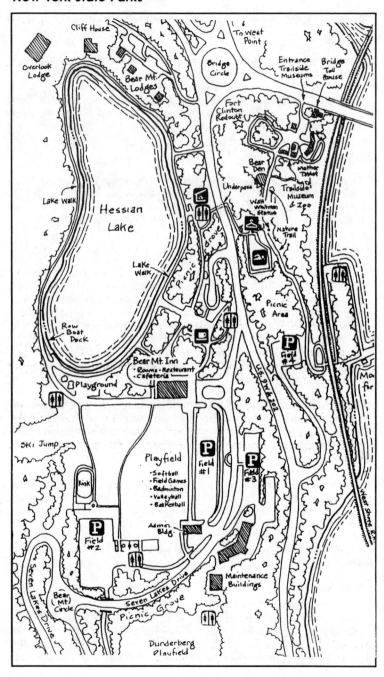

The park has huge day-use areas complete with hard-surfaced walkways, decorative lighting and shady picnic areas with grills.

Swimming pool: The busy swimming pool has five lifeguard stands, diving platform, one-foot-deep shallow end, and nearby deck benches. The pool, surrounded by a grassy shelf, is wedged in a rocky and shady valley. There are not many sunbathing opportunities at the pool. Above the pool are a concession stand, vending machines, deck, entrance and bathhouse. A small fee is charged to enter the pool and the concession stand has some tasty grill items, cold drinks and ice cream.

The pool has a ledge around the edge, offering swimmers a place to sit. The pool is open 10 a.m. - 6:30 p.m. weekdays and 9 a.m. - 6:30 p.m. weekends. The pool's capacity is 1,669. Lockers can be rented at the CCC-built bathhouse. Children under 6 years old are admitted free.

Hiking: The Palisades Interstate parks have about 300 miles of hiking trails. Many trails take only 30 minutes to hike, while others can connect to a significant network of moderate to difficult loops and spurs. You can obtain a trail map at the regional headquarters. Most trails are blazed in paint. Three blazes indicate the start/end point of a trail. Two blazes signal a turn, with the turn direction indicated by the top blaze. If a blaze is two colors, the inner color is shown on the map.

Call the park office about camping and backpacking. Cycling is permitted on most paved roads. Horseback riding is allowed on designated trails in nearby Harriman State Park by permit.

Boating: Boats are rented from behind the lodge. Yellow, orange and green paddleboats and rowboats can be taken out onto Hessian Lake. The rowboat and paddleboat concession is open on weekends. A hard-surfaced walkway skirts the lake and connects the sprawling day-use areas.

If you walk to the river boat dock from near the trailside museum, you will pass a huge copper elk's head atop the high bank looking out toward the river. Victor Berman presented the impressive head to the parks commission in 1935. Excursion boats use this dock.

Fishing: Fishermen are welcome to try their luck on the lake both summer and winter. Trout are stocked and other species in the lake include panfish, bass and rough fish.

Trailside Museum: Open 9 a.m. - 5:30 p.m. weekdays and 9 a.m. - 6:30 p.m. weekends, there is small fee to enter the shady zoo-like educational area. Access to the trail is through a tunnel under Rt. 9W. The Trailside Museum is one of the oldest of its kind in the United States. The nature trails are the oldest in existence. The trail was an outgrowth

The zoo is undergoing extensive renovations.

from an experimental outdoor education program started in 1920 at a Boy Scout camp at Lake Kanawauke. In May 1927, the Trailside Museum was opened. As a result of this pioneering effort in outdoor education, the museum concept was spread across the country and world. Today, in addition to the trailside, the park commission operates five summer regional museums and a nature center at Rockland Lake.

The purpose of the Trailside Museum is to acquaint visitors with native flora and fauna, as well as the geology and history of the park. The museum also tries to stimulate interest in nature and to help visitors understand their role in the natural world.

The shady, hard-surfaced trail winds through the low forest past rock outcroppings and many types of identified tree specimens. Trees species you will pass along the way include red oak, maple, hickory, tupelo, Austrian pine and many pioneer plants.

Along the trail are some beautiful stone buildings that house various exhibits, including the amphibians and reptile house. Exhibits in this building were made possible by state and federal grants. Inside the building are information about the glacial development of the Hudson River, historic parks, the Ionia Marsh, examples of an estuary marsh, and many tanks filled with live frogs, turtles, fish and snakes. An interesting display on lake ecology at different depths gives visitors a chance to learn about basic ecology and lake life. Some species housed in the tanks include black snake, ribbon snake, box turtle, milk snake, copperhead and timber rattlesnakes and lizards.

The zoo-like trail also features a black bear exhibit where the furry creatures roam around an outdoor space that has a pool and bear-size play structures. Black bear range through this forested region of the United States and feed on a wide variety of plants and animals including berries, nuts, insects, mice if they can catch them, and occasionally fish. Notice the American elm tree next to the black bear exhibit—-it has a huge hairy poison ivy vine climbing the mighty trunk.

Also along the nature trail are interpretive signs that teach visitors about seed distribution, erosion, wetlands, ferns (including fiddleheads, royal, New York and cinnamon ferns), skunk cabbage, blue flag wildflowers, natural history and much more.

One of the most popular animals on display is the river otter. The amusing animal is the largest member of the weasel family. River otters are uncommon, but well distributed in the park and New York state. With a sleek body and webbed feet, the otter is ideally suited for the aquatic environment. The playful mammal is sometimes seen frolicking in family groups using rivers and snowbanks as a natural slide in the winter. They feed mostly on fish. A small pond along the trail has some easily seen fish including largemouth bass, golden shiners, pickerel, carp, suckers, black crappies, sunfish and sometimes trout.

A geology display is housed in another wonderful bulging stone building with a slate roof. This lovely building was constructed in 1935 by the WPA and is like those at the Grand Canyon. Inside you will discover the tusk of an 11,000-year-old mastodon found in Balmville, New York, 14 miles north of the museum, in 1902. Also here are dozens of mineral samples including many types of crystals, information about local mines, the ice age, and interesting information about the physical properties of minerals.

The historical museum has a white flagpole flapping above the Grand Canyon-style building. Greeting you at the arched doorway of the museum are two small cannons. The Trailside Museum was built in 1935 on the site of Fort Clinton, originally built in 1777.

Look for the old barn timbers inside and the huge stepping stone at the door.

Inside the museum is a push-button display that details the history of the Hudson Highland, Fort Clinton, Montgomery, construction materials used in the fort, pioneer tools and graphic depiction of the fort. Other interpretive displays include muskets and musket balls, cannon balls, artifacts like buttons and glassware, kitchen tools, information about the lives of officers, especially Sir Henry Clinton who commanded of the British force, and camp life. There is also some information about man's trek to North America, area archaeology, and samples of stone tools, pottery making and samples, projectile points and many delicate stone and bone tools.

On the Trailside Museum grounds is part of the Fort Clinton Redoubt. The redoubt is a small, enclosed, heavily armed fortification built to protect the strategic location. In 1776, to prevent a possible assault by land, the Americans constructed the outer redoubt. But on Oct. 6, 1777, the British stormed and captured the undermanned garrison in Fort Clinton. Although the redoubt was constructed to hold 350 men, only 99 men were defending it when the attack occurred. The outer redoubt was one of the last positions to fall to the enemy. The museum has lots of information about the fort.

The museum also details the lives of early settlers to the area. The rear of the museum has lots of contact period information including photographs, a library, and details about the national Boy Scout commissioner, Daniel Carter Beard.

Back outside and near the historical museum is a small exhibit of live beaver. These common mammals are often called "nature's engineers" because of their skillful construction that often includes air ventilation, sleeping and drying platforms, tunnels and, of course, dams. Sometimes beaver also construct channels and storage piles. Notice the front paws of the beaver; these hand-like paws can achieve incredible results. Beavers have built dams more than 3,000 feet long, houses 50 feet in diameter and canals 600 feet long. Equipped with powerful jaws and teeth, they can also cut down trees up to four feet in diameter.

The nature study museum is flanked by a turkey vulture exhibit. At the door of the nature museum is an ailanthus plant, whose leaves smell like popcorn and stale butter when picked. Inside the museum are dozens of bird mounts carefully preserved in glass showcases. Bird types include songbirds, shrikes, woodpeckers, waterfowl, hawks and many study skins. The waterfowl collection is large and includes goldeneye, loons, teal, old squaw, scooters, bufflehead, scaup and others.

The egg collection is remarkable, offering visitors a chance to see hummingbird eggs, hawk's eggs and others from dozens of species. Some of the smallest eggs are those of finches and sparrows. Study skins of New York mammals include weasels, shrews, moles, squirrels, rats, flying squirrels and many types of skulls, the largest from a black

Ice and inline hockey is popular in the huge day-use area.

bear.

Behind the nature study museum are avian cages that contain crows, pheasants, owls, red-tailed hawks and a bald eagle that isn't shy, allowing visitors a close-up view. Virtually all of the animals at the zoo are injured and can't be returned to the wild. Other naturalized bird exhibits house wild turkeys and a few white-tailed deer near a small pond.

Also at the zoo, near the bears, is the lowest point along the Appalachian Trail, a mere 120 feet above sea level.

One of my favorite points along the trail is the statute of Walt Whitman.

Whitman, one of America's great poets, was born at West Hills on Long Island, New York, in 1819. At an early age he left the public school in Brooklyn and all formal education to learn the printing trade. He later became a teacher and from 1846 to 1848 he was editor of the Brooklyn Eagle. A member of the Union Army, he was a clerk, but spent almost all of this time in hospitals aiding the wounded. Whitman was attacked by paralysis in 1873 and retired to Camden, New Jersey,

The park has many interesting museums in beautiful stone buildings.

were he died in 1892. Whitman is famous for his poems of democracy and America. His best known work, Leaves of Grass of which The

Song of the Open Road is part, was published in 1855 and was received poorly, but later came to be considered a classic.

The statute of Whitman was presented to the park in 1940 by William Averrill Harriman on behalf of his brother and sister as a memorial to their mother, Mary Williams Harriman, on the 13th anniversary of her gift to the state of the 10,000 acres of land and $1 million to establish the Bear Mountain - Herriman section of the interstate park.

This passage from *Song of the Open Road* is carved on a huge boulder next to the statue:

A foot and light-hearted I take to the open road,
Healthy, free, the world before me,
The long path before me leading wherever I choose.

Henceforth I ask not good-fortune, I myself am good-fortune,
Henceforth I whimper no more, postpone no more, need nothing,

255

Done with indoor complaints, libraries, querulous criticism,
Strong and content I travel the open road.

Nature: Bear Mountain and Harriman state parks offer diverse habitats and elevation ranges. The entire area was glaciated 15,000 years ago, leaving a barren landscape that has slowly reforested. The present oak forest, mixed with birch, hickory, ash and maple, was continually burned and been heavily cut for charcoal, firewood and timber until 1910.

The large tract is an excellent place to bird watch. A birding checklist is available from the park office. The park has a good mix of avian population including two types of loons, 29 kinds of waterfowl, an occasional bald eagle, peregrine falcon, merlin, two types of vultures, nine species of bitterns and herons, 13 types of shorebirds, hummingbird, five species of owls, many type of flycatchers, wrens, thrushes and many types of wood warblers.

Winter: Cross-country skiing is popular on the park's many trails. Ice skating at the rink is also popular.

Special events: The Palisades Interstate Parks Commission offers many special events annually including outdoor concerts, history walks, living history programs, astronomy, weekly square dancing, 4-H kids programs, natural history programs and lots more. A calendar of events is available at the park office.

Insider tips: Bring your next meeting to the massive stone and timber lodge. The average yearly temperature at Bear Mountain is 48 degrees and the average rainfall is 45 inches. Hummingbirds have 1,500 feathers, while a mute swan has 25,000. Plan to stop at the Palisades Interstate Parks visitor center (call 914-786-5003) on the Palisades Parkway. It features books, gifts, fishing licenses, maps and tons of information about the unique park system.

The visitor center is near exit 17. The park is surrounded by mountains. Plan a visit during the Bear Mountain Christmas Festival. Trees are decorated, unique gifts are on sale, and Santa is always nearby. The Trailside Museum has a pair of mounted passenger pigeons.

Harriman State Park

Land: 46,000 acres (Harriman and Bear Mountain) Water: Lakes, streams

Harriman and Bear Mountain state parks span most of the Ramapo Mountains, less than an hour north of New York City. Ten million people live within an hour's drive of Harriman State Park and on some summer weekends it feels like they are all in the park. Weekdays and off-season are some of the best times to visit.

The park is one of the best hiking tracts in eastern New York. The diversity of hikes and habitat offers day-users miles of trails to explore and places to visit including scenic highlands, forested mountaintops, historic sites, small motorboat-free lakes and pristine ponds. Campers, canoeists and beach goers will also love busy Harriman State Park.

All visitors will be delighted by the eroded slopes of the Ramapo Mountains that have risen above nearby seas for nearly 600 years, making them some of the oldest land masses on the North American continent. These ageless mountains are part of the Reading Prong that reaches from Reading, Pennsylvania, to the Hudson Highlands and north to Vermont's lovely Green Mountains. The long mountainous Precambrian formation is the result of violent periods of folding and metamorphism of rich sediments laid down more than a billion years ago. Scorching intrusions of magma also helped shape the mighty land forms. More recently, the Ice Age has polished and rounded the landscape.

The dramatic Ramapo Mountains might have gotten their name from Native Americans referring to the river or the Lenni-Lenape Indians' word that means *"place of the slanting rock."* We may never know, but we do know that these beautiful mountains were saved by early 1900s environmentalists who would have made the Native Americans proud.

In 1908, the state proposed to construct a sprawling state prison at Bear Mountain. But among the protesters was Mrs. Edward Harriman, the widow of a railroad tycoon, who offered a huge land and cash donation. Since, the park has grown to include traditional state park amenities and a massive network of trails.

Information and Activities

Harriman State Park
(914) 786-2701

Directions: About 30 miles north of New York City, access from the Palisades Parkway. From New York City, take the George Washington Bridge to the Parkway north to exits 15, 16, 17, or 18.

Emergency numbers: Park police, (914) 786-2781.

Campground: Beaver Pond Campground near Lake Welch is near the center of sprawling Harriman State Park. The camping area and huge beach are about 25 miles north of the George Washington Bridge and about 10 miles south of the Bear Mountain Bridge. Beaver Pond has 198 sites (no electric or water hook-ups). A campers' recreation hall is across from the small log check-in station that has a walk-up window. The campground has some wonderful Yellowstone National Park-style stone buildings constructed by the Civilian Conservation Corps during the 1930s.

Section A has wood tent-camping platforms that are about two feet off the ground. The deck-like platforms are about 20 feet square and most have a railing around three sides. Campers actually pitch their tents on the elevated wooden platforms. Some of the sites in the teens have a partial view of the small lake. The fieldstone bathhouse has an exterior laundry sink and showers. Many sites are near steep wooded ravines and have private forested views. Sites in this loop are at least 80 percent shady and equipped with tables and fire rings. Sites 22 and 26 loop are perched on a hillside.

Section B has hundreds of basketball-size boulders scattered between sites and along the mountain base. Sites in the B30s are high and dry, excellent places for tents. Many sites in the C area are large enough to accommodate medium-sized RV's.

Areas D, E and F can accommodate medium-sized RV's and offer some views of the lake cove. This tract is 85 percent shady and under large trees. Sites D2, D12 and D14 are favorite spots for larger RV's. There are some camping platforms in these loops. On a higher elevation are D8 and D9, which are grassy sites in the open. Sites D28 and D30 receive midday sun and are grassy, perfect for tents or medium-sized RV's. For privacy, consider site D43 that is notched out of the woods and down a narrow gravel lane. Many of the sites in area F are tent platforms made of pressure-treated lumber and equipped with tables and fire rings.

The W loop has scattered boulders in the adjacent woodlands and grass pads. Sites 11 and 12 are near a modern bathhouse with gray trim and shingle roof. Site W23 is the premier site offering an oversized pad nestled between some large boulders and big trees. Site W55 is an excellent tent site situated between some large outcroppings. On slightly higher ground are sites W52-W56, which are excellent sites for medium-sized RVs. Many sites are separated by a wall of vegetation and are near thick stands of mixed deciduous trees and the occasional hemlock. Each site has its own character and many are wonderfully set off the road and private. Sites W66-W69 are especially interesting camping sites. Many sites in this area have moss-covered rocks, ferns covering the rich forest floor and medium-sized trees with a spreading canopy overhead.

Cabins: The heavily wooded, 39-cabin colony is about a mile from the Sebago Beach and is self-contained offering interesting recreation facilities and a camp store. The rustic units are on varying elevations with front door parking. Near the cabin colony are the popular recreation building, playground, ball field, horseshoe pits, soccer fields, two tennis courts, volleyball net and dirt basketball court. All of the cabins are terrific, often perched on the hillside, private and shady. The side yards are often littered with boulders and low ledge-like rock outcroppings. The showerhouse is in a terrific stone building that is centrally located and has a great lake and wooded shoreline view. Notice the carefully varnished doors and massive wrought iron hinges on the carefully maintained classic stone shower buildings.

Cabins are equipped with an electric refrigerator, two-burner hot plate, four cots with mattresses, a table and four chairs, charcoal grill and out-

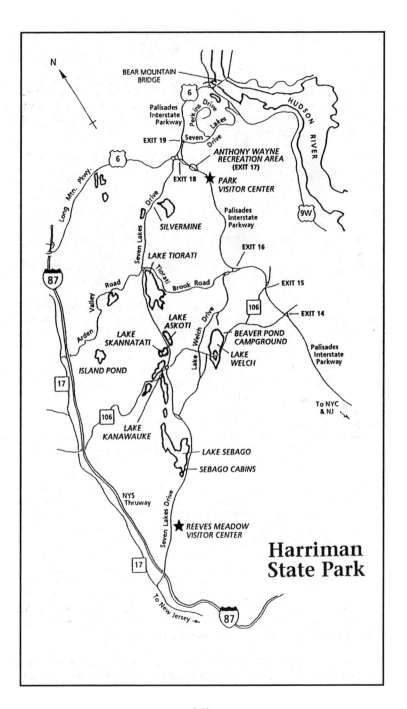

N

BEAR MOUNTAIN
BRIDGE

6

Perkins Drive

Palisades
Interstate
Parkway

Seven Lakes

EXIT 19   Seven Lakes Drive

ANTHONY WAYNE
RECREATION AREA
(EXIT 17)

6

Long Mtn. Pkwy.

EXIT 18   PARK
VISITOR CENTER

Seven Lakes Drive

SILVERMINE

Palisades
Interstate
Parkway

9W

LAKE TIORATI

EXIT 16

87

Valley

Road

Tiorati Brook Road

EXIT 15

LAKE
ASKOTI

106

EXIT 14

Arden

LAKE
SKANNATATI

Lake Welch Drive

BEAVER POND
CAMPGROUND

LAKE
WELCH

Palisades
Interstate
Parkway

ISLAND POND

17

To NYC
& NJ

106

LAKE
KANAWAUKE

LAKE SEBAGO

SEBAGO CABINS

NYS
Thruway

Seven Lakes Drive

REEVES MEADOW
VISITOR CENTER

Harriman
State Park

17

To New Jersey

87

HUDSON RIVER

door picnic table. Bring your own bedding, dishes, towels, cooking utensils and personal items.

Some of the cabins have small porches with a picnic table and wooded view. Cabin A11 is one of the nicest cabins that has a porch and elevated view. Units B13 and B14 are on the highest elevation; cabins C3-C5 have a lake view from a rugged ridge that is dotted with big boulders.

Recreation Hall: The rustic hall is sided with gray log slabs and houses an old piano, fireplace, ping pong table, bookcases, canoe camping information, store, park office and a wonderful lounge with fireplace and seating. A church and hospital directory is also posted in the rustic two-story building that can be swarming with activity. Recreation equipment available at the office includes baseball and softball bats, bases, Whiffleball sets, volleyball, kickball, tennis equipment, footballs, fishing line, board games, horseshoes, books and magazines, and ping pong paddles and balls.

The camp store sells paper products, canned goods, soft drinks and snacks. You can rent a boat there. On the walls of the stores are maps and natural history information about the park. A map of the Appalachian Trail is also posted at the store. This unique recreation building is the focal point of the cabin colony.

Day-use areas: A small stone camper's recreation hall with a slate roof is across from the campground check-in station. Sprawling, well-equipped day-use areas are offered throughout the park.

Beaches: Lake Welch Beach is believed to be one of the largest inland beaches in the country. Lake Welch is surrounded by rugged forested shorelines and distant mountain views. The busy beach is within walking distance from the campground. At parking field No. 2 is a basketball backboard. The red brick bathhouse is at parking field No. 3. A number of equipped picnic areas are scattered under shady groves of trees along the massive parking lots.

The sandy beach has about 20 white lifeguard chairs along a broad cove that is sectioned off by red and white buoys. A hard-surfaced walkway runs along the transition area between the sandy and grassy areas. The modern bathhouse has showers and more than 1,300 blue lockers. Bikes, in-line skates and skateboards are not permitted at the beach. The park manager's office and a first aid station are in the bathhouse building. The beach closes at 6 p.m. daily. Sundays are the busiest days during the summer.

The beachside concession stand serves hamburgers, hot dogs, pizza, soft drinks and ice cream. A small elevated patio is adjacent to the walk-up concession stand. Hedgerows and knee-walls outline the walkways that connect the beach amenities. There are also plenty of picnic tables near the beach.

Nearby Sebago Beach is a popular destination for families with small children. It is complete with bus parking and lots of shady picnic areas. Sebago, about half the size of Welch Beach, is outlined by a retaining wall and nearby playground and volleyball courts. The 50-yard-wide sandy beach has lots of attractive bench seats and views of mountains and beautiful rocky shores. A red and tan brick bathhouse has indoor showers. Places to picnic are on varying elevations around the beach. Families with small children will like this beach that has playground equipment nearby. Many heavily shaded day-use areas surround the beach. One of the best day-use areas is on a ridge above the beach accessed by parking lot No. 3. A lightly-used ball diamond, with lightly used base paths, is near this scenic and popular ridgetop day-use area.

Hiking: Harriman has about 225 miles of marked trails. With so many trails, serious hikers should obtain a copy of Bill Myles 500-page book, Harriman Trails: A Guide and History. The book is published by the New York-New Jersey Trail Conference, G.P.O. Box 2250, New York, NY 10116. The terrific guidebook details marked trails, gives accurate distances and lots of park history, including entire sections dedicated to historic roads, mines, lakes and important figures in the park's development.

Although Harriman and Bear Mountain are huge tracts of land, hikers seeking solitude should consider weekday treks during the off-season. Hikes offer great variety, from walking across small valleys, along slopes, through handsome hemlock groves to scrambles up steep hills and long quiet streams. Many of the hikes crest knobs and wander along the rubble of cliffs. Some of the most interesting segments can also take you past old mines, rock formations and near glacial potholes, ponds and lakes.

A 20-mile segment of the Appalachian Trail courses through the park, cutting through the Bear Mountain zoo, along the north shore of Island Pond, over Green Mountain and down to Elk Pen and beyond. Although the number of quality trails are too many to mention here, try Beech Trail, Breakneck Mountain Trail, shady Kakiat Trail, 25 -mile-long Long Path, Welch Trail, Poplopen Gorge Trail and many others.

Boating: A small boat rental and mooring spaces are near the popular Welch Beach. It offers a great view of the mountains and the lily pads that coat parts of the lake. A small boat rental is also at Sebago Beach. Rowboats can be rented from the park store at the cabin colony too. There are 36 lakes and ponds in Harriman and Bear Mountain state parks.
Canoeing at Harriman is a wonderful surprise, because no gasoline motors are allowed and boaters must purchase a boating permit. There are several gentle lakes worth exploring including Lake Sebago, Lake Tiorati, Lake Kanawauke, Lake Stahahe, Silvermine Lake and Lake Welch.

Almost all of these scenic lakes offer paddlers views of exposed rock, fragrant lily pads, stumpy and deep areas, floating vegetation and rolling forested shorelines. Clusters of islands are the homes of wading birds and paddling waterfowls, deer that will often bound away as you near. Some paddlers enjoy visiting the many lakes during the fall when colors are blazing and crowds are off the beaches and shorelines. Bring your fishing pole and binoculars! The shrub shorelines and thick grasses are homes to otters, many types of birds, muskrats and beavers. Bass and panfish are the primary species in the lakes; bring lots of live bait and small spinners for some fast action. especially in the spring.

Fishing: The steep and rocky shoreline and the edges of the small islands are places where many anglers use live and artificial baits. Anglers should also try places where trees have fallen into the water. The best shoreline fishing is from causeways and day-use areas near underwater structure. Some of the lakes have lily pad flats, fallen trees, weed beds, rocky islands and steep banks. A New York state fishing license is required.

Sebago Lake is the largest lake in the park, with six miles of shoreline and good populations of large- and smallmouth bass, panfish and chain pickerel. Many early-season anglers try to work the mountain laurel-covered bank areas. Lake Tiorati (4.8 miles of shoreline) is the second-largest body of water in the park and has the highest elevation. It offers largemouth bass and chain pickerel fishing opportunities. The many coves, island and inlets are good places to toss spinners. By mid-summer the lake has thick beds of coontail, fanwort and bladderwort that offer excellent habitat for all fish species. Look for osprey that are also known to fish these waters.

Lake Kanawauke, which means *"place of much water,"* was formed in 1947 by damming Stony Brook. The shallow, stumpy lake is thick with aquatic vegetation, and the southern shore is marshy where many species of waterfowl often nest. Fish or canoe these waters early in the season.

Nature: A number of recreation and education programs are offered. Programs include battlefield tours, guided hikes, campfire talks, astronomy programs, lantern walks, river walks and more.

The lakeside Kanawauke Regional Nature Museum (like three others in the interstate system) features a touch table, natural history and some

programming. The center is open seasonally and offers hikes. It is a 20-minute walk from the campground. Also in the tiny nature museum that is next to a boat ramp are animal skins, bird silhouettes, small nature library, rocks and minerals, wall posters and countertops covered with live aquariums and hands-on nature artifacts.

Winter: Cross-country skiing is popular on the jumbo network of trails at Bear Mountain and Anthony Wayne Recreation Area in Harriman.

Visitor Center: A comprehensive Visitor Center for the Palisades Interstate Park system is located on the Palisades Interstate Parkway. The small stone building is well signed and features travel books, regional maps, hiking maps, and supplies, charcoal lighter fluid, some fishing tackle, Golden Guides, field guides, collections of rocks and minerals, local history books, fishing books and more. The Visitor Center also has orienteering maps, postcards, vending machines and rest rooms. You many also purchase fishing licenses as well. The center is open 8 a.m. - 5 p.m. daily. Closed on Thanksgiving, Christmas and New Year's Day.

Insider tips: The CCC-built stone buildings are considered some of the men's best work east of the Mississippi River. The buildings seem to squat on the land, effortlessly blending into the rugged terrain. The protected beach is ideal for family fun. Harriman is a huge park with small lakes, trails and many facilities scattered over the 46,000 acres. It will take visitors several days to learn the area, and many more to enjoy the widely dispersed amenities. Plan to visit and learn about Doodletown and the spiral railroad. Try canoeing the area; you'll be surprised!

Minnewaska State Park Preserve

Land: 11,600 acres Water: Lake Awosting and Lake Minnewaska

Once you see the towering rock cliffs, you'll appreciate that fact that the stone base of the Statue of Liberty was quarried nearby. The sharp pinnacles, sheer cliffs, windswept knobs and huge boulders offer a special beauty that is wonderfully accessible from a network of mostly easy trails. The park is for day-use only.

These are the Shawangunk Mountains, sometimes called the *"Gunks."* These scenic mountains aren't as well-known as the nearby Catskills, but they are just as spectacular. The craggy mountains are made of durable white conglomerate that make the rugged ridges and outcroppings especially interesting and beautiful. The north section of the Shawangunk Mountain ridge is a triangular shape outlined by the Rondout Creek valley in the west, and U.S. 209 and the Wallkill River valley in the east. The elevation ranges from about 200 feet at the valley edges to 2,289 feet near Sam's Point. The total area is about 100 square miles.

One of the best parts about hiking or biking at Minnewaska is that the trails are easy. An especially good trail for families is Beacon Hill, a gentle carriageway. A wonderful view of the Wallkill Valley can be seen.

Hiking and biking are the reasons to visit. A free trail map available at check-in or the park office can guide park users around the lake, to the foaming waters of Peter's Kill at Awosting Falls, or along cliffs and wooded walks. The old carriageways in the park are excellent for biking. For hikers seeking a longer trek, try the five-mile Millbrook Trail, or for a full-day hike use the Castle Point Trail that will take you through some splendid scenic areas.

Information and Activities

Minnewaska State Park Preserve
P.O. Box 893
New Paltz, NY 12561
(914) 255-0752

Directions: U.S. 44/55, west of the village of Minnewaska, 12 miles from New Paltz. The panoramic mountain views from U.S. 44/55 are terrific. A 12-foot information kiosk near the check-in station features fire and bike safety information and a map of the park's many trails.

The park office has a variety of interesting brochures, a large park map, benches and a soft drink machine. The park opens at 9 a.m. daily and user fees and closing hours are posted.

Emergency number: Park police, (914) 786-2781.

Trails: Biking, hiking and cross-country skiing are popular on the vast network of scenic trails at Minnewaska State Park Preserve. Most of the trails have bluish-gray stone chipped surfaces that are ideal for fat tire bikes or walking. The park also has some excellent horseback riding trails that are shared by bikers and hikers. Riders must obtain a permit from the park office.

Most of the trails are color-coded and many have scenic viewpoints. Hikers should obtain a map, judge the distance and then create their own hike using connecting trails that form loops and spurs. Great views of the Catskills, Castle Point, Awosting Lake and sweeping clifftops are along many of the heavily used trails.

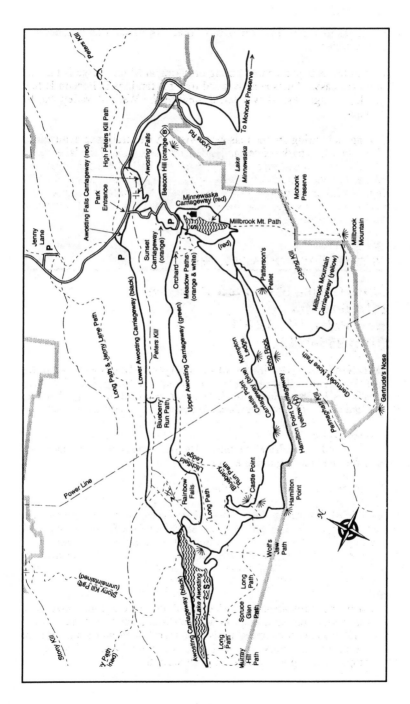

Day-use areas: Near the parking lot at the top of the mountain is the primary day-use area, complete with a small food wagon and truck-size boulders that share space with picnic tables, bikers and hikers. This day-use area offers scenic views of the lake, gray cliffs and spindly trees clinging to rocky ledges and walls. Notice how blue the lake water is.

Swimming: Lake Awosting has a guarded beach and is 3.5 miles from the park office. Lake Minnewaska also have a guarded beach.

Scuba diving: At one diving area are benches and a rack where diving equipment can be hung. There are also lots of table-top rock outcroppings from which divers stage their activities. Diving hours are 9 a.m. - 4 p.m. and you must obtain a permit from the park office. Divers must be certified and have a C card. The office can provide you with rules and special regulations.

Programs: A variety of interpretive and recreational programming is offered at the sprawling park including nature hikes, Native American studies, a snake study, plants and wildflowers, orienteering, outdoor survival, junior ranger programs, naturalist hikes and more. Steady rain cancels outdoor programs.

Boating: Boating on the lake is regulated. Hours are 9 a.m. - 4 p.m. Boaters must have Coast Guard approved personal flotation devices. Boating permits can be obtained at the park office. Do not swim or dive from your boat, and watch for scuba diver's flags. No outboard motors may be used on the lake.

Nature: Since 1928 members of the Smiley family in Mohonk have kept bird records. Dozens of groups and individuals have contributed observations that have made the third edition of the Checklist of Birds of the Northern Shawangunk Mountains possible. A copy of the four-panel list is available from the park office.

The easy-to-use list is broken down by season and frequency. The list includes 16 types of vultures, ospreys, hawks, eagles and falcons; 15 species of woodpeckers and flycatchers; 20 kinds of loons, grebes, cormorants, heron and waterfowl; and lots of warblers, finches and sparrows.

The preserve's diverse habitat also has at least 200 types of woody plants, 41 species of reptiles and amphibians, and dozens of mammals that include shrews, opossums, moles, bats, rabbits, rodents, porcupines, weasels, mountain lions, lynxes, elks, whitetail deer, coyotes, foxes and black bear.

Deer hunting: Call the park manager for hunting information.

Winter: Cross-country skiing is popular at the park.

Insider tips: Visit the small park office for natural history information. Watch your step; there are lots of apples along the trails left by horses. The Peter's Kill area of Minnewaska has been designated for climbing. Weather can change quickly in the mountains; bring warm clothing and

Rockland State Park
Land: 1,079 acres   Water: Rockland Lake, Hudson River

Rockland Lake is a spring-fed lake on a ridge of Hook Mountain above the west shore of the Hudson River just 30 miles from New York City. The lake is accessible from the Hudson through a winding break in the ridge. Since the first settlers in 1711, the lake and adjacent riverfront have provided an interesting livelihood for thousands of people.

Before refrigeration, when an entire industry was developed around providing ice, Rockland Lake was a famous producer of pure, clear ice. Busy rail lines rushed millions of tons of packed ice to thirsty New York City. Some lake ice was sent as far as India and Australia. Local workers cut block ice during the winter and worked in the quarries in the summer. In fact, a massive stone crusher, built in 1872, produced millions of tons of traprock that was used in the building of New York City. By the turn of the century, the greatest part of the riverfront at Rockland Lake was the floor of a quarry.

During this time Rockland Lake was also a celebrated summer resort. Rail lines and excursion boats on the Hudson brought a crush of summer visitors escaping the sweltering city. This tourism, quarry and ice house businesses boosted the area economically. At its peak, Rockland Lake had 3,000 residents, a post office, fire company, school, churches and bustling main street.

With the invention of the refrigerator and demise of the quarry, tourism was the sole industry for the area. Today, all that remains of the ice houses and quarry are random stone foundations, scattered buildings and small rock piles.

The Palisades Interstate Park Commission acquired and revitalized the lake and surrounding tract in 1958. Today, the day-use state park features two sparkling swimming pools, two challenging golf courses and huge picnic and game field areas. Hundreds of church, school and scouting groups visit the park from the metropolitan area yearly.

Information and Activities

Rockland State Park
P.O. Box 217
Congers, NY 10920
(914) 268-3020

Directions: 30 miles north of New York City. From the city, take the George Washington Bridge, stay in the right lanes on the bridge and get on the Palisades Interstate Parkway. Take the Parkway north to exit 4. Take Rt. 9W North for 12 miles to the park on your right.

Emergency number: Park police, (914) 786-2701.

Day-use areas: Each of the many day-use and play field areas has picnic tables and grills, they are connected by the multi-use trail. Many picnic areas are shady and offer excellent views of the lake and hilly shoreline. The south recreation area has basketball courts and bike racks. Some of the lakeside parking fields are open; others are mostly wooded, cool and shady. Parking field No. 2 is shady and offers lakeside picnicking. Sprawling day-use areas have dozens, if not hundreds, of picnic tables and grills.

Six tennis courts are open from May - November near the championship golf course.

Swimming: An Olympic-size swimming pool is at the north bathhouse area. There is a fee to swim. This pool is closed on Wednesdays, Thursdays and Fridays. The pool is surrounded by wide cement decks, elevated sunning area and a green rail fence. Six lifeguard stands and lots of benches are along the clean deck. Blue and white buoys are used to section off the pool in front of lifeguard stations.

Inside the pool complex is a small children's wading pool that is two feet deep. There is no swimming in the lake.

The food concession at the complex serves both swimmers and walk-up patrons. It offers standard grill items, soft drinks, snacks and ice cream treats. From the pool you can see the lake in the distance. A program center and the park office are in the building that surrounds the pool.

The swimming pool at the south bathhouse area, near the lakeshore, has a brown brick bathhouse. There is a fee to swim. This pool is open 10 a.m. - 6 p.m. weekdays and 10 a.m. - 7 p.m. weekends, but is closed on Mondays, Tuesdays and Thursdays. This pool complex is about half the size of the northern pool area. Surrounding the southern swimming complex are broad grassy fields and the par 3 executive golf course. The park police have offices in this bathhouse. Like the larger northern pool, this one is divided by blue, red and white buoys and offers sunning on the surrounding deck. The complex has one of the biggest lawn sunning areas in the state. Six lifeguard chairs and many benches are also carefully positioned around the popular pool. A food concession offering basic grill items serves pool users and walk-ups. Some picnic tables are on an elevated patio that is outlined by a stainless railing near the concession windows.

Near the main pool is a fenced, guarded children's wading pool.

Golf: The popular par 3 executive golf course on the south end of the park is a challenging little course with tree-lined fairways and tight greens. Bring your wedge, putter and nerve.

The championship golf course features 18 holes and is near and the northern pool complex. The challenging course is hilly with wide fairways and tight roughs. The course is open early April to November, 6 a.m. until dusk on weekends, and opens at 7 a.m. on weekdays.

Hiking: A 3.2-mile multi-use hard-surfaced walkway skirts the entire lakeshore and along the Hudson River. A marked trail up Hook Mountain is open for those who are adventurous.

Boating: You must be at least 18 years old to rent a boat. Boaters may also use their own cartop boats on the quiet lake. No gasoline-powered motors are allowed.

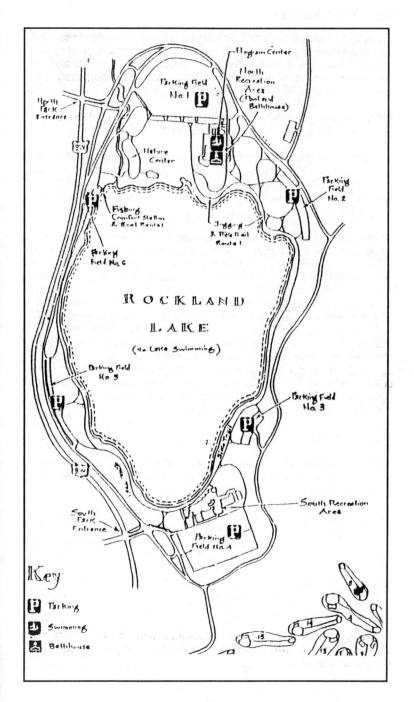

Program Center

North Recreation Area (Pool and Bathhouse)

Parking Field No. 1

North Park Entrance

Parking Field No. 2

Nature Center

Fishing Comfort Station & Boat Rental

Parking Field No. 6

Jogging & Bike Trail Route 1

ROCKLAND

LAKE

(No Lake Swimming)

Parking Field No. 5

Parking Field No. 3

South Recreation Area

South Park Entrance

Parking Field No. 4

Key

P Parking

Swimming

Bathhouse

Animal display at seasonal nature center.

Fishing: The park has a fishing station near play field No. 6. A hard-surfaced parking area and nearby boat rental offer would-be anglers a chance to explore the oval lake. The accessible fishing dock is L-shaped and the boat rental sells live bait, some tackle and soft drinks. The lake is up to 35 feet deep and some bass, perch, panfish and rough-fish can be taken.

Nature: Some outdoor and recreation programs are conducted by local 4-H organizations. The nature center building is a low board and batten-sided structure near parking field No. 2. The building has many outdoor reptile tanks, a workshop and the nature center office. The small center is open seasonally, 9 a.m. - 4:45 p.m., Memorial Day - Labor Day.

Small animals on display may include turtles, tadpoles, spotted sala-mander, red salamander, spring peepers, water snake, common toads, native fish species and others.

The habitat around the nature center is of hemlock, pine, cedar and spruce. The deciduous trees are maple, ash, elm, oak and cherry. Along some of the trails are question and answer boards and interpretive signs.

On exhibit are some spring peepers whose shrill peeping is a welcome sign of spring. Hundreds of these tiny frogs call at once during the early spring mating season. Also on display is a gray tree frog, which is fairly common in the woodlands that surround the park. Adhesive discs on their toes allow them to cling to the bark of trees. They feed mainly on insects.

"Man and nature must walk hand in hand. The throwing out of bal ance of the resources of nature, throws out of balance also the lives of men," **Franklin D. Roosevelt**.

A nature trail, which has several raised boardwalks, departs from the center and extends about one-half mile. The trail offers access to wetlands rarely seen on an ordinary walk. The Lakeside Bog Trail is dominated by many flowering shrubs that blossom from early spring through the summer. An observation deck offers a fine panoramic view of Rockland Lake and the palisade hillsides which surround it.

Center Trail tracks through an open field and supports a large diversity of wildflowers and suitable habitat for a large number of birds, mammals and insects. The Woodland Swamp Trail is dominated by trees. The swamp forms the natural dam and only outlet for Rockland Lake. The wetland acts as a giant sponge during periods of heavy rainfall and helps to alleviate flooding and destruction by erosion.

If the lake doesn't freeze, many types of waterfowl winter on the lake. Some species that often stay during the winter include widgeon, bufflehead, merganser, mallards, canvasbacks, goldeneye, ruddy ducks, shovelers, gadwalls, wood ducks and, according to staff, many robins.

Also at the side of the nature center building is a tanbark wheel. The heavy stone was once used in the area to grind tree bark for the removal of tannin, which was used to prepare hides and skins for the tanning process.

Winter: Cross-country skiing and sledding are offered in designated areas.

Insider tips: Look out for the large resident flock of Canada geese, and please, do not feed the geese—it only encourages them. The park has a wonderful trail that circles the scenic lake, taking hikers along the rolling, rocky shoreline and across broad day-use areas. Call ahead for picnic permits. No alcoholic beverages are allowed in the park.

PALISADES REGION

PHONE	PARK — PALISADES REGION	Tent/trailers sites (h = hookups, e = electricity)	Trailer dump	Showers	Camper recreation	Cabins	Food	Store	Picnic tables	Shelters (• reservations)	Swimming beach (• bath house)	Swimming pool (• bath house)	Recreation programs (• performing arts)	Hiking	Biking	Nature trails	Fishing	Playground	Golf (•clubhouse)	Tennis	Pond or lake (• power boats ok)	River or stream (• power boats ok)	Launching site (• hand launch only)	Boat rental	Marina (• anchorage)	Pump out	Ice skating (•rentals)	Cross-country skiing (• rentals)	Snowmobiling	Sled slopes
914 786-2701	Bear Mountain			▶			▶		▶			•▷	▶	▷	▷	▶	▷	▷			▶	▷▶		▶			••	▷		▷
914 786-2701	Blauvelt													▷	▷															
914 786-2701	Goosepond Mountain*													▷																
914 786-2701	Harriman			▶	▶	▶	▷		▷		▷•			▶	▷	▷	▷	▷	▷			▷	▷	▷	▶			▷	▷		▷
914 947-2792	Beaver Pond Campgrounds	e		▶										▷			▷	▷			▷		••							
914 351-2583	Lake Sebago Beach						▶		▶		▶•			▷		▷	▷				▶		••				▷	•		
914 351-2360	Sebago Cabin Camp					▶			▶		▶			▷							▶								▷	
914 351-2568	Silver Mine						▷		▶		▶			▷			▷				▶									
914 351-2568	Lake Tiorati Beach	▷	▷				▶		▶		••			▷			▷				▶							▷		
914 942-2560	Anthony Wayne								▶			▷	▶	▷	▷		▷					▷								▷
914 947-2444	Lake Welch Beach						▶		▶		▶	▷		▷	▷	▷					▷							▷		
914 634-8074	High Tor											▷		▷	▷	▷														
914 786-2701	Highland Lakes*													▷	▷															
914 786-2701	Lake Superior*													▷	▷		▷				▷		•							
914 255-0752	Minnewaska*						▷		▷		▷			▷	▷		▷				▷	▷	••					•▷		
914 358-1316	Nyack Beach																▷					▷								
914 268-3020	Rockland Lake						▶		▶		▶	••	▶		▷	▷	▷	▷	•	▷	▶		••	▶			▷	••	▷	
914 786-2701	Storm King																													
914 359-0544	Tallman Mountain											••	▶		▷	▷		▷									••	▷	▷	▷
	STATE HISTORIC SITES																													
914 561-5498	Knox's Headquarters																													
914 561-1765	New Windsor Cantonment																													
914 338-2786	Senate House																													
914 786-2521	Story Point Battlefield																													
914 562-1195	Washington's Headquarters																													

Visit the Revolutionary War headquarters for Generals Knox, Gates and Green.

Military drills, camp activities, and exhibits recall the final encampment of Washington's Army.

Visit the meeting place of the state's first senate in 1777. View the collection of Washington's paintings.

Exhibits and walking tours explain American light infantry's daring midnight raid on this British post.

Tour the house which served Gen. George Washington as headquarters from April 1782 until August 1783.

▷ Availability of service or facility   ▶ Handicapped accessible   *Bridle paths

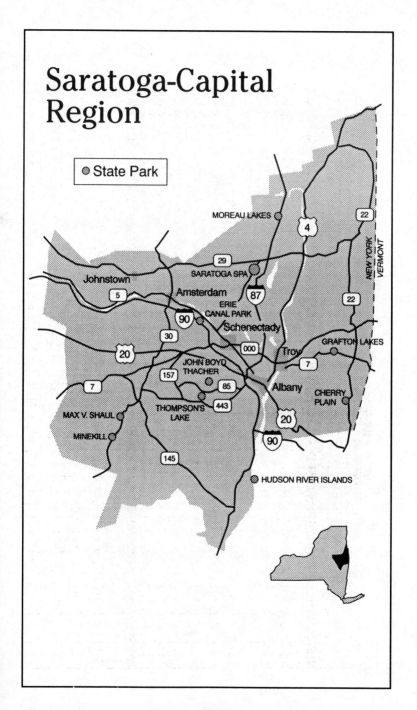

Saratoga-Capital Region

◉ State Park

MOREAU LAKES ◉

22

4

29

SARATOGA SPA ◉

Johnstown

NEW YORK
VERMONT

5

Amsterdam

87

ERIE
CANAL PARK

22

90

Schenectady

30

000

GRAFTON LAKES ◉

20

Troy

7

JOHN BOYD
THACHER ◉

157

Albany

7

85

CHERRY
PLAIN ◉

443

MAX V. SHAUL ◉

THOMPSON'S
LAKE

20

MINEKILL ◉

90

145

HUDSON RIVER ISLANDS ◉

Saratoga-Capital Region

For generations people have flocked to Saratoga for the waters. Today, great numbers of peple are traveling throughout the entire region to enjoy the blend of old and new, rustic tranquillity to world-renowned performances of the New York Ballet, Philadelphia Orchestra and other top-name stars at the Saratoga Performing Arts Center.

The timeless charm of the famous Gideon Putnam Hotel, spas and world-class golf at Saratoga Spas State Park and the panoramic vistas of John Boyd Thacher State Park prove the unique balance that is prevalent in this region.

Visitors will love the rustic camping and hiking parks at the foothills of the Adirondacks, majestic waterfalls and elegance in one of New York's most popular 10-park regions.

The region also hosts nine state historic sites, fishing and winter outdoor sports.

Grafton Lakes State Park
Land: 2,357 acres Water: Five lakes

This cozy park on the forested mountain ridge between the Taconic and Hudson valleys is dotted with five scenic lakes. The tree-lined lakes offer good access, fishing, canoeing, swimming and nearby day-use areas. Grafton Lakes is an easy drive from Troy or Albany.

Grafton's lakes are undeveloped and surrounded by deciduous trees that grow thickly to the water's edge. Native tree species include red oak, beech, four types of birch, black cherry and red and sugar maple. Also along the shoreline of the ponds are blueberry bushes that fill with fruit and birds in August. Many types of songbirds can be seen along the shoreline and throughout the varied habitats.

The city of Troy used the reservoir for its water supply until the 1960s, when the land was acquired for the park. Today, the park's most popular features are the sandy beach and sprawling high quality day-use areas. The unit has two reservable picnic shelters, hunting, fishing, summer sports and some terrific family canoeing. Day-users will enjoy the easy trails that link the ponds, play areas and picnic spaces. Bring your softballs, bats, flying discs and other field game equipment when you visit. The park is heavily used for family reunions and corporate outings.

The park has several special events each year. One of the most popular is the long-running Run for the Roses 5K foot race (there is a kid's one-mile Fun Run). The event features age divisions, T-shirts, beach showers and refreshments. The fun event helps support local Big Brothers-Big Sisters.

Grafton Lakes State Park opened in 1971.

Information and Activities

Grafton Lakes State Park
P. O. Box 163
Grafton, NY 12082-0163
(518) 279-1155

Directions: The park is 12 miles east of Troy on Route 2, which bisects the park.

Emergency numbers: Park police, (518) 584-2004, or state police, (518) 279-3403 or 911.

Day-use areas: Some of the most pleasing day-use areas are near the beach. They are equipped with pedestal grills and picnic tables, often under shade or near rolling grassy areas. A quality timber-style playground, ball field and basketball goal are near the beach parking field at the Deerfield Day-use Area. The Shaver Pond Woodland Trailhead is also here.

Beach: The sandy beach on Long Pond has nine wooden lifeguard chairs, and is 300 yards long wrapped along a gentle cove at the west end of the lake. Swimming areas are roped off with red, orange and white buoys. The beach has a railed ramp for access to the water for persons with disabilities. The reddish-brown brick bathhouse is clean and near a hard-surfaced walkway that connects the beach to the boat launch. One sand volleyball court is near the beach, where lots of smaller children can often be seen playing with sand buckets at the water's edge.

The relaxing beach has bench seats, a bike rack, flapping flags over the angular bathhouse, tidy concession stand and a reservable picnic shelter. The concession stand features outdoor seating on round red tables and a great view of the sandy beach and wooded lakeshore. Mowed spaces between the beach and concession stand also offer soothing places for snacking and sunning along a split-rail fence and busy walkway.

The sparkling clean concession stand has walk-up service, a wall of windows and a vaulted tongue and groove ceiling. A variety of grill foods including hamburgers, French fries and hot dogs, ice cream and soft drinks are served. A small gift counter sells sand pails, visors, hats, T-shirts, film, batteries and sunscreen. The candy counter is the most popular part of the concession stand. Youngsters swamp the glass-front counter buying candy bars, lollipops and chewing gum. Try the sauerkraut dogs and Italian ice.

The beach is open daily from Memorial Day to Labor Day, 10 a.m. to 6 p.m.

Hiking: Grafton Lakes has a great 12-station self-guided nature trail along Shaver Pond beginning at the Nature Center. Pick up a guide from the park office that details the dozen natural history learning stations.

At station No. 1, walkers will learn about 80-foot-tall sugar maples and why the dense, heavy wood is best suited for flooring and furniture making. It takes 30-40 gallons of sap to make one gallon of maple syrup! You'll also learn about the helicopter-like seeds that are food for chipmunks, squirrels and mice.

At station No. 2, learn about hair cap moss, one of more than 14,000 species of moss in the world. Station No. 3 teaches about ferns, which have been living for 345 million years. At station No. 4 you'll see the forest floor covered with club mosses, a plant that is also known as ground pines. They grow about six inches high and run along the surface of the ground.

Station Nos. 5 and 6 depict gnarled trees and a shadbush, also known as Juneberry or serviceberry. The shadbush is a member of the rose family and the white flowers are said to look like shad (fish). Station No. 7 tells how the black cherry is eaten by 70 types of birds and the pits are gathered by chipmunks and deer mice and stored for winter food.

Near station No. 8 is a witch hazel shrub with smoothly rippled leaves and bright yellow flowers that appear in the fall. The witch hazel's tough, powerful seed cases burst like popguns in the fall when the cold dries them. The cases pop open and shoot seeds up to 20 feet.

Tree-lovers will like station No. 9 where a smooth and silvery bark beech stands. The triangular beech nut is a favorite of squirrels, deer,

turkey, black bears and blue jays. Beech wood is hard and strong, but not durable. It is often used for railroad ties, furniture and broom handles. The beech is closely related to maples.

Station Nos. 10 and 11 have examples of shelf fungus, lichen and ferns. You'll learn that lichen is a both a fungus and an algae. Did you know fungus (mushrooms) can't make its own food—it must live on a decaying old plant, like a stump. It draws nutrients from the rotting material.

Finally, at station No. 12, is information about those pesky black flies, New York's most discomforting pests. Fortunately, black flies don't live very long and they die off in the early summer.

Deer Run Trail is three miles long and various trails circle the lakes and connect the park's amenities.

Boating: The launching ramp is at the Rabbit Run Picnic Area (Long Pond) down a gravel two-track road. Boat launching is by permit only. Boats are rented from a small shack with three small floating docks bobbing at its doorstep. Rowboats are rented by the hour. Each of the ponds has access points.

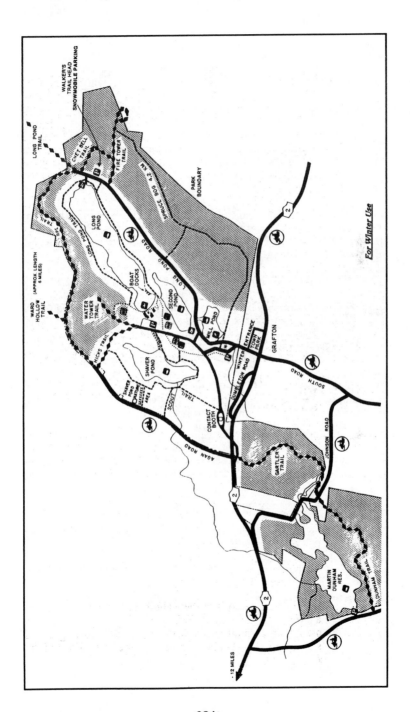

For Winter Use

Boaters are reminded to remove all aquatic plants and shellfish from their trailer frame and boat exteriors. Dispose of these materials on dry land. This helps prevent the spread of nuisance aquatic weeds and zebra mussels. Electric motors are permitted on Dunham Reservoir.

Shaver Pond and Dunham Reservoir are great places to canoe. They have easy access (about a one-half mile carry to Shaver), interesting shorelines and better than average fishing. The eastern end of Dunham has a winding inlet stream that can be explored for more than a half-mile before reaching water and rocks. At the other end of Dunham are a dam and berming. The reservoir was a water source for the city of Troy until the 1960s.

Fishing: Shaver Pond used to be a designated trout pond. There are no longer any live bait restrictions on the pond. Mill and Second ponds are the best fishing. Nearby Martin Dunham Reservoir (100 acres) offers excellent fishing lake for walleye and bass.

Tiny Mill Pond (18 acres) is up to 25 feet deep in the middle and has a good population of large- and smallmouth bass and pickerel. Second Pond (31 acres) features rainbow trout (stocked annually), small- and largemouth bass and pickerel. Long Pond (122 acres) has a boat livery and good populations of bass and trout. Shaver Pond (44 acres), an excellent trout pond, is up to 55 feet deep.

Nature: Bluebird nesting boxes and stands of pines line the entrance to the park. The Junior Museum program, a visiting outdoor education program, sometimes visits the park offering youth and adult programs, mostly on weekdays. A small interpreter's office is next to the life-guard office. The modest nature-oriented office has some educational posters and houses a seasonal naturalist that offers limited programs for youth.

Beaver are overrunning some of the ponds. Look for their logging operations and other activities during the evening. During the day, look for osprey hovering over the lake looking for a fish lunch.

Winter: Cross-country skiing and snowmobiling are popular during the winter. The park maintains 10 miles of ski trails and 10 miles of snowmobile trails. Night skating is offered on Fridays and Saturdays as weather permits.

Insider tips: Try the annual Run for the Roses foot race held each August. Visit the Shaver Pond nature area. Day-use amenities (beach, boat rental, food) are concentrated at Long Pond. Bring your fishing rod and try the four ponds. Grafton has some of the most developed playgrounds in the park system. Nearby Cherry State Park has a beach, boating and fishing. The park hosts a winter festival every January.

Moreau Lake State Park
Land: 900 acres   Water: 120-acre lake

Moreau Lake State Park, in the foothills of the Adirondacks, is for campers and day-users. The large wooded campground is shady, rustic, private and popular with visitors from Albany and many out-of-state travelers. The park is a wonderful mix of hardwood forests, pine stands, scenic pothole lake and rocky ledges. Visitors will enjoy lakeside picnic areas, a swimming beach, trout and bass fishing, hiking trails and boating.

The round, bowl-like lake was formed over the past two million years. During this span, four glaciers moved south during the Ice Age, covering this area with many feet of ice. After the retreat of the last glacier about 10,000 years ago, a huge block of ice was left behind, covered with rocks, gravel and soil. As the ice melted, it left a deep depression called a kettle hole, which filled with water and became Moreau Lake.

The park is about a 20-minute drive south of 32-mile-long Lake George. Lake George was formed the same way as Moreau Lake, but unlike the quiet park, the Lake George area has become a hub of year-round business and vacation travel. The region offers an endless list of leisure activities including swimming, boating, hiking, fishing, hot air balloon rides, scenic drives, dinner theaters, fine lodging, Fort William Henry, golf, tennis and many winter activities.

Moreau Lake State Park is the perfect place from which to day-trip to the high-energy Lake George area or to other nearby natural places, scenic mountains, hiking, biking or fishing destinations.

Information and Activities

Moreau Lake State Park
605 Old Saratoga Road
Ganesvoort, NY 12831
(518) 793-0511

Directions: In northern Saratoga County, 10 miles from Saratoga Springs and 15 miles from Lake George. The park is off of Rt. 9, near Exit 17S on I-87.

Emergency numbers: Park police, 584-2004; 911 system for medical and fire emergencies.

Campground: A hard-surfaced road winds through the rolling campground that is covered with many young trees and patches of thick vegetation. The seven main loops that comprise the 148-site campground is 95 percent shady, and each site has a block and stone ground-mounted fire box and picnic table. Each loop has centrally located rest rooms. The campers' shower is near the entrance to Loop E.

Virtually all of the sites are flat and dry, covered with a combination of gravel and grass. The quiet wooded campground is along the east shore of the lake, across from the bathhouse and swimming beach. A footbridge and narrow causeway offer access to the beach from the northern camping loops. The campground is open from mid-May to mid-October.

Sites 6 and 7 (A Loop) are excellent tent sites on a bed of pine needles. Site 8 can accommodate a large RV rig. Sites throughout the campground are separated by small caliper trees and low shrubs. Sites in the high teens are on a ridge with a view of a densely wooded valley. Sites 20-23 have a view of the lake when the leaves are off the trees. Site 31 is oversized and near the firewood shed and recycling station. Site 28 is handicapped accessible.

Most of the sites here are notched out of the woods. Sites 33 and 34 are in a grove of pines and near the comfort station. If you would like some midday sun, try site 38. This site is also near a water hydrant that has a convenient pedestal where you can set your bucket while filling it. Water hydrant spigots are also painted bright yellow for easy visibility—a great idea. Sites 36 and 43 have plenty of privacy, while site 45 is flat and ideal for a small pop-up camper.

Loop C's sites are on higher ground and the trees that shade the tract are larger. Site 51 is open and sunny, while most of the other sites are totally shaded. Many sites are private and on a ridge line above the lake. Site 55 has a partial view of the lake.

Sites 63-77 is the D Loop and next to loop C, enjoying mature trees and rolling terrain. A few sites are on high elevations and have an obscured view of the lake. Sites in the high 60s have a partial view of the back bay of the lake. Sites 71-73 are perched against the hillside and look down into a wooded hollow.

Loop E features sites 78-93. The brown block showerhouse (shower hours are posted) is close to this loop that has sites on many different elevations. The showerhouse is well-lit for night use and two benches are nearby. The building has four shower stalls and a baby changing table in both the women's and men's areas. The loop is shaded, but a few sites in the high 70s are under a grove of airy pines. A mixture of

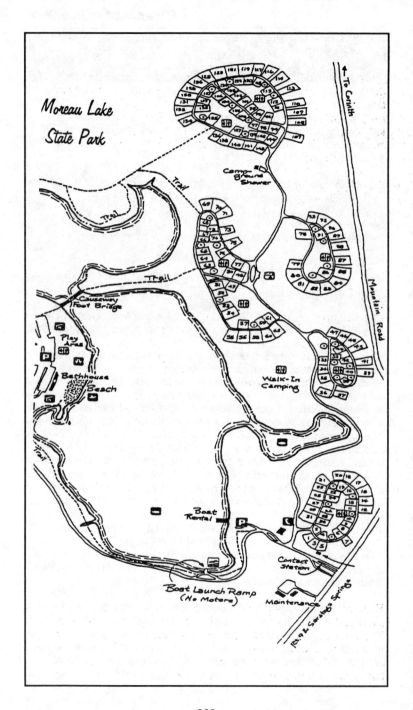

Moreau Lake State Park

RV types can be found in this private loop. Sites 88 and 89 accommodate any size RV.

Sites 94-144 comprise the F and G loops and is the northernmost area. Some of the front sites, those in the 90s, are a bit more airy and open than others. The rest of the section is heavily shaded and outlined by natural fences made of tree trunks. A trail along the north shore of the lake connects this loop to the beach. There are two rest rooms in this larger loop. Site 105 is oversized and all of the sites are separated by a wall of vegetation.

Site 130 is one of the biggest sites in the campground. Sites 100 and 101 offer some sunlight during the middle of the day. Sites 113 and 114 are excellent, airy tent camping sites. Site 131, on a curve along the bumpy road is private. Site 134 is oversized and site 135 is near the rest room.

Firewood is sold at the recycling station. Campers are issued recycling bags and expected to use the recycling station. A sink is also at the small garage-like station.

Day-use areas: Benches dot the accessible shoreline around the entire lake. The park's three horseshoe courts are separated by a four-foot-tall chain-link fence near the beach. Lots of equipped day-use and picnic areas roll off in each direction from the popular beach. A small picnic shelter is near the beach and one larger shelter is located on the north part of the beach. Also there is a volleyball and playground area.

Swimming beach: The sandy beach is deep and carved out of the woodlands. It has four lifeguard chairs and is at the foot of a mountain. The tan bathhouse is along the hilly shoreline. During the summer the beach is open 10 a.m. - 6 p.m. Several shady picnic areas are near the beach. A snack concession can be a popular place on hot summer days. Inside the clean small store/snack bar is an inventory that includes charcoal lighter fluid, marshmallows, charcoal, mustard, bags of snacks and cold drinks. From the grill you can order hot dogs and hamburgers. Candy, ice, some toiletries and playing cards are also available.

A hard-surface walkway passes by the beach connecting the nearby day-use areas that have scores of picnic tables. A sandy peninsula is a favorite place to walk and view the tree-lined shore.

Hiking: Some rolling trails connect amenities and skirt the lake. A short self-guided trail that has signed learning points is maintained. The trailside interpretive signs teach walkers about lichen, emerging vegetation, glaciers, geology and natural history. Pink lady's slippers are sometimes seen along the trails. The rugged .8-mile Overlook Trail has some excellent places to view the entire lake and surrounding foothills. The trailhead is at the back of the parking lot near the pavilion. The nature trail can also be accessed from here.

Boating: The single-lane gravel launch is best for small fishing boats. A pair of park benches at the boat launch are often occupied by guests watching the action, or anglers tossing lures into the lake. A rowboat rental operates on the lake.

Fishing: Many campers and other anglers try the thickly vegetated narrow bay between camping loops A and B, especially for bass in the spring. This small bay has lilypads, various floating vegetation and a soft shoreline. The bay is accessed by small boats, and a tiny parking lot serves the scenic little body of water.

The upper bay is three to five feet deep. A few largemouth are taken from the upper bay in the spring and early summer.

The deepest part of the spring-fed, bowl-shaped lake is 50 feet, and it's stocked with rainbow trout. Perch, sunfish, bullhead and largemouth bass are also in the lake.

Winter: Ice fishing and cross-country skiing are popular when weather permits. Some years, 11-pound rainbow trout are taken through the ice. Try simple minnow rigs on the trout during the winter.

Insider tips: Enjoy the mountain views. The park has a large campground with many private sites. Limited special events and programming are offered by the staff. An annual Kid's Fishing Derby is held at the end of each May. The park is also planning some annual fall arts and crafts shows. A large 3,800-acre addition may come in the future. Deer hunting is offered on lands west of the lake.

Saratoga Spa State Park
Land: 2,200 acres   Water: Geyser Creek

Stately trees, sometimes called the *"Avenue of Pines,"* greet you at the entrance to New York's most elegant state park. The historic landmarks, arched promenades, reflecting pools and classical buildings give visitors the feeling that time has finally stood still. The park has a wonderful history that can be enjoyed by reading some of the books written about the area or walking the handsome park.

For centuries, the Iroquois Indians knew about the healthy properties of the many springs found in the Saratoga area, but not until the 18th century did settlers make this discovery. It was then that Iroquois brought their trusted friend, Sir William Johnson, to sample the soothing waters of High Rock Spring. These naturally carbonated waters, found nowhere else east of the Mississippi River, originate in layers of limestone 100 to 1,000 feet below the park and surface through the narrow Saratoga fault.

During the late 18th century, Gideon Putnam settled in the area, opened the first inn, and laid out a village around the recently discovered springs. In 1863, with the beginning of serious horse racing, Saratoga became a famous summer resort of the wealthy. Just a few years later, artificially carbonated water became popular and gas companies began recovering carbonic gas from some of the springs, seriously decreasing the natural flow of spring water.

To stop this, the New York State Legislature passed a bill creating the State Reservation in 1909, which enabled New York State to keep forever the flowing mineral spring of Saratoga. In 1911, the Lincoln Baths opened, and at one time, was the largest bath building in the world, able to give 4,500 soothing mineral baths daily. Much of the popularity of the springs was due to noted hydrotherapist Dr. Simon Baruch, who encouraged the Reservation to develop treatment centers modeled after European spas.

During the 1930s the Saratoga Spa was created and financed through the Reconstruction Finance Corporation. With formal opening ceremonies taking place in July 1935, the "spa" became the first major program to be completed under the "New Deal." Additional buildings included the Gideon Putnam Hotel, Hall of Springs, Recreation Complex, Roosevelt I and II, Administration Building and the Little Theater.

Saratoga Spa became a state park in 1962.

Information and Activities

Saratoga Spa State Park
19 Roosevelt Drive
Saratoga Springs, NY 12866
(518) 584-2535 park office
(518) 583-2880 Lincoln Bath
(518) 584-3000 Gideon Putnam Hotel
(518) 584-2008 golf course

Directions: The park is one mile south of downtown Saratoga Springs and can be reached by traveling three miles north on Rt. 9 after exiting I-87 (the Northway), Exit 13N. Amtrak and bus lines serve Saratoga.

Emergency number: 911 system.

Gideon Putnam Hotel and Conference Center: The elegant Georgian-style hotel has 132 rooms in the center of the 2,000-acre park, near the golf course, clay tennis courts, hiking trails, pools, mas-

sages spa and world famous mineral baths. The hotel is also a short stroll from the Saratoga Performing Arts Center. The Saratoga Harness Racing Track is also nearby, just outside the park, for those who like to wager on the pacers and trotters. The hotel has a strong old-world charm and a traditional but relaxing atmosphere for business, social functions or unforgettable vacations.

The hotel, which is on the National Historic Register, has 20 private rooms, a fine Grand Ballroom that can seat 500 guests, full conference services including audio-visual equipment, banquet menus and conference packages. It operates 18 luxury rooms with graceful parlors and screen porch suites with a delightful view. Guests will also enjoy the inspired cuisine in the Georgian Room, featuring regional specialties and attention to service. Dinner is serviced 6 p.m. - 9 p.m. The Sunday brunch is set for 10:30 a.m. - 2 p.m.

Inside the radiant old hotel is a gift shop that features many golf-themed items, T-shirts, books, post cards, maps and typical hotel items. The lovely lobby has overstuffed chairs, flora wall covering and long halls to quiet rooms, shops or restaurants. Notice the ceiling to floor wall mirrors, arched windows, huge fireplaces, colorful vases, outdoor seating and classic oil paintings. While walking the halls, duck into an old-style phone booth and notice the tiny fan in the upper corner, pol-

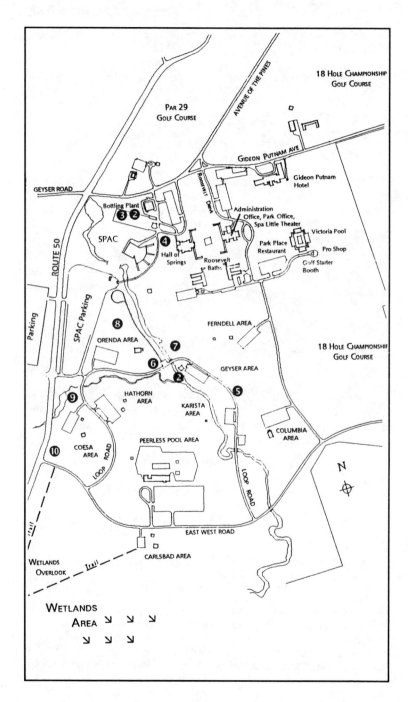

ished wood and tin wall coverings. You might expect to see Humphrey Bogart crouched inside one of the dark little booths.

There are always marble floors under foot and crown moldings and brass lights overhead. The hotel also features a second upscale gift shop that stocks wonderful scents, dishes, glassware, jewelry and quality wall hangings.

The Cafe in the Park, at the front entrance to the hotel, is open 10 a.m. - 10 p.m. daily. This outdoor seating area offers comfortable green chairs with a view of blooming flowerbeds and the rolling park, golf and mature trees touching at their canopy level. Bikes can be rented at the hotel for rides in the deep hemlock shade or along the certified running courses.

Lincoln Mineral Baths: Saratoga Springs is famous for its mineral springs, European-style baths and massages. During the summer the bath is open late June to September, 9 a.m. - 7 p.m. weekdays, 9 a.m. - 5:30 p.m. on Saturday and 9 a.m. - 9 p.m. on Sunday. Appointments aren't necessary for mineral baths, but you must make an appointment for massages and spa treatments. Call 583-2880.

During your bath, you submerge in a deep soothing tub of naturally carbonated spring water heated precisely to body temperature. The effervescent water creates a feeling of warmth and relaxation which continues after your bath while you're wrapped in warm sheets and left to rest. If you choose to complete your experience with a massage, a professional massage therapist will ease muscle tension and fatigue away. Either invigorating choice will leave you feeling revitalized and refreshed. It is wonderful!

Herbal and seaweed wraps, foot reflexology and other spa services are also available during the summer. The Lincoln Bath building is sparkling clean with marvelous three-over-three windows, wrapping tables, shiny ceramic tile and a quiet feeling of relaxation and humble professional service.

Day-use areas: Near the Victoria Pool are eight tennis courts, mature trees and a large theater with six huge columns that guard the entrance. The Hall of Springs is a huge performance center with a wonderful jazz bar and ornate fixtures. Notice the huge planters, fountains, marble floors and crystal chandeliers. The giant marble columns and towering ceiling have been used over the years for many types of special functions. The hall is nearly 200 feet long and the ceiling is too high to judge.

The park offers some reservable picnic areas. The park has a baseball backstop and enclosed picnic shelters that are large enough for corporate outings or family reunions.

Performance theater: Near the Hall of Springs, the geometric-shaped theater has brown vertical siding and colorful accent trim. Along the hard-surface walkways that surround the visually interesting theater are often tents placed for special events and activities. There are lots of shady day-use spaces between the performance theater and the closed Roosevelt Baths. The theater often hosts the New York City Ballet, Newport Jazz Festival and the Philadelphia Orchestra. Call the SPAC box office at (518) 587-3330.

Regional office: The Saratoga-Capital Region office is in a building called the Simon Baruch Research Laboratory. The wonderful building has a sprawling courtyard and fountain, with repeated arches and wonderful columns supporting a copper-clad roof. Inside the building are elegant office spaces, ornate detail from ceiling to floor, quiet sitting spaces, a brochure rack and polished woodwork.

The laboratory opened in 1934 in honor of Simon Baruch, a pioneer in hydrotherapy. In fact, Dr. Baruch developed a program of cardiac therapy based on the Nauhiem regime using Saratoga mineral waters. Up until this point, mineral water was used largely for gastrointestinal complaints, rheumatism and related diseases. Remember, this was in the early 1900s.

297

Swimming: The park has two swimming pools (fee). The Victoria Pool Complex is on the east side of the park, off North Shore Road, near the championship golf course. There is no prettier pool and surrounding arched promenades in the state. The Victoria Pool is smaller than the Olympic-size Peerless pool, which has a separate diving and wading pools.

The ornate promenades around the Victoria Pool feature arched windows (some of the windows have lace curtains), iron lamps and a red brick building. The pool is in an almost courtyard-like setting, outlined by lamps and a stately building with slate roofs. A blue and white floating buoy divides the pool. The deep end is 10 feet deep and crystal clear. There are many blue deck chairs and lounges around the deck of the elegant swimming pool, which tends to be the quieter of the two swimming pool facilities.

Take a walk in poolside area that was once a Victorian parlor. The rooms have a spectacular fireplace, brass chandelier, mirrors and polished marble floors. The old-style clock with gold leaf trimming is a wonderful reminder of the time, and times gone by. Also notice the interesting inlaid patterns of the marble and tile floors throughout the enclosed space.

Snacks and food can be ordered from the 19th Hole Restaurant and eaten poolside at several umbrella-covered tables.

The Peerless Pool, built in 1962, is in a red-brick complex and is surrounded by a chain-link fence. The almost neighborhood-like Olympic-size pool has a diving well, some shade structures with benches and wide grassy and cement sunning decks. The pool has four lifeguard chairs around the main pool. The pool is open 10 a.m. - 6 p.m. during the summer. The concession features routine grill foods, snacks, cold drinks and ice cream.

Inside the pool complex are also a small enclosed children's wading pool and lifeguard station.

Golf: The park has two wonderful golf courses, a championship 18-hole and a nine-hole course. The courses are open late April to early November.

The challenging and beautiful 18-hole course is near the Victorian Pool Complex (Park Place Restaurant and 19th Hole). The high manicured greens are guarded by kidney-shaped sand traps, fairway bunkers and mature conifers that guard the rough. The pro shop, in a brown clapboard-sided building nestled in a grove of conifers, sells golf clubs, golf videos, customized coffee mugs, golf wear and shoes, and offers information about tournaments and league play. From the blue tees the course is 7,078 yards long and has two holes with water hazards. The fairway has markers to the middle of the green. The 18-hole golf course wraps around the hotel and along the edge of the New York state nursery. A PGA pro offers lessons at the course.

Electric golf cars are available for use on the cart path. The starter shack is next to the pro shop. Many of the tees have planting pockets that are outlined by timbers and filled with colorful annual plants.

The par 29 nine-hole course has tightly clipped fairways and features sloping greens. The tough course has wide fairways and tall pines that are known to eat golf balls. The course is near a red brick bottling plant.

Winter: Bring your ice skates for use on the rink near the Victoria Mall.

Insider tips: Notice the high-quality directional signs, huge columns and ornate details throughout the park. If you like big Victorian-era buildings, plan a visit. There is an almost campus-like feeling to portions of the park. Notice the inscriptions on some of the fine buildings in the park. Some of the promenades have white marble walkways. The regional park office is at resort-style Saratoga Spa State Park. A network of often shady walkways connects park amenities. Look for pileated woodpeckers. Saratoga is the most elegant of the New York state parks.

Near the bottling plant is a running well where you can fill your jugs with mineral water. Kids can fish in Geyser Creek. Try the China Bowl restaurant near the park entrance. Some history and environmental education programming are offered.

Stop by the Geyser Pavilion area to see one of the few geysers east of the Mississippi River. Also in the area are polo, Saratoga National Historical Park, National Museum of Racing, Saratoga Harness Hall of Fame, Children's Museum, Grant Cottage, Brookside History Center, National Bottle Museum, Saratoga Battlefield, covered bridge, Petrified Garden and lots more.

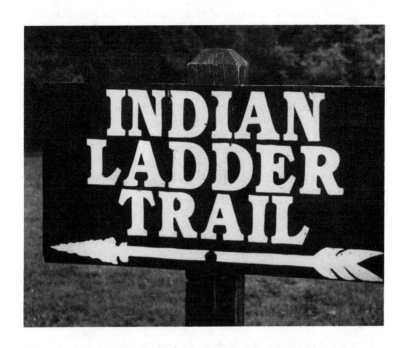

John Boyd Thacher
State Park
Land: 2,300 acres Water: Streams

The scenic day-use park is along six miles on the windy rim of the Helderberg Escarpment. The sheer-wall escarpment takes its name from the word "helder," which means bright or light, and "berg" meaning mountains. The limestone cliff-face was formed several hundred million years ago and is classic for the study of geology and stratigraphy (the arrangement of rock in layers or strata). The area is acknowledged as one of the richest fossil-bearing formations in the world. It's also one of the prettiest places in New York.

Millions of years ago, the cliffs were uplifted and then eroded by rushing streams and harsh weather. As softer rock was worn away, undermining the harder limestone above, huge blocks broke off the cliff along weak vertical joints, leaving a perpendicular wall. Two limestone formations, the Manilus and the Coeymans, which date from the Paleozoic Era period nearly 450 million years ago, make up most of the escarpment.

The altitude of the cliff varies from 800 to 1,300 feet above sea level. On a clear day it is possible to see the Adirondack foothills, the Taconics in Massachusetts and the Green Mountains in Vermont.

The park is rich in cultural history, too. In fact, names of various sections of the park commemorate much of the area's rich history and ownership following the arrival of the first Europeans in the late 17th century. Pear Orchard and Hop Field remind today's visitors about the early settlers' crops—and the struggle they had farming the poor soils. Knowles Flat, LaGrange Bush and Hailes' Cave were named for previous owners or explorers of the area. Mine Lot refers to an area once thought to be rich in gold, but was found to contain only iron pyrite. The iron pyrite was later used to make paint in Revolutionary times, hence the name Paint Mine, another park feature.

During Colonial times a well-worn pass over the cliffs was used by Mohawk Indians as they journeyed on trading missions to Albany. Part of the pass, known as Indian Ladder, is accessible to visitors today.

Nearby Thompson Lake State Park has a terrific campground and 128-acre lake with beach. Thompson is a great base camp from which to explore the region's fascinating geology and rugged trails. For more information about Thompson Lake State Park, see below.

Information and Activities

John Boyd Thacher State Park
R.D. #1, P. O. Box 238
Voorheesville, NY 12186
(518) 872-1237

Directions: In Albany County on Rt. 157, 16 miles west of Albany and 17 miles south of Schenectady. The park is along the Helderberg Escarpment and named after former Albany mayor and New York state senator.

Emergency numbers: Park police, (518) 872-0625 or sheriff, (518) 765-2351.

Day-use areas: The park has a number of wonderful observation points and picnic areas along the rim of the soaring escarpment. The main viewing point, called the Cliff Edge Overlook, is outlined by a stone knee-wall across from the Knowles Flat Picnic Area. From the overlook you can see the sheer cliff walls, a pattern of farm fields,

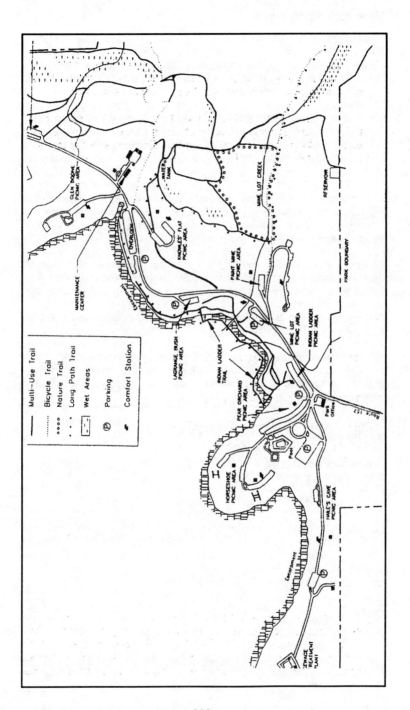

302

wooded tracts and the tops of houses and buildings in the distance. Mountain views are to your right. The two coin viewers are worth the pocket change to see the mountains, fertile farm fields and the sweeping broad valley.

Many of the day-use areas are outlined by split-rail fences and have views of the distant valleys and towering cliff faces. Some picnic areas are under an airy grove of pines. The Paint Mine Picnic Area has a reservable shelter. The Pear Orchard Picnic Shelter is near the pool and a colorful playground that sits on a sand base. The park has two main playgrounds.

Swimming pool: The entrance to the Olympic-size swimming pool and game area is near the park office. A small round concession and modern play equipment serve walk-ups and pool users. The brown, vertical, clapboard-sided bathhouse is behind the white lifeguard chairs and hard-surfaced deck. A small kiddies wading pool operates during the summer. The water is divided by red and white buoys in front of the lifeguard stands. Parents will like the bulky wood benches that surround the pool. The pool is open 10 a.m. 6 p.m. daily. The concession stand sells ice cream, hot dogs, French fries and soft drinks. A few blue tables are scattered inside the pool area, where you may eat your snacks and enjoy the atmosphere.

The bathhouse has a popular balcony with few sunning chairs that overlook the busy pool and wide deck. The pool is sunny, but the general area is flanked by shady day-use areas, a flag pole, bike rack and flowerbeds.

Behind the pool, on an old tennis court, are basketball goals and colorful play equipment.

Indian Ladder Trail: The trail is open from May 1 - Labor Day, 8 a.m. - 8 p.m. and Labor Day to Nov. 15, 8 a.m. - 5 p.m. The trail is closed the rest of the year. Proceed with caution on the rough walking trail; beware of the falls and loose rocks.

Narrow stairs take you down the face of the cliff where hikers often see chipmunks scurrying into the dense vegetation. While on the stairs and along many areas, examine the many layers of rock, as well as the many joints and cracks that comprise the limestone wall. The trail is .5 miles long and takes about 30 minutes to hike.

Along the trail are wooden boardwalks, tall tumbling waterfalls, streams, slippery spots, boulders, wonderful views of the valley, wooded sections and wildlife, including lots of songbirds.

According to the Indian Ladder self-guided brochure: "Geological and human history at John Boyd Thacher State Park have been running on

The popular Indian Ladder Trail.

different clocks for millions of years." The forces acting to create the huge escarpment happened long before man. The towering wall has been an impediment to human travel and continues to fascinate visitors.

Why the name Indian Ladder? Verplanck Colvin, one of the earliest men to write about the Helderbergs, in 1869 wrote: "What is this Indian Ladder so often mentioned? In 1710 this Helderberg region was a wilderness; nay, all westward of the Hudson River settlement was unknown. Albany was a frontier town, a trading post, a place where annuities were paid and blankets exchanged with Indians for beaver pelts. From Albany over the sand plains, "Schenectada" (pine barrens) of the Indians...led an Indian trail westward. Straight as the wild bee or the crow, the wild Indian made his course from the white man's settlement to his own home in the beauteous Schoharie Valley. The stern cliffs of these hills opposed his progress: his hatchet fells a tree against the stumps of the branches, which he trimmed away and formed the round of the Indian ladder."

The old Indian ladder used to lean against the cliff where the trail now descends.

Learning stations along the scenic trail discuss fossils, Manlius and Coeymans formations (colorful limestone layers), fissures and the dynamics of cracks and joints, caves and sinkholes, creeks, underground streams and the talus slope.

Nature: The sea that once covered the area was abundant with marine life, including millions of tiny hard-shelled animals that thrived in the shallow waters. As these creatures died, their shells settled to the bottom and slowly compacted into limestone. Today, the area is also rich with flora and fauna including salamanders, several types of snakes, many types of fish and minnows, dogwoods and a mixed deciduous forest.

The woodlands on slopes above the escarpment provide excellent habitat for many species including wild turkey, deer, raccoon, skunks, songbirds, raptors and an active beaver colony.

Caves: The area has some interesting caves including Tory Cave, which was used in 1777 by Jacob Salsbury, a spy during the Burgoyne Invasion, as refuge from settlers. The caves found at Thacher were used as meeting or hiding places for loyalists during the revolution.

Winter: Cross-country and downhill skiing (no lifts) are offered south of Rt. 157. You may also sled and snowshoe the trails. Limited snowmobile riding is offered. Check with the park office.

Thompson Lake State Park: Four miles from John Boyd Thacher State Park on Rt. 157, Thompson has camping (140 sites on 125 acres) and recreation areas. Call (518) 872-1674 for more information. The beach is open during the summer from 10 a.m. - 6 p.m. daily. Firewood is sold to campers and rowboats are available for rent.

The sinkhole lake is up to 60 feet deep and contains good fishing for pike, pickerel, perch, bass, bullhead, trout and panfish. Many docks and private cottages line the lake and offer places to fish.

The park is for campers. Sites have blue gravel pads, ground-mounted fire rings and picnic tables. Some sites in the teens are deep, while sites in the 30s and 40s have partial lake views (these are preferred sites). Many sites in the 50s are great for pop-up campers or tents.

Sites in the 70s and 80s are notched out of the woods and private. Sites at Thompson Lake are some of the most private in the system. Site 106 is oversized. Sites 119 and 121 are the closest to the water. The small beach has a volleyball court and a single lifeguard chair. Sites in the 20s are near the beach.

Some recreation programming is scheduled for campers at Thompson Lake State Park.

Insider tips: From the Cliff Edge Overlook, looking northeast toward Albany, you can see the state university campus and the Empire State Plaza. There is no fishing in the park (try nearby Thompson Lake State Park). Hike the rugged Indian Ladder Trail, then go for a swim and snack near the park office. The view at the Outlet Falls is terrific.

The highlight of the park is Indian Ladder Trail (remember to stand behind the waterfalls, but be prepared to get a little damp!). Bring your canoe to Thompson's Lake State Park and camp for the weekend. Thompson is a complementary park to the day-use Thacher State Park. A 7.4-mile section of Long Path traverses Thacher State Park (along Indian Ladder Trail).

PHONE	PARK	Tent/trailers sites (h = hookups, e = electricity)	Trailer dump	Showers	Camper recreation	Cabins	Food	Store	Picnic tables	Shelters (• reservations)	Swimming beach (• bath house)	Swimming pool (• bath house)	Recreation programs (• performing arts)	Hiking	Biking	Nature trails	Fishing	Playground	Golf (•clubhouse)	Tennis	Pond or lake (• power boats ok)	River or stream (• power boats ok)	Launching site (• hand launch only)	Boat rental	Marina (• anchorage)	Pump out	Ice skating (•rentals)	Cross-country skiing (• rentals)	Snowmobiling	Sled slopes
518 584-2000	**SARATOGA-CAPITAL REGION**																													
518 733-5400	Cherry Plain								▷					▷		▷	▷	▷			▷		▷				▷	▷	▷	▷
518 279-1155	Grafton Lakes*								▷	•	▲			▷		▷	▷	▷			▷		▷				▷	▷	▷	▷
	Hudson River Islands								▷								▷						▲							
518 827-6111	Mine Kill						▲		▲	•		•	▲	▷		▷	▷	▷	•		•		▲				▷	▲	▷	▷
518 793-0511	Moreau Lake	▲	▲	▲	▲		▷		▲	▲	▲		▲	▷		▷	▷	▷			•	•	▲				▷	•	▷	▷
518 584-2535	Saratoga Lake								▲								▷				•		•							
	Saratoga Spa						▲		▲	▷		•	▲	▷		▷	▷		•	•							▷	▲	▷	▷
518 827-4711	Max v. Shaul	▲	▲	▲	▲				▲	•	▲		▲	▷		▷	▷	▷												
518 872-1237	John Boyd Thacher								▲	▷			▲	▷		▷		▷									▷	▷	▷	▷
518 872-1674	Thompson's Lake	▲	▲	▲	▲				▷	•	•		▲	▷		▷	▷	▷			•		•					▷	▷	▷
518 664-5261	Canal Parks: Champlain - Lock 4								▷																					
518 237-4014	Erie - Lock 6 (boat launch)																▷						•							
518 829-7516	Erie - Lock 9								▷																					
	STATE HISTORIC SITES																													
518 279-1155	Bennington Battlefield	— see note																												
518 463-0738	Cralo																													
518 597-3666	Crown Point																													
518 597-8277	Grant Cottage																													
518 762-8712	Johnson Hall																													
518 829-7516	Schoharie Crossing																													
518 434-0834	Schuyler Mansion																													

State Historic Sites descriptions:

- **Bennington Battlefield** — Enjoy a picnic lunch at this historic hilltop where American militiamen defeated the British in 1777.
- **Cralo** — See early Dutch life in the upper Hudson River Valley reflected in this unique museum.
- **Crown Point** — Visit the ruins of Fort St. Frederic (1734) and His Majesty's Fort of Crown Point (1759).
- **Grant Cottage** — Here at the summit of Mt. McGregor, former President Ulysses S. Grant died in 1885.
- **Johnson Hall** — Twenty acres of grounds and scented herb garden surround Sir William Johnson's 1763 mansion.
- **Schoharie Crossing** — Walk along the original Erie Canal and the enlarged Erie Canal with its impressive stone aqueduct.
- **Schuyler Mansion** — Tour the gracious 1761 hillside home of Philip Schuyler, the noted Revolutionary War general.

▷ Availability of service or facility   ▲ Handicapped accessible   *Bridle paths

307

Taconic Region

Scenic vistas from mountaintop trails, fishing, woodland cabins and history are some of the highlights upon a visit to the state parks on the east side of the Hudson River.

Hikers can choose from challenging mountain trails with breathtaking views of the Hudson Valley, or panoramic views of Hudson River and other wonderful areas.

The region has 12 parks and includes one-third of the historic sites in the state. The region is known for warm summers and gentle breezes, to showy autumns and crisp snow-white winters.

Anglers will find plenty of launch sites, while campers will enjoy five parks with campsites and four with shady cabins.

From horseback riding to a sanctuary for flora and fauna, the Taconic Region has one of the nation's largest swimming pools and excellent golf courses.

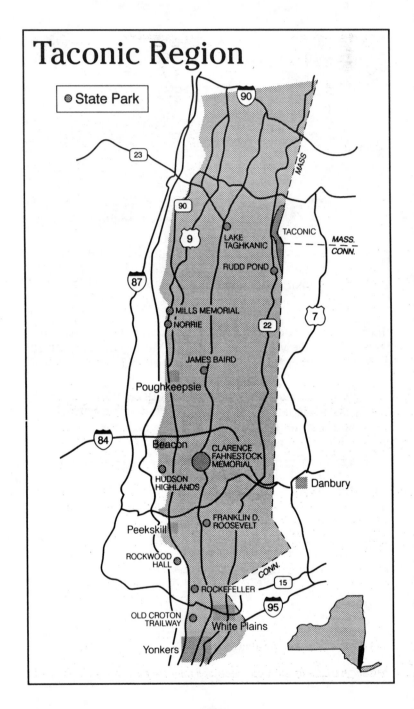

Taconic Region

⬤ State Park

90

23

MASS

90

9

LAKE
TAGHKANIC

TACONIC

MASS.
CONN.

RUDD POND

87

MILLS MEMORIAL

NORRIE

22

7

JAMES BAIRD

Poughkeepsie

84

Beacon

CLARENCE
FAHNESTOCK
MEMORIAL

Danbury

HUDSON
HIGHLANDS

Peekskill

FRANKLIN D.
ROOSEVELT

ROCKWOOD
HALL

ROCKEFELLER

CONN.

15

OLD CROTON
TRAILWAY

95

White Plains

Yonkers

Fahnestock Memorial State Park

Land: 6,532 acres   Water: Lakes and streams

In the highlands of Putnam County, the Fahnestock Memorial State Park began as a gift in 1929 of Dr. Ernest Fahnestock in memory of his brother. Clarence Fahnestock added 6,200 acres to the original 2,700 acre parcel in the 1960s.

The densely wooded park includes six lakes, a hemlock stream ravine and limited marshlands. Elevations are 600 to 1,308 feet above sea level. Trails along the higher elevations offer some awesome panoramic views of the broad and fertile Hudson Valley. Much of the old forest is oak and mixed hardwoods, but a significant area of Eastern hemlocks is near the park headquarters.

Although traces of old iron ore mines are now hard to find in the park, the general area was once a major supplier of quality ore. In fact, the Sunk Mine was the source of iron ore for the West Point, N.Y. Foundry. The ore was turned into Parrot guns the Union army. From points on the parks trail you can see railroad beds that once provided the overland route for long trains of ore-laden cars.

Originally, the park lands were purchased by Adolphe Philipse in 1691 and established as the Philipse Grant six years later by King William III. The rugged wilderness along the vast mountain range could not be farmed and was settled only lightly. Little ore was found in the area until Richard Hopper opened a mine in 1820. Most of the mines closed in the panic of 1873 and much of the land was obtained by Dr. Clarence Fahnestock in 1915, after many intervening land sales.

Information and Activities

Clarence Fahnestock Memorial State Park
RFD 2
Carmel, NY 10512-7207
(914) 225-7207

Directions: In Putnam County, on both sides of Route 301. The park is adjacent to the Taconic Parkway.

Emergency number: (914) 225-7207.

Campground: The campground entrance is directly across from the entrance to the popular beach. An informational bulletin board is at the entrance of the intimate campground offering notes on tick safety, park rules and public programs. Movies are offered in the campground at 7 p.m. on Saturday evenings throughout the summer. Most camping sites have grass, dirt and gravel pads and all have a grill or stone fire ring and picnic table. The pay phone and park office are one-half mile from the scenic campground. A basketball goal is near the campground Dumpsters. Hot showers are at the beach bathhouse that was built in 1981.

The rolling and shady campground has some walk-in tent sites and many of the sites are on varying elevations. Site 15 is near the rest room and pleasantly shady. The stone rest room has a soft drink machine stationed at the entrance. Sites 17 and 18 are excellent tent sites also near the rest room. Sites 20-22 are ideal tent sites outlined by large rock outcroppings. Site 26 has a dozen hemlocks offering airy shade and a bed of short needles underfoot. Sites 30-33 are under a grove of evergreen trees and tucked between rock outcrops that are the size of trucks.

The small nature center has displays and offers natural history programming.

The lake is in view from some of the sites in the 40s. Site 42 has some huge rocks surrounding the shady respite. Many of these sites are well separated by vegetation and rock formations. A newer play area is near sites in the 60s.

Cabins: The Taconic Outdoor Education Center has lodging; call (914) 265-3773.

Day-use areas: Day-use areas are on various elevations and are often dotted with rock outcroppings.

Beach: The compact, full-service beach down a gravel road is served by a clean bathhouse that has a flag flapping nearby. The food concession, is open 10 a.m. - 5 p.m., has grill foods, ice cream, simple camping supplies, paper plates, chips, insect repellent, soft drinks and sells firewood and rents umbrellas. A small patio has a few tables available for outdoor eating.

The cove-side sandy beach is about 200 yards long and 75 yards wide.

A smooth cement sidewalk outlines the sweep of the cove where benches are carefully placed. At the back of the beach are a scattering of picnic tables under a thin grove of trees. Swimming areas are marked and the water is shallow near the shore and safe for small children. The views from the beach include rocky shorelines and tree-covered mountains.

Hiking: Mountain biking is offered on designated trails; contact the park office for information. Riding on trail paths is not permitted.

The Appalachian Trail can be accessed from the park's trail system. Great views of the Hudson Valley are also along some of the easy to moderate color-coded hiking trails. The Blue and Red trails offer terrific overlooks. Some of the trails are steep, climbing to 1,000 feet and back down to the valley floor.

The lily-pad covered Pelton Pond has a wonderful picnic pavilion with two fireplaces. From the ceiling of the rugged shelter are interpretive signs that discuss the work of the Civilian Conservation Corps. The plaques also include a poem by the CCC worker Charles Pierce:

"We are hopeful that those who are to follow through years, that shall pass just as these will derive a bountiful blessing from our temple building of trees. The trees are a boon to the Nation regardless of how great or how small. Rich gems of nature's adornment extending solace to all."

This massive shelter was built by enrollees in the CCC. The 1930s CCC workers were paid $30 monthly. By the end of the CCC in 1942, it had employed more than 3.2 million men who planted two billion trees and constructed hundreds of facilities on public parklands throughout the United States.

The Pelton Pond Nature Trail starts at the picnic shelter. Follow the yellow markers around the pond to the right. A three-panel self-guided brochure is available at the park office. Numbers in the guide correspond to wooden numbers on trees along the trail. The trail is 1.5 miles long and takes less than an hour to walk.

Along the trail, hikers will learn about organisms that decompose dead trees into soil, common species of evergreens, woodpecker holes, a small dam, swallows, trees growing on rocks and more.

One of the most common trees in the park and along the trail is the Eastern hemlock. They are easy to identify by the short (less than one inch) needles that grown in two rows. The hemlock cone is only the size of the tip of your finger and can be susceptible to woolly adelgid, an insect that lives in the needles sucking sap from young twigs, stunting the tree's growth.

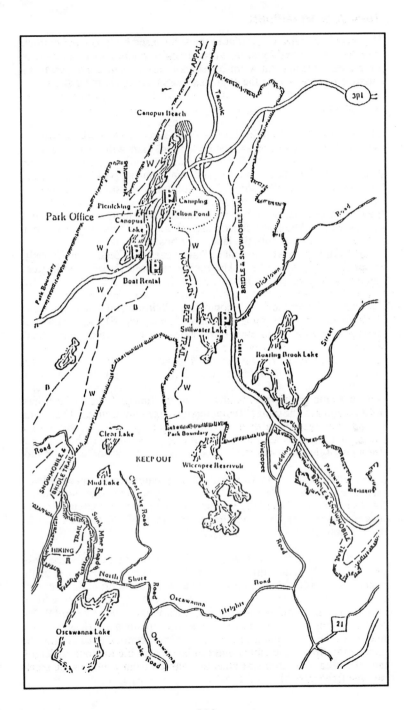

The high iron and acid content in the soil caused by the thick hemlock forest caused Pelton Pond to be called "Poison Pond" by farmers. The pond water was unhealthy for livestock to drink. The small pond was enlarged by the CCC in the 1930s by damming an ore mine shaft.

Fahnestock has little, big and brown bat species. In some places around the park, bat houses have been installed. The interpretive trail teaches a number of interesting bat facts, such as: A single brown bat can eat 3,000 - 7,000 mosquitoes each night. Bats will not land in your hair. Bats are not blind. Bats are mammals, which must nurse their young. Less than .005 percent of bats have rabies. Bats are very helpful to have in the park and they help control the insect population.

Boating: Near the end of a single-lane gravel launch is a boat rental on Canopus Lake. Boat rentals are offered from mid-June to Labor Day. A few sailboats ply the lake. The boat rental is open 8:30 a.m. - 4 p.m. You must have a permit to launch canoes. Electric motors only are permitted on the lake. The rocky and treed shoreline will greet paddlers along the scenic lake.

Fishing: Try your luck on Canopus Lake, Pelton Pond, Allen Pond and Duck Pond for bass, perch, sunfish and pickerel. Stillwater Lake is managed for trout; thousands of rainbow and brook trout are stocked annually.

Nature: The Taconic Outdoor Education Center is on Rt. 301 west of the main park area. It offers environmental programs for visitors to the park and Hudson Highlands area. The multipurpose center also has meeting spaces, lodging and recreational programming. For more information call (914) 265-3773.

The small seasonal stone and wood nature center in the campground offers a variety of outdoor education programs including guided hikes, low-impact camping, outdoor skills classes, nature crafts, map reading, bird identification, Sunday strolls and youth programs. The nature center is a beautifully designed structure that has benches built under multiple pane windows. Programs are posted weekly. The nature center is near camping site 37.

Inside the nature center are a number of mammal and bird mounts, wall displays, skulls, snake information, a display on wingspans and a small historical display about the importance of ironworking and mining in the area. The interesting display talks about the conditions of the mines, mining techniques, lifestyles of the employees and the culture of the mining era in this part of the state. The display includes photographs that depict the smelting of iron, blacksmithing and the making of charcoal. In fact, many farmers spent two weeks of the fall making charcoal. This activity added substantially to their income. Twenty-five cords of wood equaled about 35 bushels of charcoal.

The small center also has a nine-hole touch box and various bits of natural history information about the park lands.

Ask for a handy birding checklist at the park office. It details bird sightings by season and abundance. The list also breaks down the recorded avian sightings by types. It includes 29 types of wood warbler, six species of vireos, 10 kinds of finches, 11 species of waterfowl, falcons, owls, hawks, shorebirds and hummingbirds.

Winter: The park is a top cross-country ski destination. Fifteen kilometers of trails are groomed and tracks are set. The park also rents skis and maintains food service and a warming lodge. Lesson are also possible by calling in advance. Snowshoeing and snowmobiling are also offered at the park.

Hunting: Archery deer hunting is allowed.

Insider tips: Plan a visit to the city of Nelson where there are plenty of small shops and interesting restaurants. Bring your canoe. The beach, rocky outcroppings and good hiking trail are a treat at this getaway state park.

Taconic State Park
Land: 5,000+ acres Water: Ponds, creeks

The large park has two developed areas. There are camping and day-use areas and a wonderful waterfall and natural area.

The rugged beauty of Bash Bish Waterfalls contrasts pleasingly with the soft undulating terrain that is Berkshires County. Mountain slopes on both sides of the dramatic falls are heavily forested with maple, beech and hemlock. In the spring, wildflowers carpet the forest floor and hikers take to the many miles of moderate trails. Among the wildflowers at the park are pink lady's slippers, purple burgeons bowers and false yellow foxgloves. Interesting tiny liverworts and mosses thrive in the constant spray of the falls.

Open rocky ledges in the Bash Bish gorge also provide ideal habitat for the timber rattler. Good numbers of the snake live in forested hilly terrains of south New England. They are frequently seen in the gorge, particularly as they sun themselves on the ledges in the spring and fall months. Check a field guide for the distinctive marks of the black and dull yellow reptile. To avoid the normally timid snake, keep hands and feet out from under ledges and stay on the trails.

Many birds also inhabit the tract. Perhaps none are as spectacular as the peregrine falcon, which has nested in the gorge for centuries. These dramatic birds of prey whirl and veer through the gorge at speeds of more than 160 mph with their wings wet from the spray of the falls. Use of DDT in the 1950s destroyed the population here, but there is hope more of the birds will return to the area.

Many other mammals are also in the area including bobcat, black bear, porcupine, deer, beaver, raccoon and squirrels.

Long before the Ice Age, the Berkshires underwent three major periods of mountain building. The last of these took place 225 million years ago during a period when the Appalachian Mountain system was formed. The four glacial periods that came much later changed the course of streams, rivers and mountain peaks without radically altering the landscape. Generally speaking, waterfalls were short-lived and unimportant geologic phenomena compared to the events like the formation of the sprawling mountain ranges.

Bash Bish Brook, like all other streambeds in New England, is only as old as the retreat of the last glacier that covered the region 10,000 years ago. During the melting of the last glacier, mounds of glacial debris blocked streambeds. When dammed streams finally broke through, they water cascaded down mountains, often following joints and weaknesses in the mountain, creating waterfalls.

A white quartz dike which angles across the gorge halfway up the falls, is the result of hot silica-rich liquid escaping from within the earth 400 million years ago. The liquid forced itself upward along a weakness in the gorge. The water of the brook has now cut away enough of the rock to make the seam visible.

Sediment in the water erodes the streambed. Bash Bish, like all falls, is slowly destroying itself—but it will take thousands of years. You've got plenty of time to visit the pleasant cascade and especially clean state park.

Information and Activities

Taconic State Park
Copake Falls, NY 12517-0110
(518) 329-3993

Directions: In Columbia and Dutchess counties, along 11 miles of

318

border separating New York from Massachusetts and Connecticut. The Bash Bish Falls are on Falls Road off of East Street in Mt. Washington, Mass., 14 miles from Great Barrington via Rts. 23 and 41. The falls are four miles from Copake Falls, NY on Rt. 34. The falls are actually in Massachusetts.

Emergency number: 911 system.

Campground: Section A of the campground has 37 sites; 55 sites are in section B, 22 in section C and 16 trailer and RV sites in the shady area D. Areas A and B are tents only. Charming stone bathhouses have hot showers and flush toilets. Cut firewood is available at the campground. All sites have steel fire rings, nearby water hydrants and picnic tables. Many sites have a firm gravel pad, ideal for parking your RV rig.

Near sections A and B are several amenities for children including mowed field spaces, a basketball goal and play equipment. Plantation pines growing in straight rows offer a soft bed of needles at many campsites.

Sites in Section A are mostly shady and filled with many wooden platforms scattered among the tall, 18-inch caliper pines. Site A6 is near the stone shower building, open spaces area and volleyball court. Sites 20 and 25 are platform sites, private and near the day-use amenities. A small playground is near sites 34 and 35.

Tent sites are offered in the B section mixed among straight pines. The best platforms in the B section is 46 or 48. At the top of the hill is a terrific site No. 54. Many sites in this section are nestled against a hillside and natural area, often looking down on other camping sites.

Camping areas C and D are for small to medium-size trailers. A CCC-built showerhouse serves campers in this grove of airy pines. Sites D3-D16 are in a more densely shaded area. Most of the sites in the pines get more sunlight, especially in the late afternoon. These sites tend to warm up and dry out quickly too.

Cabins: The quiet park operates duplex cabins that are along Rt. 344 on your way to the Bish Bash Falls. The cabins are vintage rustic two-story structures that contain two or three rental units in each building. Depending on the size of the unit, four to six people can be accommodated. All of these units provide regular beds, hot and cold running water, flush toilets, in-unit showers, fireplace, electric stove, refrigerator, tables, and chairs or benches on an open, common porch. You must provide linen and eating and cooking utensils. Notice the interesting stone bridge just past the house-like units.

Five more secluded cabins are about one-half mile from the large

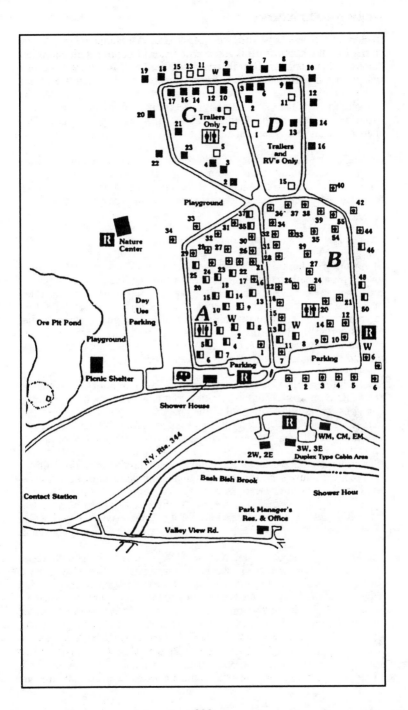

duplex units down a shady and quiet road. A rushing rocky stream courses by the cabins, offering a scenic experience rare in most parks. A mowed open space is near this colony of rustic private cabins. A centrally located bathhouse serves guests of these terrific cabins that are tucked along a steep hillside above the stream, near the waterfall. Although rustic, the cabins do have electricity, stove and refrigerator. Trout anglers should book these cabins in the spring and fall. The shaded stream in this section has a gravel bottom and pools are nearby.

In the Copake Falls area are 12 unheated cabins that have cold running water and accommodate up to four people. They have bunk beds, flush toilets, electric lights, refrigerator, stove, table and chairs or benches on the screened porch. A clean central shower building serves the guests.

Day-use areas: Near Ore Pit Pond are a baseball backstop, basketball goal, volleyball net, swings and picnic shelter.

Swimming: The Ore Pit Pond swimming site is an interesting platform with a small changing house near a tiny wading pond. This area is north of the contact station near the main campground entrance. The improved shoreline has three lifeguard chairs, three ladders and a diving platform. The shady swimming area has some grassy surrounding the small pond. The swimming area is roped off with large red buoys at each corner. There is deep water at the swimming area. In fact, in front of the floating platform it is 40 feet deep.

Small children will love the neighboring wading area that has a smaller lifeguard chair and nearby drinking fountain. The cool water slowly moves through the tiny pool to the creek.

The Rudd Pond area has a grassy beach and is east of the park on Rt. 62 in Dutchess County. Rudd Pond has 40 trailer and tent camping sites under deciduous trees. A small rowboat rental and primitive gravel launching site are on the nearby pond. The pond is getting weedy and increasingly difficult to fish.

Bash Bish Falls: From the parking lot it is a three-quarter mile walk to the scenic falls. There is also an upper parking lot in Massachusetts.

The history of the falls is interesting. The waters of Bash Bish Falls begins at a spring high on Mt. Washington and tumble into a dark, clear pool at the bottom of a deep snail-like gorge. After the 200-foot plunge, Bash Bish Brook continues on a winding course through New York state until it finally joins the Hudson River on its way to the Atlantic Ocean.

The falls is made up of a series of cascades that twist between the cliffs of the gorge. The beauty of Bash Bish changes with the seasons. Fall might be the best time to visit when the leaves have turned to crimson

and gold.

Legend has it that a beautiful Indian woman called "Bash Bish" lived in a village near the falls. According to lore, she was a cheerful sister to all. Yet one day a jealous friend accused her of adultery. She pleaded innocent before the village council, but the stern elders sentenced her to death. The Indian woman was to be strapped to a canoe and turned loose upstream from the falls. The moment before her execution, the rays of the sun formed a perfect halo around her body and a ring of colorful butterflies softly fluttered around her head. Suddenly the canoe plunged into the falls and smashed on the rocks below. The shattered canoe was retrieved at the base of the falls, but there was no trace of Bash Bish's body. Villagers concluded that Bash Bish was a witch and the memory of her execution haunted them for years to come.

The story might have ended there if Bash Bish had not left a young daughter, "White Swan." White Swan grew to enjoy health, beauty and the love of Whirling Winds, the great chief's son. But unexplainable loneliness often caused her to climb to the edge of the gorge above the falls. When she discovered she was unable to give Whirling Wind children, she decided to end her life by plunging into the turbulent waters of the rushing falls.

Whirling Wind, without her knowledge, had followed her up to the gorge—and followed his love into the thundering water. Once again the villagers searched the north pool. Although they found Whirling Wind's battered body, they never found any sign of White Swan. It is said that the images of Bash Bish and White Swan sometimes appear fleetingly in the falls.

Hiking: Ask the staff for directions to the Appalachian Trail.

The Bash Bish Falls trail has about 100,000 hikers annually. The trails are open for cross-country skiing in the winter. Pick up a trail map at the office that details the trail system. Nearby Cedar Mountain has an elevation of 1,883 feet. Mt. Prospect is 1,919 feet tall.

Try the Sunset Rock (elevation 1,788 feet) hiking trail for a great view. From mid-June to early July, mountain laurel that lines the trail is in bloom and for more than a half-mile you can walk between the pink and white blossoms before stepping into a clearing that offers a breathtaking 50-mile view across the Hudson Valley to the Catskill Mountains.

The walk to Bash Bish Falls wanders along the rushing stream that is littered with car-size boulders. Once at the falls, a series of 47 steps takes you to its base that is littered with boulders and smooth driftwood logs.

Notice how the waterfall is cutting its way right through the mountain. There are some large rounded boulders that you can climb on near the frothing base of the falls. Look for ducks swimming in the pool at the base of the falls. Notice the J rock that has been slowly carved away near the crest of the roaring falls. The rock is about 30 feet tall and is skirted by a moss-covered wall and overhanging plants.

Boating: Try paddling Rudd Pond. Its shoreline is lined with oaks, paper birch, hickory, Norway spruce, red pine and tamarack. These trees offer a colorful autumn. The pond has heavy vegetation.

Fishing: Brook and rainbow trout are in the Ore Pit Pond and the stream. There are four small ponds that you can fish: Ore Pit, Weed Mines Pond (3 acres), Rudd Pond (10 feet deep) and Iron Mine Pond (five acres). The small, cold ponds typically have trout, largemouth bass, panfish and bluegills. A few perch are taken from Rudd Pond.

Furnace: Near the park manager's office is an old brick furnace, once part of the Copake Ironworks. The company produced about eight tons of ore per day between 1845 and the turn of the century. What little remains of the once-busy factory offers valuable insight into local industrial history.

On an interpretive board near the old furnace are some samples of slag, a waste product of the blast furnace. The glassy slag can be found in many areas of the park because it was used as a fill material. Slag can be found in many colors ranging from shades of blue and green depending on the temperature of the furnace and the ore. There is also an example of an iron bar bolted onto the interpretive sign.

Much of the iron that was produced here was cast into bars. The heavy bar was shipped to other factories to be remelted and made into the finished product. There is also information about wrought iron, the blast furnace, fuel and ironmaking, the birth of the modern iron and steel industry, how iron casts were made and the lifestyle of ironworkers from the 1870s, which is called the "Age of Steel."

A charcoal iron furnace required a community of many skills. Some skills included wood cutting, which was easily learned and relatively low paying, and others were complex and represented knowledge that was passed along for centuries. Among skilled workers were charcoal makers, miners who dug the ore, foundrymen, molders who cast the hot iron, clerks and ironmasters.

Charcoal is a partly burned wood product produced by a slow smoldering process that takes up to two weeks to complete. The wood was carefully stacked in mounds and covered with turf to control air pressure and ensure that it didn't burst into flames. Quality charcoal making was critical to the blast furnace operation.

Blast furnaces were developed in the 14th century and revolutionized iron making technology. The significant change was the increase in the height of the furnace. The iron had more time to work its way down the furnace, absorbing more carbon from the charcoal than sponge iron made in bloomeries.

Because carbon-rich iron melts at 350 degrees, lower than sponge iron, it became liquid and was much higher quality. Therefore the blast furnace produced liquid iron, in contrast to semi-liquid iron bloomery. The first blast furnaces were built in England in 1490. The first in the United States was in 1646.

Nature: The tiny hut-like nature center has screen-covered windows with small history displays inside. On the white interior walls are various posters, insect collections and photographs. A small display about the endangered timber rattlesnake also reminds visitors not to disturb the generally timid snake.

In the back room of the little building is a small activity room where children often do projects. On the counters are touch items, furs, information about animal tracks and some recreation equipment. The center also has a small collection of field guides.

Staff offers a daily nature hike during the summer, craft programs, recreational programs, guided hikes to Sunset Rock, kickball games and other programs. The nature center is surrounded by day-use areas and is near the campground.

Winter: Cross-country skiing is popular at the mountainous park.

Insider tips: Bring your bike; the park roads are rolling and quiet. The park is a low-key, clean and rustic park. Families with small children are drawn to Taconic State Park. The park does not have a camp store, but there is a party store (Depot Deli) at the entrance to the park that sells ice, beer and food. The falls are a must see.

The 10-foot-wide trail to the falls is gravel and of medium difficulty. Many riffles, cascades and water shoots are along falls trails. Climb on the big boulders at the base of the Bash Bish Falls. The water is crystal clear. Grab a bite at the nearby friendly Taconic Inn on Rt. 344.

Lake Taghkanic
State Park
Land: 1,569 acres Water: 162-acre lake

Lake Taghkanic is a wonderful little park that draws heavy crowds of down-staters to the placid lake, shady campground, cottages, beaches and lush natural areas. The 800 acres of original tract were donated to the state in 1929 by Dr. McRae Livingston with the caveat that it be named Lake Taghkanic. Just four years later, the Civilian Conservation Corps established a work camp at the site and set about building all types of amenities including: beaches, camping area, cabins, water tower, roads and scenic stone walls.

The lovely park is in the rolling hills of the Hudson Valley, nestled amid lush woodlands and next to a cool lake. The park is heavily used and well-designed, complete with lots of private day-use and picnic areas, ball fields, a campground, cottages, cabins, fishing, hiking and beaches.

The park is an easy drive from the New York City, off the Taconic State Parkway, one mile south of Rt. 82 near Hudson. The park is oriented around the clear lake, offering lots of access points and shoreline views.

The park is open year-round and bow hunting is offered in the fall. Many of the busy day-use areas are surrounded by oaks, tall tamaracks, hickory and red pine—the perfect place for a family reunion. A favorite area is the east end of the lake where a blanket of aquatic vegetation contains flowering plants, muskrats, lots of songbirds and fishing opportunities.

The biggest and best attraction of the park is the many quality cottages and cabins. The lakeside cottages are in high demand and offer wonderful views, water access and peaceful surroundings.

Information and Activities

Lake Taghkanic State Park
1528 Route 82
Ancram, NY   12502-9731
(518) 851-3631

Directions: Adjacent to the Taconic State Parkway in Columbia County. Depart the parkway between Jackson Corners to the south and Route 82, Hudson exit to the north. Trailer access is via Route 82, three miles south of the town of Taghkanic.

The park office is at the east beach in a gray fieldstone building. The park office is open mid-May to the end of October, 8 a.m. - 9 p.m. daily.

Emergency numbers: 911 system; park police, (914) 889-4100.

Campground: The popular campground is near the east beach. Firewood and food are sold at the small concession stand at the nearby beach. The stand is open 10 a.m. - 6 p.m. during the summer. The campground is open the first Friday on or after May 10 and ends the last Sunday in October. Like most state parks, the peak camping season is mid-June to Labor Day. Many sites are private. Sites toward the front of the campground get more sunlight and a breeze.

A large timber-style climber is near the entrance to the rolling campground. If you would like to camp near the play area, choose site No. 6. The campground has elevated wood platforms 16' X 20' as well as grassy camping sites. The tract is 85 percent shady, hilly, and the sites are on varying elevations. Site 7 gets some midday sun. Site 8 is one of the more private platform sites, near the parking lot that services the east beach.

The bathhouse is a wonderful CCC stone building that is centrally located. Camping platforms 16 and 17 are high, dry and have wood railings on three sides. They are also close to the bathhouse. Near site 29, at the top of a hill, are a comfort station and brown clapboard-sided recreation hall. Inside the recreation hall are tables and chairs, white rafters, fireplace and knotty pine paneling. The adjoining comfort station has showers. Site 33 is near the comfort station.

Several camping sites have a cement slab for a picnic table. Platform sites 21, 22, 25, 26 and 28 are accessed by a gravel lane.

Cabins: The park's cabins and cottages are attractive and heavily used. All cabin and cottage patrons must provide their own cooking and eating utensils, and linens. All units are equipped with stove, refrigerator, electricity, picnic table, fire ring and screened porch.

There are 15 wonderful cabins in the woods at the east end of the park. The cabins have two, three or four bedrooms with stone chimneys, screened porches and rough-sawn siding. Each has a small gravel parking spot, picnic tables and grills. Cabins 11 and 12 are on a ridge, near cabin 16. These, and others, have neighboring rock outcroppings.

None of the cabins has hot water or heat. They do have fireplaces and cabins 6, 7, 8, 9 and 10 are closest to the showerhouse. Cabins 1-5 are in close proximity. The most private cabin is C-15, a one-bedroom unite and C-8, a four-bedroom unit. C-14 is up some timber stairs and is private, shady and scenic.

Cottages: There are 17 cottages. Almost house-like, the various cottages are lined up along the west lakeshore. There is no heat in the cottages, but many have fireplaces. Most of the units are two or three bedrooms, but there are three cottages with four bedrooms. Units that are close together are 155, 158, 159, 160, 168 and 169. Cottages 158, 159, 163 and 171 sleeps eight.

The cottages comes in all shapes and sizes. Some are small and quaint with a tiny screened porch; others are large with metal roofs and big porches. The units have parking for two cars. The view across the lake is of rock ledges that catch the late daylight and melt it into many colors and reflections. These cottages are an easy walk to the west beach.

Pencil-straight pine trees dot the shoreline and punctuate spaces between the cottages. Many of the cottages are two-story and have clotheslines with bathing suites flapping the breeze. Each unit has a picnic table, and many have direct shoreline access and volleyball nets.

Shoreline fishing can be very good from along this west side of the lake.

Many of the cabins are well-separated and near the lapping shoreline. Cottage 158, with a red-brick chimney, has a wonderful view of the widest part of the lake. Cottage 157, a smaller unit, also has a view of the wide lake and sandy beach in the distance. Next to cottage 157 are a small playground and day-use area.

Day-use areas: The park has a variety of outdoor recreation opportunities including ballfields, volleyball, picnic areas, playgrounds and open fields. Picnic Area A, near the big beach, is a wonderful place for a family outing that is surrounded by trees and low rock outcroppings. Picnic Areas B has a comfort station and lots of picnic tables scattered under trees. Picnic Area C, D and E are up hills in the rolling park and offer private day-use areas. In some places, picnic tables are along a rocky ridge shaded by a thin grove of pine trees. Picnic Area F is on a downhill slope that reaches toward the lake where some backwater fishing could be done. Try shoreline fishing in this area during the spring.

The park is known for intimate picnics that are private, grassy and often near the lake.

Swimming beaches: The park has two swimming areas from which you have views of the rounded mountains and tree-lined lakeshores.

West beach: Many people bring umbrellas to the open beaches (you can also rent umbrellas). No alcohol is allowed on the beaches. The bathhouse and general area are well-maintained and clean. Lots of folks set up chairs along the walk on hot days and enjoy the limited shade provided by small caliper trees.

Vending machines, pay phones and coin viewers are at the bathhouse. Umbrella tables are next to the concession stand on a hard-surface patio. The concession stand sells limited fishing equipment, sand toys, inflatable water toys, soft drinks, ice cream, draft beer, firewood, charcoal, lighter fluid and grill items. There are five walk-up windows. A single volleyball court is also at the west beach near a grassy slope and shady area.

East beach: Both beaches have clean sand and clear, sometimes cold, water. The bottom of the swimming area is firm. A small stone concession built by the Civilian Conservation Corps is at the older-style bathhouse across from the office. Take a close look at the interesting building that is above the small beach. It has capstones, milk-glass light fixtures and a partial copper roof that has turned a wonderful green color over the years. Near the concession window (ice cream, toys, film, sunscreen, batteries, soft drinks and grill items) is a small display about the CCC and its efforts in the park. Also here is a bulletin board that features information about boat rentals, safety tips, park programs, regulations, camping rules and maps.

The cove-side beach has grassy sunny areas with picnic tables, a nearby retaining walk and a single lifeguard station. The intimate east beach has coarse sand and is a great place for families with smaller children. Some older-style play equipment is also near the beach complete with benches for adults. Young children will love the dog spring ride that has neatly painted whiskers and big ears.

Civilian Conservation Corps: CCC camp No. 302 built many of the fine structures in the park and worked in the park for several years until 1937. Photos in the display depict workers, the spartan mess hall, simple barracks and completed projects. The typical schedule for the workers was up at 6 a.m. and lights out at 10 p.m. Workers ate a diet of canned corn, spaghetti, pickled beets and fruit for the evening meal. Some interesting photos from 1935 include views of the stone bathhouse, almost Gothic-like water tower, wood cabins and many other amenities.

State park development was in its infancy in the early 1900s. By 1921, only 19 states had state parks. With the newfound ease of car travel, there became a real demand for state parks and campgrounds. By

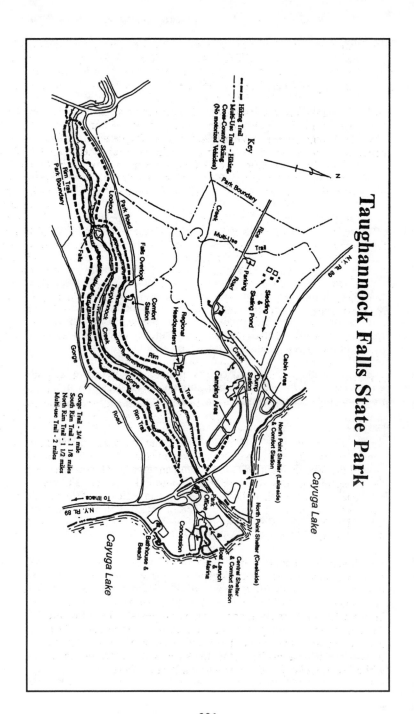

Taughannock Falls State Park

Key

Hiking Trail

Multi-Use Trail - Hiking
Cross-Country Skiing
(No motorized Vehicles)

Park Boundary

N.Y. Rt. 89

Park Boundary

Rim Trail

Lookout

Falls

Park Road

Taughannock Creek

Falls Overlook

Comfort Station

Regional Headquarters

Rim Trail

Gorge Trail

Gorge

Gorge Road

Gorge Rim Trail

Gorge Trail - 3/4 mile
South Rim Trail - 1 1/8 miles
North Rim Trail - 1 1/2 miles
Multi-use Trail - 2 miles

To Ithaca

N.Y. Rt. 89

Camping Area

Creek

Creek

Multi-Use

Trail

Parking
Road

Sledding
& Skating Pond

Dump Station

Cabin Area

Park Boundary

Rice

Cayuga Lake

North Point Shelter (Lakeside)
& Comfort Station

North Point Shelter (Creekside)

Central Shelter
& Comfort Station

Park Office

Boat Launch
& Marina

Concession

Bathhouse &
Beach

Cayuga Lake

1925, all 48 states has started some type of development. By 1930, the Depression has virtually stopped all the building. With the establishment of the CCC, state park development resumed. Many of New York's state parks were built by the CCC.

In 1932, Franklin Roosevelt was elected president, after the stock market crash in 1925, which left the country in depression. Roosevelt vowed to revitalize the economy and end the Depression. FDR took office in early 1933 and on March 31, 1933, he established the CCC. The original concept of the CCC was to put unemployed youths to work on natural resource projects. The projects were confined to forestry, park development and soil erosion projects.

The enrollee had to be unemployed, 18-25 years old, unmarried and come from families on government relief. The enlistment period was for six months with the possibility of re-enlistment for up to two years. Each enrollee was paid $30 a month; $25 was sent home to his family, leaving only $5 monthly to spend on the camp canteen. In those days, a candy bar cost five cents. The CCC provided room, board and tools. In the nine years of the CCC from 1933-1942, more than 3 million people worked from in 4,000 camps in all 48 states.

Hiking: The park maintains a four-mile hiking and biking trail that begins at the boat launch and circles the lake.

Boating: The small boat rental is at the west beach. V-bottom rowboats and red johnboats are offered by the hour and half-day for a cruise around the placid lake. A floating dock and small shed are at the shoreline.

Bring your canoe to paddle Lake Taghkanic or nearby Rudd Pond (south on Rt. 62). The lake's small size means you can leisurely go around the lake in about an hour. From canoe or kayak you can study the 12 species of oak trees (red oak, white oak, scarlet oak, swamp white oak, chestnut oak and others). Botanists believe that the mighty oaks evolved over millions of years and radiated south and north from here. The United States has about 50 species, fewer as you approach the northeast.

Tree lovers will enjoy the shoreline and view from the water. Oaks have two main families: red oaks and white oaks. You can tell the difference by examining the leaves. Red oaks have bristles at the tips of their leaves, while white oaks are rounded. White oak acorns mature in one year, while red oak acorns take two years. These tree provide valuable food for turkey, grouse, squirrel, deer, wood ducks, bear and many other small mammals. The heaviest crops of acorn seem to come in two- or four-year cycles. Other trees you will see include black gum, white cedar, hickory, red and sugar maple and others.

There are two boat launch areas, one at the west beach, the other on the east end of the lake. No gasoline motors are allowed.

Fishing: Sunfish, bass and pickerel are commonly caught. The deeper areas of the 168-acre lake contain species like cisco. However, low oxygen levels limit their abundance.

The lake is clear and cold. Vegetated shallow areas may hold good numbers of fish. The maximum depth of the lake is 42 feet.

Sport fish include chain pickerel, large- and smallmouth bass, bluegill, pumpkinseed, rock bass, yellow perch, brown bullhead and American eel. Near the boat launch, along the floating aquatic vegetation, is a popular place to shoreline fish. From this area at the southeast end of the lake, you can cast into 20 feet of water. There are many other shoreline access sites, but some are down a fairly steep grade. Day-use Area A has some good shoreline fishing places. Shoreline anglers might also want to try areas near the east beach.

Nature: As budget conditions allow, environmental programming is offered during the summer.

The lake has good populations of nesting songbirds, visiting waterfowl, deer and many small mammals that can often be seen from the trails. On the marshy east end of the lake are some large patches of water shield, various lilies, pickerelweed, purple loosestrift, buttonbush, fanwort and pondweed. This part of the lake is wonderful to explore by canoe. Many aquatic animals and insects are also found in this transition zone from lake to shoreline.

Winter: Activities include cross-country skiing, ice fishing, snowmobiling and ice skating.

Insider tips: The park has more than the average number of playgrounds (many of the play areas have wonderful little spring animal rides for toddlers). Paddle the east end of the lake. Try camping on a shady wooden platform in the hilly campground or enjoy a furnished lakeside cottage. The lakeside cottages are some of the most modern in the state park system. Enjoy both sandy beaches. Day-use Area E has good access for visitors with disabilities. The lake is scenic and has rocky shores with plenty of fallen trees offering excellent panfishing from the bank.

PHONE	PARK	Tent/trailers sites (h = hookups, e = electricity)	Trailer dump	Showers	Camper recreation	Cabins	Food	Store	Picnic tables	Shelters (• reservations)	Swimming beach (• bath house)	Swimming pool (• bath house)	Recreation programs (• performing arts)	Hiking	Biking	Nature trails	Fishing	Playground	Golf (•clubhouse)	Tennis	Pond or lake (• power boats ok)	River or stream (• power boats ok)	Launching site (• hand launch only)	Boat rental	Marina (• anchorage)	Pump out	Ice skating (•rentals)	Cross-country skiing (• rentals)	Snowmobiling	Sled slopes
914 889-4100	TACONIC REGION																														
914 452-1489	James Baird						▷		▷				▷	▷	▷	▷	▷	▷	••	▷								▷		
914 225-7207	Clarence Fahnestock*	▷		▷					▷	•	•		•	▷		▷	▷	▷			▷		•	▷				▷	▷	
914 225-7207	Hudson Highlands													▷		▷	▷											▷		
518 851-3631	Lake Taghkanic	▷	▷	▷	▷	▷	▷		▷		••		••	▷	▷		▷				▷		•	▷			•	▷	▷	▷
914 889-4646	Margaret Lewis Norrie*	▷	▷	▷	▷	▷	▷		▷					▷			▷					▷	▷	▷	▷	▷		▷		
914 889-4646	Ogden Mills & Ruth Livingston Mills*						▶		▶	▶	•	▶	••	▷	▷	▷	▶	▷			▷	▷	•	▷			•	▷	▷	▷
914 245-4434	Old Croton Trailway													▷	▷		▷											▷		
914 631-1470	Rockefeller*						▷		▷					▷	▷	▷	▷				▷							▷		
914 631-1470	Rockwood Hall													▷	▷													▷		
914 245-4434	Franklin d. roosevelt													▷	▷		▷					▷			▷	▷		▷	▷	▷
518 329-3993	Taconic: Copake Falls	▷		▷	▷		▶		▷	▷			•	▷		▷	▷	▷			▷	•	▷				▷	▷	▷	▷
518 789-3059	Rudd Pond	▷	▷	▷	▷		▷		▷	••	▶•		••	▷		▷	▶	▶		▷	▷		••	▷			▷	▷	▷	

STATE HISTORIC SITES

PHONE	PARK																													
518 537-4240	Clermont*						▷		▷					▷	▷	▷	▷	▷			▷			▷			▷	▷	▷	
914 471-1630	Clinton House																										•	▷	▷	▷
914 232-5651	John Jay Homestead																													
914 889-8851	Mills Mansion																													
518 828-0135	Olana																													
914 965-4027	Philipse Manor Hall																													

Enjoy beautiful views of the Hudson river and Catskills, trails, and picnicking at an estate of the Livingstons.

Explore the history of Dutchess County in this 18th-century house.

View furnishings, portraits, and memorabilia at the retirement home of this patriot and founding father.

Vistas of the Hudson River adorn this estate and its opulent 1895 Beaux Arts classical mansion.

Marvel at the panorama, romantic landscaping, and Persian-style villa created by artist-owner Frederic Edwin Church.

Exhibits of history, art, and architecture and housed in one of New York's finest Georgian structures.

▷ Availability of service or facility ▶ Handicapped accessible *Bridle paths

334

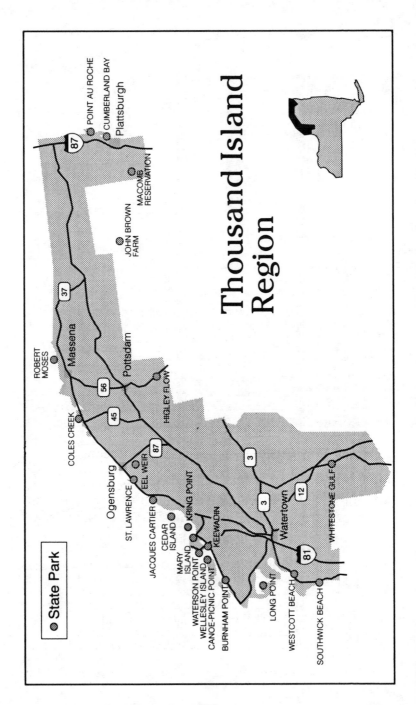

State Park

Thousand Island Region

Thousands Islands Region

The vast maritime region has 17,000 acres and 26 state parks, including Wellesley Island State Park which has 18 miles of shoreline along the St. Lawrence Seaway.

This park has also been rated by *Family Circle Magazine*, as "one of the 20 best campgrounds in America."

The huge park has a terrific nature center, top-notch fishing, 430 campsites, boating and marina, and is along the Coastal Seaway Trail; a 454-mile byway starting at Lake Erie and along Lake Ontario's southern shoreline.

Most of the region's state parks offer excellent camping and almost all have a beach, swimming, winter sports and some of the best fishing in the world.

Many visitors hike, bring their canoe, rent a cabin or just relax in this northernmost state park region.

Keewaydin State Park
Land: 179 acres Water: St. Lawrence River

The small rolling park has inspiring views of rocky islands, passing freighters and scenic rock outcroppings. It is dotted with groves of straight pines and gladsome picnic areas. The park also boasts a small modern marina, shoreline fishing, swimming pool and campground with two sites accessible by persons with disabilities.

Geologists say that the Thousand Islands have many characteristics of a "drowned landscape." Before the last series of glaciation, the Great Lakes drained southward, but changes in the land form resulting from this glaciation forced the Great Lakes to drain northeastward, creating the immense St. Lawrence River. The waters of this new river flooded the existing landscape and isolated the higher ground, creating the Thousand Islands.

Humans have inhabited the area for 4,000 to 5,000 years. These people called the area *"Manatoana,"* the Garden of the Great Spirit. I like that.

The mighty St. Lawrence was discovered in 1535 by Jacques Cartier and named in honor of a martyred third century saint. Soon French settlers came to the area and signed fur trading deals with the Algonquins and later treaties with the Iroquois. Within the next 100 years, the area saw an increase in British presence along the river, culminating in the War of Independence. The first settlers to the area after the war were farmers, mainly dairy farmers. It wasn't until the mid-1800s that vacationers began coming to the area. As more people discovered the charming expanse, wealthy visitors began building seasonal cottages, almost all located near the water—and many on rocky islands.

Keewaydin State Park was once a private estate owned by James Wesley Jackson of New York City. Jackson built a large summer home in 1894. Since, the property has been owned by the New York Sun, The Mohican Chain, the Munsey Publishing Company and John K. Wallace of St. Louis, Missouri.

In the mid-1950s the property was leased to the Keewaydin Point Club. The state bought the scenic tract in 1961 and has preserved some of the estate's old features.

Information and Activities

Keewaydin State Park
43165 NYS Route 12
Alexandria Bay, NY 13607
(315) 482-3331

Directions: On the St. Lawrence River, three miles north of the Thousand Islands Bridge and I-81. The park is on Route 12.

The cedar-sided regional office for the Thousand Islands district is at Keewaydin.

Emergency number: 911.

Campground: The mostly open campground has 41 sites (no utilities). The campground is open mid-May to Labor Day. The park is open year-round.

If you would like to camp near the pool, consider sites 7, 8, 9 and 10. Sites 15, 17, 19, 21 and 23 are on a rocky bank above the river. The view from these sites is of a wonderful large Victorian house built on an island in the middle of the slow-moving river. Campers will notice that the garage is actually a boathouse. These island houses have boat-only access.

Sites on the interior of the loop are backed up against natural vegetation. Some of the sites in the loop are on an incline. Each site has a ground-mounted steel fire box and picnic table. Sites 1-3 are the most shaded in the intimate campground. In a smaller loop, site 35 allows tent campers to pitch their tent on a ledge rock. Sites in this loop have a river and island view. Sites 36, 38, 40 and 41 are grassy and nestled under some maple trees.

Day-use areas: A volleyball court and lots of grills and picnic tables surround the popular swimming pool. A basketball court is near the boat trailer parking area.

Picnic pavilion: Next to the regional office, is a terrific gazebo-like shelter. The four stone columns and white pillars of the pavilion offer a million-dollar view. Be sure to check out the ceiling of the pavilion.

Swimming pool: Near the campground, the Charles J. Elliot Swimming Pool is open 10 a.m. to 7 p.m. during the summer. The yellow bathhouse has individual changing stalls. Blue and white sunning chairs are scattered around the cement deck that surrounds the clean pool. A ramp provides access to the shallow water for persons with physical disabilities. A set of timber-frame play equipment is next to the pool complex. The pool has nine lanes and depths from 3.5 to 5 feet. The medium-size pool measures 75 by 164 feet.

Boating: There aren't many marinas with as delightful a view as Keewaydin. The small marina (120 slips total) has some big slips where larger boats rest at their moorings. From large cruisers and houseboats to long pontoon boats, this park offers boaters an excellent place from which to explore the Thousand Islands area.

The small gray marina building sells gasoline, soft drinks, ice and some limited bait. Seasonal and overnight slips are offered. A walk around the marina reveals some delightful low stone buildings, scurrying chipmunks and a view of a passing freighter in the distant river channel, called the American Narrows. Some 700-foot "lakers" pass through this section of the St. Lawrence Seaway.

Several stone buildings near the marina remind you of mushrooms perched above the river under a shady canopy. The stone building are very handsome and date back more than 100 years.

The rest room at the marina has a shower and a bulletin board.

Fishing: Some sections of the shoreline are steep. Access to the shoreline fishing area is available from the marina parking lot. The clear

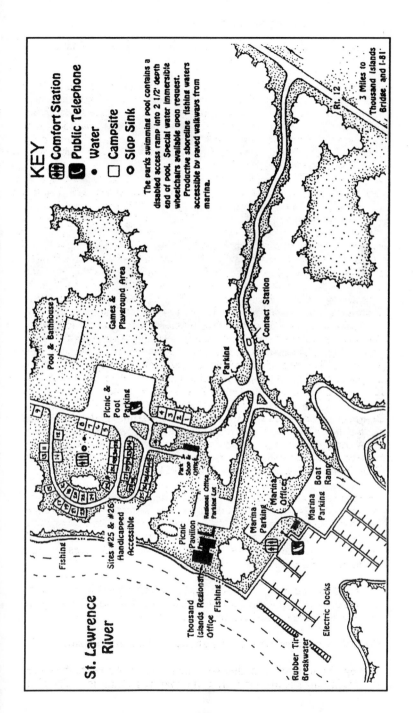

St. Lawrence River

KEY
- 👬 Comfort Station
- 📞 Public Telephone
- • Water
- □ Campsite
- ○ Slop Sink

The parks swimming pool contains a disabled access ramp into 2 1/2' depth end of pool. Special water immersible wheelchairs available upon request. Productive shoreline fishing waters accessible by paved walkways from marina.

Pool & Bathhouse

Games & Playground Area

Picnic & Pool Parking

Sites #25 & #26 Handicapped Accessible

Fishing

Thousand Islands Regional Office

Picnic Pavilion

Fishing

Park Shop & Office

Regional Office Parking Lot

Rubber Tire Breakwater

Electric Docks

Marina Parking

Marina Office

Marina Parking

Boat Ramp

Parking

Contact Station

Rt. 12

3 Miles to Thousand Islands Bridge, and I-81.

water gives up lots of panfish and bass.

Nature: State parks in the Thousand Islands region are near or on some of the 60 miles of shoreline that have a mixture of habitats where 260 species of birds have been recorded over the years. The regional office at Keewaydin has a birding checklist for the Thousand Islands area.

Insider tips: There's lots to do in the area—try a boat or helicopter ride, floating restaurant, Remington art Museum and much more. Sackett Harbor Battlefield is a wonderful history site within an easy drive from the park.

Robert Moses State Park
Land: 2,322 acres   Water: St. Lawrence River

Robert Moses State Park is the second largest state park in the Thousand Islands region and is along one of the largest rivers in the world, the mighty St. Lawrence. It is located both on the mainland and Barnhart Island, featuring quality campsites, cabins, nature center and programs, swimming beach, 66-slip marina and ramps, hiking trails and spacious day-use areas. The park is also a wonderful place to fish and gain access to the wide river.

The St. Lawrence River is more than 760 miles long and reaches from Lake Ontario to the Atlantic. Because of its high volume (246,000 cubic feet per second) and a 3 million-square-mile drainage basin, it is ideal for hydroelectric power generation. The huge dam and switch yards are easily seen from many places in the park.

In the 1930s, the state Legislature authorized that the International Rapids section of the river, near Massena, be harnessed for its hydroelectric potential. In 1953, the Federal Power Commission issued a license to the state to construct, operate and maintain the U.S. portion of the St. Lawrence River Project. The project began in 1954 with Robert Moses as chairman of the Authority.

The result was a joint project that produced an effective hydroelectric source along the international seaway. During these years the park was also developed. The area has a variety of rich natural communities that offer habitat for coyote, whitetail deer, beaver, bobcat, small mammals and many types of songbirds and birds of prey. This is a nature lover's park.

Anglers will find excellent fishing near the park where smallmouth bass, pike, muskie and panfish are abundant.

Information and Activities

Robert Moses State Park
P.O. Box 548
Massena, NY 13662
(315) 769-8663

Directions: Off Route 37, three miles north of Massena.

The park office/information center has tall glass windows and features considerable information about the park and northern area. Firewood, soft drinks and ice are sold at the center.

Emergency numbers: Park police, (315) 769-0127. The park is also on the 911 system.

Campground: The spacious, flat and dry campground has 168 sites, 38 with electric hook-ups. The covered pavilion/rest rooms has campground recreation programs from 10 a.m. - 10 p.m. during the summer. Ping pong, games and many programs are offered to campers. Near the tidy pavilion are basketball goals, a fenceless tennis court, volleyball courts and mowed open spaces that once contained a mini-golf course. Large RV rigs have an easy time at this campground and often set up near the entrance and pavilion. Each campsite has ground-mounted fire rings and wood picnic tables. The tract does have some sites that are accessible for campers with disabilities. The campground is about 65 percent shady.

Sites 10-15 get a half-day of sun. Site 20 allows for larger RVs rigs to park under shade and near a small natural area. Sites 24, 26, 28 are also near the natural area and equipped with electrical hook-ups. Sites in the 40s and 50s have a river view. Sites 49 and 51 are two of the best sites in the sections. They are shaded with grassy pads and enjoy a sweeping view of the wide river. Although not very private, sites in the 70s through 90s are backed up against natural areas.

Sites in the 140s are along a linear road and will enjoy a half-day of sun. These sites have a wall of vegetation that separates you from your backdoor neighbor. Tents, small trailers and pop-up campers are best along this part of the flat campground. For big RV rigs, check out sites in the 160s that are on a short spur.

Cabins: The park operates 15 small, clean and spartan cabins, with cabin 8 accessible for guests with disabilities. The simple cabins have wall-to-wall carpeting (except in the kitchen), bath with flush toilet and hot shower, living room, dining room, refrigerator and stove. The cabins are on a spur from the campground access road. Each unit has a small bay window, side yard and picnic table.

Units are gray with vertical siding and adjacent parking. Cabins 1-5 are along the river, offering splendid views. All of the cabins are near the water. Cabins 12 and 13 have excellent river views and are near a small grove of birch and sumac. Cabins 14 and 15 are at the end of the loop and private. Some say cabin 12 is the best of the group. All of the cabins have space for parking an additional vehicle or boat trailer.

Cabin guests should bring linens, bedding, cooking and eating utensils, and lawn chairs. The cabins are equipped with four single beds, stove, sink, hot water and table with four chairs.

Beach: The bathhouse is gray and have a concourse walkway around them. Although there is no food concession, soft drink machines are near the bathhouse. The bathhouse has lockers; bring your own lock. The coarse sand is about 300 yards long and 75 yards wide, and is scattered with yellow litter barrels and many sun-drenched people on warm weekends. The beach, corded off by orange and white buoys, along a scenic cove with expansive views of the river and small island in the distance.

Parents will enjoy the many park benches and kids will love the nearby ballfield, older-style play equipment and picnic tables.

Hiking: Hikers often flock to the wooded nature trail at the park, using snowshoes in the winter. Cross-country skiing is offered on five main trails that are well-marked.

The park has a terrific self-guided nature trails that takes about one hour to complete. Follow the white markers and beware of poison ivy. The trail has 16 learning stations; a guide booklet is available from the nature center.

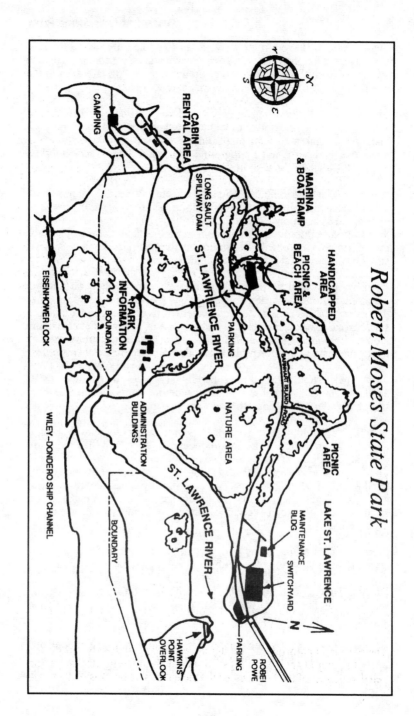

Robert Moses State Park

CAMPING

CABIN
RENTAL AREA

MARINA
& BOAT RAMP

LONG SAULT
SPILLWAY DAM

HANDICAPPED
AREA

PICNIC &
BEACH AREA

ST. LAWRENCE RIVER

PARKING

EISENHOWER LOCK

PARK
INFORMATION

BOUNDARY

ADMINISTRATION
BUILDINGS

BARNHART ISLAND ROAD

NATURE AREA

PICNIC
AREA

LAKE ST. LAWRENCE

ST. LAWRENCE RIVER

BOUNDARY

MAINTENANCE
BLDG

SWITCHYARD

WILEY-DONDERO SHIP CHANNEL

HAWKINS
POINT
OVERLOOK

PARKING

ROBE
POWE

N

The nature center is filled with natural history displays.

Along the easy nature trail, you will learn about forest and field communities, mosses, ferns, hop hornbeam trees, white pine, fungus, woodchucks, staghorn sumac, beavers, Robinson's Bay and see some huge beech trees.

Boating: The 66-slip (three electric slips are kept open for transient use) marina has overnight accommodations. The tiny white marine store sells ice cream snacks, limited bait, gas, oil and other marine supplies. The scenic marina is accessed by a steel bridge (there is no bike riding on the bridge). From the bridge you can see the huge dam and the bottomlands below.

The marina is on Barnhart Island and near a small picnic shelter that is often used by boaters. Sheeks Island is directly in front of the marina, where many anglers try their luck. A number of ledges and dropoffs attract anglers to this section of the river. A small fee is charged to launch from the ramp near the marina.

The marina is colorful and sheltered, with many sailboats and powerboats tugging at their moorings. Some of the floating docks are carpeted and most of the boats moor for the entire season. Inside the marina building is a large navigational chart

From the marina you may rent a 14-foot aluminum boat equipped with a 9.9 hp engine. Boats are rented by the half or full day. Campers may rent the boat by the week, and they may moor the boat at the campground if they choose.

A single-lane launch and basin are at the end of Hawkin's Point Road, which lies under the forest of towers of high-voltage wires from the generation plant. From the boat ramp you can see the dam, switch yard and electrical plant. Anglers often drift this section of the river. This is a deep-water launch with an industrial view. A small gravel parking lot and shelter are near the launch.

Fishing: Game fishing is excellent for walleye, northern pike, a few muskie and bass. The muskie are usually taken near the dam. Muskie guides operate near the park (Muskie Magic charter is one of the most popular). Zebra mussels are cleaning up the river and causing anglers to explore new methods. Area bait and tackle shops provide information on hot spots and the best lures.

Nature: In the end of a green building, the nature interpretive center started humbly many years ago as staff began collecting mounts and nature objects. Today the center is filled with many interesting natural history items and chances to learn about the environment.

Look for the hummingbird feeder near the entrance. The nature center is open year-round.

Inside the center are many bird mounts, maps, field guides, skull collection, huge moose head, nesting box samples, old wood skis, hawks and owl mounts, and waterfowl behind glass. Individual mounts include woodcock, snipes, hooded merganser, snow owls, pheasant, bufflehead, osprey, Canada goose, coyote, skunk, fox, rabbit and deer.

The middle room at the center features a live observation honeybee hive, some aquariums tanks filled with native fish, insect collections under glass, rocks and minerals that are expertly labeled, a large fossil collection (learn how trilobites can reach two feet in length), butterfly chart and edible plant chart. Did you know you can eat cattails or wood sorrel, milkweed, knotweed, birch, clover, dock, popular, spring beauty, slippery elm, sow thistle, taro, tall fireweed, sugar maple, wild onion, canna lily, arrowroot and many others?

At the far end of the nature center is a cozy space that offers touch tables filled with materials including a bobcat and coyote pelt, raccoon skin, pieces of fungus, twigs, skulls, feathers and rocks. Next to the touch tables are a seating area and children's library. The walls are covered with nature photographs and interpretive posters about air quality, land use, nocturnal animals, astronomy and geology. Also near this part of the jam-packed interpretive center are carefully displayed geology samples, delicate fossils and a relief map of the state.

The nature center also offers information about North America's endangered species including the gray wolf, American peregrine falcon, Florida panther, Everglades kite, Key deer, black-footed ferret, California condor, whales, woodland caribou and others. Nature buffs can also examine dozens of leaves and learn about wisps and tiny wildflowers.

Programming at the park is excellent and includes nature camps, arts and crafts, animals in the north country, bird hikes, terrific tree programs, scary silly spider, weeds and wildflowers, the wonderful world of weather, painting, scrabble tournaments, scavenger hunts, soccer, busy beavers and the history of the St. Lawrence Seaway.

Winter: Snowshoes are checked out for guided nature hikes. Cross-country skis may be rented to try on the marked trails.

Insider tips: Take time to learn about the Eisenhower Lock and stop at the dam's visitor center that includes a viewing deck, gift shop and restaurant. An annual carp shoot is one of the biggest in the eastern United States. In fact, the carp fishing is so good, some Europeans are known to visit for the fast action.

Robert Moses is one of the few state parks in the system that racks brochures from other state parks. The nature center, near the park police office, is comprehensive and shows loving care. The park has some excellent environmental education programs. Nearby Cole's Creek State Park is managed by Robert Moses staff and features camping and hiking. A large aquarium is proposed for development in the park.

The park is part of the *Seaway Trail* that stretches west along Lake Ontario's southern coast.

Point au Roche
State Park
Land: 825 acres Water: Lake Champlain

Point au Roche means "rocky point," of which there are many. Cliffs and plunging rock shorelines are everywhere, framing vistas and offering wonderful vantage points along Lake Champlain, which is also known as the *"queen of great lakes."* The focal points of the day-use park are the trails, bike riding, nature programming, fishing and swimming.

In the 1920s, a large parcel of the park was a youth camp. Along some of the trails you will still see remnants of old camps, called Camp Red Cloud and Camp Red Wing. The woodframe lecture center, which is at the waterfront, is the last building from those days still in use. The building is used by guest speakers and for slide shows. Summer concerts are also featured at the scenic center.

Over the years, most of the park was used for agriculture or pasture. For a time, a theme park called "Fantasy Kingdom" operated near the beach. During the 1960s some sections of the park were partially developed. Roads and utilities were installed, but nothing further happened.

Point au Roche is one of the state's newer state parks, occupying a wonderful mixture of open and forested areas along one of America's most beautiful lakes. Its boat access allows intrepid anglers a chance to get on the vast lake for some of the best fishing in the world. The 121-mile-long lake is 12 miles across at its broadest point and has more than 60 fish species. The lake is blessed with deep, clean water, cradled between two magnificent mountain ranges—Vermont's Green Mountains and New York's Adirondacks. Some say the lake is in a league with Lake Tahoe or Lake Geneva. When in the area, consider taking the Champlain Trail, a wonderful route that includes many scenic and historic destinations. For more information call (518) 563-1000.

There is no camping at Point au Roche State Park.

Information and Activities

**Point au Roche State Park
19 Camp Red Cloud Road
Plattsburgh, NY 12901
(518) 563-6444
(518) 563-0369**

Directions: On the northwestern shore of Lake Champlain, off I-87, north of Plattsburgh. The check-in station is a modern building with a flat roof and cedar siding.

Day-use area: The entire park has hard-surfaced bike and walking trails and picnic sites near the beach. The day-use area has a baseball backstop that is accessed by a footbridge that arches over a shallow stream. The park has a nice playground with a newer slide, stepping stone-like bollards and other play equipment.

Swimming beach: The small, guarded sandy beach is on the west end of the park and outlined by a low retaining wall. There is a fee to use the day-use area and beach. The bathhouse is a modern log-style building near the gravel parking lot. The grassy picnic area is equipped with pedestal grills and tables. The beach is along a cove and is sectioned off by white and yellow buoys in front of three wooden lifeguard stations. Bathers must swim between the green flags. A single coin viewer and drinking fountain are near the open beach. A few pieces of play equipment are also scattered around the day-use area.

The knotty pine concession stand features grill foods, soft drinks, ice cream and snacks. It has a terrific view of the beach and sometimes windy open spaces. There is indoor seating around white tables where you can enjoy a snack and the aroma of the grill. Menu items include cheese steak sandwiches, quarter-pound hamburgers, cheeseburgers, fries with gravy, beer sticks, candy, coffee, light breakfasts and cold beer. Try an egg and cheese bagel in the morning while watching the fish rise to the surface of the cold, clear lake.

Fishing: The rocky shorelines and clear waters offer scenic but sometimes difficult angling. Most of the shoreline is wooded to the water's edge, and many rocky points extend into deep water. For up-to-date fishing information, call the regional fishing hotline at (518) 891-5413. The line is always open and updated each Friday afternoon.

Lake Champlain is the sixth largest freshwater lake in the continental United States and is nicknamed the "sixth Great Lake." Fishing here is much like fishing Lake Erie. The lake is generally narrow and is more than 400 feet deep in many places. To the west of the deep water channel, a New York fishing license is required; to the east an Vermont license is necessary. To the north of the Champlain Islands and in the Richelieu River and portions off Missisquio Bay, a Canadian license is needed. Know where you are; fishing, the lake is patrolled.

Spring walleye fishing is terrific throughout the lake. Between ice-out and mid-May, most anglers cast slowing-moving lead head jigs tipped with a minnow. Simply cast the jig, let it sink to the bottom and slowly pick it up and retrieve by lifting the rod tip in a gentle, consistent lift and drop manner. Be ready to feel the light tap of a feeding fish.

These fish move to offshore bars and mid-lake reefs from June to October. Most anglers slow troll a bottom bouncing three-way rig trailing a chartreuse or silver spinner blade and worm, a Rapala or active crankbait in 20-40 feet of water. Medium-sized plugs can work well at dawn and dusk.

For smallmouth bass, try drifting or bouncing a live crayfish near rocky shelves in 12-25 feet of water. Daytime action can be good using a variety of artificials.

During the summer largemouth are found along edges of lake marshes and in shallow weedy coves and bays where structure is found. Try a weedless spoon tipped with pork or grape-colored plastic worms. Lots of anglers also do well with pig and jigs, Wiggle Warts and lead head jigs and trailers. At night, move to deeper water and try surface lures in dark colors. Fly rod poppers can bring up some big lunkers. For smallmouth, cast over rocks, reef tops and rocky bottoms.

When you are in the early season weedy area, bass anglers often pick up some pike, especially in the upper reaches. For pike try 10-inch suckers off a wire leader and a big bobber. In the summer, the fish move in and out of deep water, when casting spoons tipped with pork strips can trigger hits. Anglers who troll consistently in the summer for pike will sometimes catch a muskie. For the best muskie action, stay near the Champlain Islands. They are difficult to catch. Try trolling in your wake at night.

All pan fishermen need to do is find a shallow bay and use worms, minnows or small spinners. These bays can be extremely productive in April and May. As the water warms, look for brush tops, under docks and along weed edges.

Lake and brown trout offer year-round fun. In the spring, cast near the shore with live bait of Little Cleo-type spoons and retrieve slowly. In mid-summer, you need to fish the bottom flats using downriggers, wire line, flutter spoons and a variety of divers.

Ice fishing is terrific in the frozen bay throughout the lake. Almost all species can be taken through the ice. When ice fishing, learn to move, find the fish and jig grubs for panfish and big minnows, suckers and chubs for pike. Perch taste great in the winter.

Boating: The park operates two boat launches. The main launch is in the day-use area (you may park overnight here by permit). This launch is a single lane with a courtesy dock and comfort station with vault toilets. There is a terrific view of the protected cove which often has a sailboat moored in the middle.

Boat rentals and charter fishing are offered in the area.

Hiking: Two of the park's trails (Western and Eastern loops) are paved and biking is encouraged. You may also bike on other trails, except the Middle Point Trail, which is experiencing some erosion problems. The Middle Point Trail tracks along the shoreline and is a wonderful quiet hike. The park has a total of 12 miles of trails.

A self-guided nature trail begins at the nature center, and there is a brochure available. In the winter the park provides groomed cross-country ski trails and also rent equipment for use on the marked trails. The hiking loops are color-coded and easy walking. The Eastern Loop skirts Corner Bay. The Middle and Long loops trace along the bay and point. Many of the trails are hard-surfaced and lined with buckthorn, milkweed, young trees, bushy cedars, wet areas, sumacs, chicory, birch trees, grapevines climbing up ash trees and some wooded valleys.

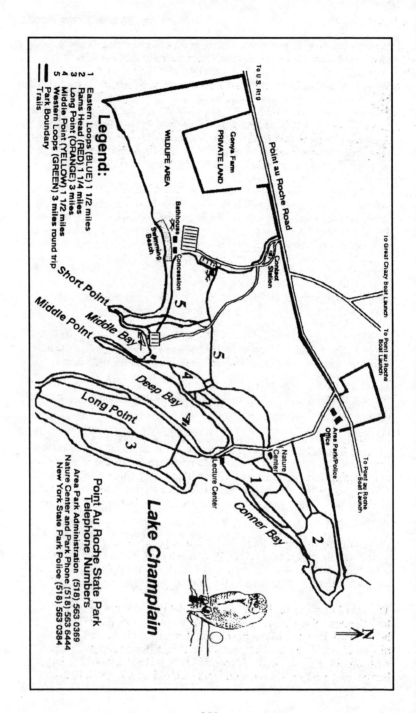

Legend:

1 Eastern Loops (BLUE) 1 1/2 miles
2 Rams Head (RED) 1 1/4 miles
3 Long Point (ORANGE) 3 miles
4 Middle Point (YELLOW) 1 1/2 miles
5 Western Loops (GREEN) 3 miles round trip
— Park Boundary
═ Trails

Point Au Roche State Park
Telephone Numbers
Area Park Administration (518) 563 0369
Nature Center and Park Phone (518) 563 6444
New York State Park Police (518) 563 0384

Lake Champlain

WILDLIFE AREA

Gonya Farm PRIVATE LAND

Point au Roche Road

To U.S. Rt 9

To Great Chazy Boat Launch
To Point au Roche Boat Launch

To Point au Roche Boat Launch

Contact Station

Bathhouse
Swimming Beach
Concession

Short Point

Middle Bay

Middle Point

Deep Bay

Long Point

Conner Bay

Nature Center

Area Park/Police Office

Lecture Center

N

353

There are good views of the lake from many trails. Fireplugs you may see are remnants of an old camp or a failed development. The bike path is 2.5 miles long.

Nature: The small red wood nature center building, next to a gravel parking lot, is the focal point for many environmental education programs and the nature trail system. Many nature center users come from neighboring communities and Cumberland Bay State Park. Lots of school groups use the center and participate in programming. Access to the nature center and trailheads is free. The beach area requires a fee.

Programming might include fossil hunting, scavenger hunts, fitness walks, reptile programs, feathered friends nature walk, seine the beach, bike hike, sand castle building and others. During the summer, the park advertises its programs in the Sunday newspaper.

The small displays in the nature center detail a number of natural history themes. You can learn how fossils were formed, gathering fossils, how fossils are clues to our past, and information about area mammals, birds and wildflowers. Notice the excellent trilobite sample, complete with bits of ancient shell. Mounted birds include a northern harrier, barred owl (the only owl with dark-colored eyes), red-tailed hawk, green heron, ruffed grouse, common screech owl, kestrel, snowy owl, great horned owl and a full skeleton of a white-tailed deer (the deer skeleton was donated by Park Manager Gary Parrott).

The small nature center also features a number of interpretive posters, a relief map of New York state, a cluster of pesky zebra mussels, nature books and field guide library, and various printed information.

One of the most fascinating birds detailed in the nature center is the great horned owl, the largest of the long-earred owls. Like other owls, it has special adaptation that helps it survive. The owl has its eyes on the front of it head, rather than the upper part of their head. In order to compensate for this eye position, owls have the ability to turn their heads 180 degrees both left and right.

Great horned owls hunt mostly at night when it is quiet in the fields and meadows. For owls to sneak up on their prey undetected, they are equipped with a special feather along their wing's edge. These fuzzy feathers break up the air moving over the wings and allow the owl to approach its prey almost silently. The owl is the original stealth aircraft. Other adaptations include protective coloring, strong talons and the ability to see and hear well in limited light. Great horned owls will attack any medium-size mammal or bird, porcupine, snake or duck.

Great horned owls begin to breed in the cold of the winter when they typically reuse the nest of a hawk. They also nest in hollow trees or caves, depositing two eggs. Sometimes the big birds will also nest on the open faces of ledges. Owls often eat tiny prey whole. They can't digest the bones and fur, so they regurgitate these in pellets, which can sometimes be found under roosting places. By taking the sometimes furry capsules apart, you can tell what the great birds have been dining on.

The park has some active beaver which can often be seen working in nearby wetlands. Beaver were important to Indians as a source of food and fiber. Their thick fur was valued for warmth and the fatty meat of their tails was considered a delicacy. This was before the Big Mac. The animals had no particulate trade value to the Indians. With few natural predators, beavers prospered along Lake Champlain and nearby ponds, rivers and brooks. The beavers cut trees and built ponds anywhere there was water, prospering throughout the region.

Europeans crossed the Atlantic Ocean in search of gold, spices and even the fountain of youth; instead, they found natural treasures. King among the natural resources was the busy beaver. In fact, the animal has been credited with opening up the North American continent for exploration and settlement. Europeans used the beaver's soft under fur for making popular beaver hat. At the time of the Pilgrims, no fashionable man could be seen without his beaver felt hats. In fact, Charles

I of England issued a proclamation in 1638 prohibiting the use of any material except pure beaver wool in the making of such hats.

There were so few beaver in Europe that it was not profitable to trap them. Image the settler's delight to find an abundance of beaver in New York. About 60 million beaver inhabited the United States when the settlers arrived. That's more than three times the number of people living in New York state today.

When the Pilgrims stepped ashore in the New World in 1620, they spotted the rich beaver furs worn by Chief Samoset. Through sign language, the Europeans let him know that they wanted to trade for the furs and that he should bring more. Desiring the glass beads, copper kettles, steel knives and brandy offered by the settlers, Indians were quick to trade beaver pelts. White men also discovered they could earn a handsome living by trading trapped beaver. Thankfully, I guess, today's fashion is baseball hats worn backwards. Save the beaver. Today, beaver are still important. They create wetlands necessary for a variety of other animals such as waterfowl and many aquatic species. Beaver can be a mixed blessing, however; their work can result in floods that can damage homes and crops. Beaver alter their surroundings more than any animal, except man. According to staff, beavers account for almost half of the time spent by wildlife biologists on nuisance wildlife complaints. Nevertheless, the beaver is the official mammal of New York state. In many ways it is a living symbol of wise resource management and, hard work, and it reminds us of the rich past.

Insider tips: Try the log-style bed and breakfast near the park entrance. Look for the active beaver lodge near the road to the nature center. The theme of the park is nature; there is no camping. Although collecting fossils is restricted, certain areas have many examples. Look for concerts on the lawn, behind the waterside lecture center. Look for the booklet in the nature center entitled "Fossils of Lake Champlain." Bring your bike; there are lots of trails for them. Plan a trip to the corner bookstore in downtown Plattsburgh.

Nearby state park: Cumberland Bay State Park

South of Point au Roche, near Plattsburgh on Cumberland Bay, the state park has a huge but tightly packed campground with 200 sites. The park also features picnic areas and a 2,700-foot beach. There are a number of prime camping sites that have a view and direct access to the water. The camping park has a store and recreation room.

The campground is about 50 percent shady with many sites tucked under groves of pine trees. Most of the sites have gravel pads and are along a gravel road. The park is an excellent point from which to explore the region, fish the lake or enjoy the many beaches.

Southwick Beach
State Park
Land: 500 acres   Water: Lake Ontario

Some of the finest—and most popular—beachside camping sites in the state are at Southwick Beach State Park. The park's white sandy beach is one of the best on the shores of Lake Ontario. Another reason Southwick is so great is that it abuts the Lakeview Wildlife Management Area to the south. The large natural area offers hikers and nature lovers plenty of marked trails, dunes and wetlands to explore. All of this, and more, is along a scenic 17-mile stretch of sand dunes, wetlands, ponds, creeks and woods known as the Eastern Lake Ontario and Wetland Area.

Reaching from the mouth of the Salmon River to the outlet of Black Pond, the area supports a diversity of plants and wildlife. Five state-owned or managed properties offer access for outdoor recreation including Southwick Beach State Park, Deer Creek Wildlife Management Area (WMA), Westcott State Park, Sandy Pond Beach

Natural Area and Black Pond WMA. There's lots of nature to explore, and Southwick and nearby Westcott state parks are perfect places to use as your base camp for exploring the region.

Southwick State Park was named for the Southwick family, who owned the waterfront property from 1870 to 1960. The beautiful beach was popular in the 1920s, when a bawdy dance hall was shaking with jitter-bug dancing and roaring fun every Sunday night. It mysteriously burned to the ground in 1925. Soon after all of this excitement, promoter Albert Ellis leased the land and developed what came to be called the "Coney Island" of Northern New York. Ellis built a roller coaster, new dance hall, pavilion, bathhouses, merry-go-round, midway and a baseball stadium that once boasted huge crowds.

The Depression stopped the fun in 1938. Nevertheless, over the next 20 years the natural beauty and visitors returned to the waterfront. In 1960, the Leesi Management Corporation bought the land from the Southwicks and operated the beach for five years. In 1965, the state purchased a 3,500-foot section of the lakefront, and opened the day-use area and camping the next year.

Information and Activities

Southwick Beach State Park
8119 Southwick Place
Woodville, NY 13650
(315) 846-5338

Directions: Off Rt. 3, two miles west of Woodville. The main park office is located at Westcott State Park, (315) 938-5083.

Emergency number: Park police, (315) 938-7354; and 911 system.

Campground: The campground has 112 sites; 44 trailer sites have electrical hook-ups. The neatly mowed campground is comprised of loops and a waterfront spur. Loop B is the premiere camping area along the lakefront. Once school is out, you will need a reservation to get into Southwick and nearby Westcott state park campgrounds.

Many sites in Loop A (30-60) are open and sunny. Sites 32-34 and 48 have a perfect mix of shade and sun. Site 35 is a terrific site for medium-sized RV rigs. Site 36 can get wet during the early part of the season. For a bigger site near some trees, consider site 38. Sites on the perimeter are against a natural wall of vegetation. Sites 39-43 are good for larger RV units. Larger rigs have plenty of room to maneuver.

Loop B, sites 1-30, are on the water with direct access to the sandy waterfront. They are wonderful camping sites—and very popular. About half of the sites have some shade; the rest are sunny and sandy, equipped with ground-mounted fire rings and picnic tables. Sites 1-15 are very much like camping on a sandy beach. Site 15 is under two trees and on the beach, just steps from the cool Lake Ontario water. A wooden boardwalk arches over the delicate dunes in this area. Sites 16-30 are against the base of a low shrubby dune and only yards from the water's edge. This loop is near the camp store and concession. Beach camping at Southwick is so popular that the park conducts an annual lottery for these sites.

A small playground is near sites in the 80s. Sites 89 and 90 are sunny; if you want shade, try site 91. Large RVs will like the sites in the 90s because they can pull in and park parallel to the park road. Site 99 is a great site. Others nearby are on the outside perimeter and are backed up against a natural area. Site 102 and a couple of large trees offer partial shade. There is lots of room for larger RV rigs in sites 31-112. A baseball backstop is behind site 111.

The showerhouses that serve the camping loops are especially clean and well-designed.

Day-use areas: A golf putting green is at the park. The park has hundreds of picnic tables and ample day-use amenities.

The bocce ball court in the campground is unique in the state park sys-

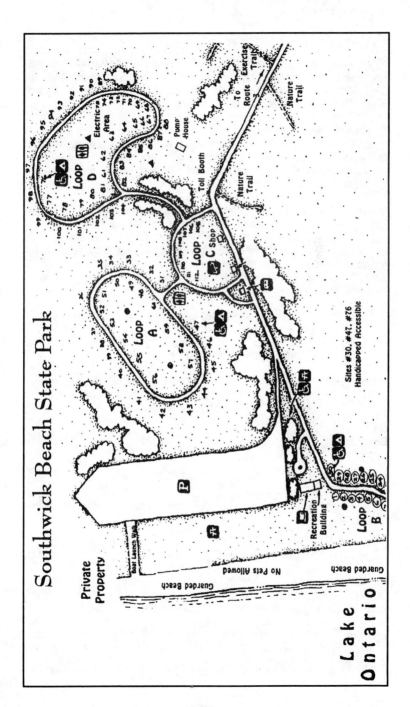

Southwick Beach State Park

Lake Ontario

Private Property

Boat Launch Walk

Guarded Beach

No Pets Allowed

Guarded Beach

Recreation Building

Loop B

Loop A

Loop C

Loop D

Electric Area

Camp Shop

Toll Booth

Pump House

To Route Exercise Trail

Nature Trail

Nature Trail

Sites #30, #47, #76 Handicapped Accessible

tem.

Beach: A sign at the beach says, "Enjoy Your Day." We did. A blond-brick bathhouse stands behind the busy sandy beach. Hundreds of picnic tables are also near the beach. The beach is several hundred yards long. No dogs are allowed there.

Concession/store: The large park store and concession have a set of video games, six tables and two walk-up windows. Simple grill foods are served and the store sells basic camping items, grocery items, simple hardware items, RV supplies, small sporting goods, fishing equipment and toiletries.

Hiking: Within the park are many short trails that connect the campground and day-use amenities. The main shoreline trail travels the entire length of the park and can access the Lakeview natural area on the south. The neighboring state-owned Lakeview area is great for long or short hikes. There is much to see along the trails for birders, naturalists, hikers, backpackers or canoeists. The state park is a good base camp for hikers to explore the Lakeview tract.

Trails in the Lakeview area include places where you will pass by dune vegetation, high spots, barriers, stabilized dunes, small brooks, flat sand, natural shoreline, meadowlands and old uncultivated fields. The trails are terrific places to see many bird species.

Boating: At the corner of a beachside parking lot, windsurfers have a small staging area from which they can launch their humble craft and ply the waters of Lake Ontario. Nearby Westcott State Park gets more windsurfers than Southwick does. A small launch is at the north end of the large parking lot. Consider bringing a canoe to paddle nearby Cowell Pond or along the big lake on windless days.

Fishing: The park has significant shoreline access to Lake Ontario.

Nature: Southwick has a significant dune restoration project underway.

Sand dunes are long ridges of sand and other sediments piled on the shore by wind and wave action. The sand is held together by plants, such as American beachgrass. This plant's leaves trap sand and its branching roots prevent the sand from blowing away. The dunes grow as sand is blown onto them and trapped by plants or snow-fencing, building them higher and higher. American beachgrass is especially important since it can survive being covered with sand. As the dunes get larger and more stable, plants such as artemisia, Eastern cottonwood, poison ivy and sand dune willow take root and add to the staying power of the dune.

Another dune may form in front of the older stable dune and the whole process is then repeated. In fact, a series of dunes may form parallel to the shore with the primary dune, or foredune, closest to the lake. The inland dune is called the secondary dune.

There are many dunes in this area because along the eastern coast of Lake Ontario is an underwater sandbar that formed thousands of years ago, when the shoreline extended further into the lake. Sand from the dunes comes from this ancient, now-underwater beach. Eventually, all the sand will be washed ashore.

As you will learn when you visit the park or Lakeview, sand dunes are fragile and easily eroded away. The tough beach grass and other plants holding the dune together are able to survive in the harsh environment—boiling summer heat, freezing winters and constant wind. But step, sit or pick them, and they can't survive. In places where the plants have been destroyed, the sand is loose and easily blown away. A small footpath over the dune becomes a gaping hole as the wind eats away the loose sand. These large holes are called dune blowouts.

Sand dunes are important. They act as a buffer or barrier, protecting the wetlands and other inland areas from the effects of high water, waves and currents, as well as severe coastal storms. Without the dunes, property near the coast of Lake Ontario, including homes and farmland, would be damaged by spring floods and storms. Damage to wetlands can lead to loss of habitat for wildlife and fewer recreational opportunities for people.

When hiking the area look for bullhead-lily, broad-leaved arrowhead, fragrant water-lily, leopard frogs, shorebirds, purple loosestrife, beaver lodges, jack-in-the-pulpit and many other flora and fauna unique to this wetland and beach environment.

Nearby state park: Westcott Beach State Park is the headquarters for three parks along the coast of Lake Ontario—Southwick, Westcott and Long Point. There are 159 camp sites at Westcott, 40 of them are on top of the ridge and pet-free. A hard-surface ramp provides access to the lake. Hiking trails are easy and the guarded beach is large and sandy. The Westcott beach is less windy and maybe safer than Southwick's long beach.

Nearby Long Point State Park is a rustic park for fishermen. The park has 32 boat slips and 97 camping sites.

Insider tips: Don't forget Murphy's Restaurant. You can't miss it; it has an ice cream cone on top. The Lakeview area has several access points. An annual beach and bike run is held at Southwick each year. Southwick has one of the best beaches in the region. Enter the lottery for the beachside camping in loop B.

Wellesley Island
State Park

Land: 2,636 acres   Water: St. Lawrence River

Wellesley part of Island State Park was once owned by the distiller of Old Grand Dad whiskey, Edison Bradley. Bradley was a horseman and early back-to-land advocate who, after purchasing the land in 1906, promptly named it *"Archadia,"* and set about making the tract as self-sufficient and independent as possible.

For a time, the sprawling parklands supported herds of Ayrshire cattle and Shropshire sheep, as well as numerous chickens and pigs. Corn, grain and hay raised on the northern part of the land fed the livestock and supported the farming effort. Bradley also raised timber, planting hundreds of chestnut, maple and poplar trees.

Bradley was a busy guy. In 1911, he began construction of a seasonal residence the area newspapers called a "bungalow." It turns out the bungalow had 40 rooms and was 240 feet long! It also had an 80-foot-tall tower, wraparound porches and two rooms that measured 30-by-50-feet. Bradley also had his own Delco plant that supplied electrical power to the bungalow. Unfortunately, as was the case with many estates in the Thousand Island region, it was leveled by fire in 1922. It's reported that sparks from the chimney set the roof ablaze and in just two hours the entire house was reduced to ashes.

After the fire, Bradley built only small structures on a small island off the point, and as time went on, he lost interest in the farm and estate. The property was eventually sold to Paul Houghton, a dairyman who furnished the island with milk and other products. Houghton also started the island's first rescue service, towing mired cars that had wandered off the muddy one-lane island roads. Finally, in the early 1950s, the state purchased the farm and other parcels to develop the park which now includes camping, cabins, top-quality fishing, swimming, marina with boat rentals, a wonderful nature center, winter sports, golf course, camp store and ample day-use areas.

Information and Activities

Wellesley Island State Park
44927 Cross Island Road
Fineview, NY 13640
(315) 482-2722

Directions: The park is about four miles from the toll bridge to Wellesley Island. The park is 39 miles from Ogdensburg, 300 miles from Buffalo and 360 miles from Niagara Falls.

In front of the park office is a kiosk that has considerable information about the Seaway Trail and island attractions. DeWolf Point and Waterson Point state parks are administered by Wellesley Island State Park staff.

Emergency number: 911 system.

Campground: The park offers 429 camping sites. Waterfront sites 58-80 and others are prime sites and often requested, according to staff. Park staff also reports that many families request Loop D because it is near the beach and playground. Loop E is also often requested. Sites are scattered and not in the usual perfectly circular loop pattern. Many sites are next to the water and offer wonderful fishing access along the rocky shoreline.

Loop A, on the west end of the park, is hilly and has many sites on varying elevations. This is a rocky and hilly area that stretches along the river's high banks. Sites 44, 46 and 47 are private, accessed by a two-track lane. These sites are nestled under a wispy grove of pines, next to the slow river and showerhouse. Sites in the high 50s and 60s are open, grassy and good for large-size RV rigs. Sites 31-40 face an open field. Sites 68-78 are backed up against a natural area while facing out on a large grassy field. These are high and dry sites and out of the wind.

Loop B, sites 1-50, is rolling and open. Site 8 has a stone fire pit and is above the river. Sites 9-13 are along a dead-end spur with a view of interesting rock outcroppings. A showerhouse with two black lampposts is central to all sites in the loop. Sites 16 and 17 are oversized, while up the hill sites in the 20s enjoy plenty of sunshine. Sites 18-20 are private and near rock outcroppings and pillow-like boulders. Sites in the high 20s are large and flat, perfect for big RVs. Site 35 is near the water.

Loop C, sites 1-5 is open.

Loop E has a small boat ramp and docks. Except for sites on the perimeter, the loop is open and sunny. The rolling loop has a few potentially soft sites. Most sites back up against a rocky hill and some sites have a river view. Site 48 is on the water and has a view of a tiny island that grows a single pine tree. The spur, sites 41-51, has some great views of the sandstone shore and islands that dot the wide, almost lake-like river corridor. Site 62 is off the road and near the shoreline, offering considerable privacy for family camping. Many sites in the 60s offer a pretty view. Site 75 has a view of the busy marina. Site 90 is a firm site under a large tree.

Loop F has full hook-ups and is generally open and sunny. Sites along the perimeter are backed up against natural vegetation. The flat campground is excellent for large RV rigs. If you would like to camp next to a big rock outcropping consider sites 14, 16, 18 or 39. Site 20 is on an incline; be careful. Site 33 is flanked by two pines offering some shade. This mostly open loop is near the camp store, mini-golf and recreation barn.

Loop H, near the nature center, has several sites with a water view. Sites 1-10 are on a 40-foot-tall bank above the water. Most of the other sites are wide open, grassy and receive all-day sun. Only sites 28-30 are shady. A tan brick showerhouse is in the center of the small, open loop.

The camp store features simple grocery supplies, basics for camping, limited fishing supplies, candy, soft drinks, propane, cots, sleeping bags, knives, toiletries, ice cream and general grill items at the concession counter. You can also buy pre-formed hamburger patties. Simply take them back to your camp and slap them on the hot grill.

Group camping is offered to non-profit organizations.

Cabins: Most of the cabins have a refrigerator, wood stove and two bunk beds that sleep four. Bring a small gas camp stove for cooking, as well as utensils and linens. Outside are a fire pit and picnic table. Several cabins have been recently been built. Cabins are open year-round.

Cabins 1-4 are near the rocky shoreline. These cabins are within walking distance of the guarded beach. On a rock ledge, cabin 5 is near cabins 6 and 7 that are nestled above the river and near the bathhouse. Cabin 8 is tucked into an area of rock outcroppings, while cabin 9 is down a winding two-track road to a wonderful view of the shoreline and river islands. This is an excellent cabin and great place for some scenic shoreline fishing.

Most of the cabins have space around them for parking extra vehicles or trailers.

Day-use areas: The broad day-use areas are complete with lots of picnicking sites, shuffleboard, game fields and volleyball court.

Recreation barn: The red barn near the mini-golf course opens in mid-June. The barn is staffed on a part-time basis and offers game tables. A few nature and recreation programs are offered through the summer. A shuffleboard and rest room building is near the large gable barn.

Swimming: The small, 100-yard-long guarded beach opens in mid-June and closes on Labor Day. Several white and wood benches are positioned around the grass and sand beach. The brown stone bathhouse is next to large mowed spaces and is attached to the store. There is a nice view of two of the Thousand Islands from the beach.

Golf: The nine-hole course is about 2.5 miles from the park office. Golf clubs and carts can be rented from the small pro shop. A few water hazards and hilly fairways are the biggest challenges on the course. The small course is rumored to have been on the professional tour in the early 1930s.

Mini-golfers might want to try their luck at the course near the recreation barn. The putty golf course has carpeted fairways, a small windmill, flower beds and other obstacles. One hole has blue carpeting, creating the illusion you are putting on water. The course is lighted for night play.

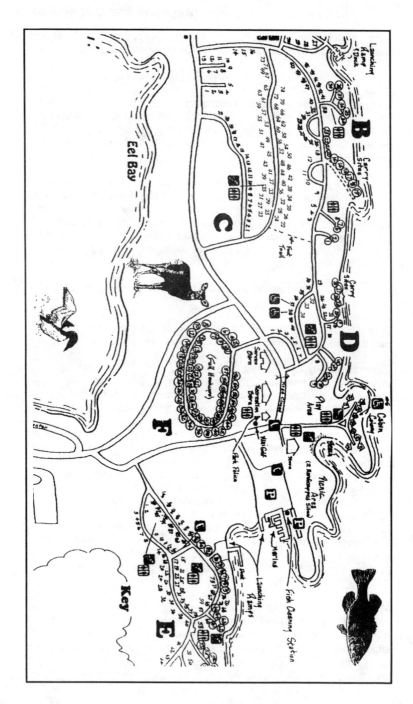

367

Hiking: Eel Bay Trail starts as a hard-surfaced trail near the nature center, then traces along the shoreline and up to the high rock. Along the way are glacial potholes, two scenic overlooks and a great place to observe the geology of the area.

North Field self-guided nature trail: The first part of the half-mile loop is across a sandstone plateau that gives way to the river. Hikers should pick up a booklet to learn about the numbered stations along the easy, winding trail. The walk has 16 learning stations and takes about 45 minutes to walk. Hikers will learn about the shallow soils that support only certain plant species, an old field undergoing succession, animal homes, geology, killer caterpillars, what role dead trees play, old farm fields, a moist bottomland forest, a towering mature forest, a talus slope of sandstone and a walk along shallow Eel Bay. The easy trail also has some rock outcrops and exposed boulders along the path.

Sand Cove Loop (1.5 miles) is mostly forested with many spring wild-flowers. Hikers will enjoy the East Trail Loop (2.5 miles) that travels over a rocky knob and beaver swamp near a pond. It's one of the best trails to see wildflowers, ferns, waterfowl, beaver, deer, songbirds or turtles. The Round-the-Peninsula Trail (3.5 miles) is along The Narrow, with two-thirds of the loop tracing the shoreline. It also passes a beaver swamp.

Boating: Several private marinas are near the park. The park operates four launches, including one at the marina that rents small 14-foot boats, with or without an engine, canoes and paddle boats. Simple live bait, gasoline and ice also sold at the marina. One slip at the 104-slip marina has a water hook-up for transient boaters. The small marina also sells ice and has a fish cleaning station near the wood courtesy docks.

The Eel Bay launch is small, best suited for cartop boats. Finger docks and a small ramp are in Loop A of the campground.

Fishing: The St. Lawrence River is the only outlet for the 300,000-square-mile Great Lakes system. There are places where the mighty river is deep, up to 600 feet at some narrow channels. In general, the shoals, most shorelines and around islands are rocky. The downstream end of most islands have sand and silt build-up. Deep water sites usually have a silt bottom, as do most bays and river channels.

The wide river has little temperature changes and is moderately fertile and clear. Aquatic vegetation is thick in fertile, soft bottom bays. Some species of aquatic vegetation grow 30 feet in the main channel.

The primary species in the river are small- and largemouth bass, northern pike, muskie, pumpkinseed and yellow perch. Secondary types include walleye, rock bass, bluegill, channel cats and carp. A few lake and brown trout, steelhead and chinook salmon are taken.

The river, especially near the park and throughout the Thousand Islands, supports the biggest self-sustaining muskie population in the world. There is a 44-inch size limit on the toothy denizens. The world's record muskie comes from the waters, a whopping 69-pounder. The average smallmouth bass is about two pounds with some up to five pounds, while largemouth can reach six pounds. Lots of four-pound northern pike are taken, as 30 percent of anglers target these fish.

Maybe the biggest success story of the river is the increasing population of walleye. Old marble eyes are becoming more widely distributed, and six-pound fish are common. Panfish in the shallows near the state park are abundant.

Anglers must keep in mind that the river offers ever-changing fishing opportunities due to seasonal conditions and natural movement. Early spring, for example, after ice-out, is an increasingly popular time to seek lake and brown trout using stickbaits in 15-30 feet of water. Walleye and pike opening day in early May is also a terrific time to stalk pike in the weedy shallows, bays and flats. Predator pikes are feeding heavily as the water temperature increases. Try drifting and casting over the tops of weedbeds in 6-10 feet of water. Chartreuse and black or yellow and black spinners, stickbaits and spoons can produce lots of hard-fighting pike. By the end of the month, most northerns have moved to dropoffs and weed edges in 15-25 feet of water. Try drifting with the current here for the rest of the season using simple live bait rigs on or near the bottom.

Walleye fishing is best the first two or three weeks of the season and in the early fall. Casting jigs and crankbaits or trolling stickbaits and fluttering spoons, especially at night, can be a killer technique.

Bass season opens in June, and anglers go nuts for smallmouth. These fish are still on their nests in the shallows until mid-July and can be taken by casting many types of small crankbaits. In about mid-July, these fish move to 25-30 feet of water and will chase a soft-craw until late September. Largemouth are shallow-water species in the river. Although less abundant than smallmouth, lots of them can be found in shallow weedy areas like those habitats around nearby Lake of the Island and many other bays. Fish the weedy edges with pig 'n jigs, topwater spinners, plastic worms, spinnerbaits or natural-colored crankbaits.

Although you can catch muskie in the summer, September and October is when the fish congregate along shoals near deep water. Most anglers flat-line troll, but downriggers can work too. These fish stay deep (25 or more feet) in areas of little current. Keep your lure 15-35 feet deep, and don't hesitate to go deeper. Anglers should try night trolling. The average muskie caught is 40 inches and 15 pounds. Lots of 50 pounders are caught each year using big plugs (often silver and black) in deep water. Remember to carefully release the fish to ensure a quality fishery.

Shoreline and boat access is excellent from the park.

Most ice fishermen congregate off the gravel launching ramp at camping loop H in Eel Bay. Near the park, use perch eyes or mousies for good panfish action.

Minna Anthony Common Nature Center: Complete with eight miles of hiking trails, the center encompasses a 600-acre peninsula and contains a building furnished with many quality natural history displays. A large outdoor display board has a map and other nature center information. Behind the interpretive building is a lighted amphitheater with sound system and bench seating for 75 along the St. Lawrence River. Also here is the floating dock where interpretive canoe tours are launched. Rocky outcroppings along the shoreline are near the shady cove-side floating dock.

Minna Anthony Common was a leading authority on birds, flowers, trees, animals, herbs and grasses of Northern New York State. Her nature writings and pen-and-ink illustrations were published for 25

years in the Watertown Daily Times before her death in 1950. Common was a summer resident of the Thousand Islands area, where she developed and maintained a 1.5-mile nature trail adjacent to her property where school children often visited. The nature center was dedicated in her name in 1964.

The primary purpose of the center is to provide environmental education, especially for visiting school children. The vaulted-ceiling museum has a small sales counter that features field guides, rubber snakes and frogs, erasers, arrowheads, necklaces, stickers and other fun educational items. A free-standing fireplace, made possible by the Friends of the Nature Center, is a wonderful feature in the winter. Along the walls of the building are glass-front display cases that contain animal mounts, a waterfowl mount collection, raptors, Eel Bay diorama, wetland diorama and other displays.

Children will enjoy the center's Discovery Room where aquariums filled with frogs, snakes and fish are labeled and positioned at children's level. A cluttery touch table has feathers, clam shells, rocks, antlers and many other natural objects. A small nature library is next to the touch table. A variety of mounts are also in this colorful room. Binoculars, microscopes, a stump cut by a beaver, puzzles, books, diorama of the Thousand Islands area, flip chart quiz, crystals and mineral samples, wall posters that detail nature themes and several 150-gal-

lon tanks that contain a gar are in the room.

One of my all-time favorite displays is a large replica of a muskie hung from the ceiling in the Discovery Room. The colorful fish is made of all types of trash and litter carefully sculpted in the form of a 50-inch muskie. The impressive artwork was made in Ohio. Another fun display is the collection of Gary Larson's wacky "Far Side" cartoons that have nature themes and ecology principle. Also, don't miss the beautiful common loon carving by Donald W. Morely.

Also on the property is a chain of beaver ponds along seasonal creeks. Some of these beaver ponds can be seen from the North Field self-guided trail. Also in the nature center is a classroom that can seat 51. On the wall of the large classroom are bird silhouettes, nature posters, relief map of the area, wonderful view, audio-visual equipment and other educational materials. Also in this room is some beautiful water-color river art (ships, waterfowls, etc.) by Hans Junga and Zena Bernstein.

The nature center hosts a number of annual events including an autumn festival, which is a country fair-style event each Columbus Day weekend. Other events include an art show, trim-the-tree party, winter festival, Earth Day festival, plus 5K and 10K runs. The oak-maple forested center also features a high viewing point on the peninsula of the bottomland forests and wide riverlands.

The museum is open 8:30 a.m. - 4:30 p.m. Monday - Saturday and 10 a.m. - 4:30 p.m. on Sunday. The trails are open sunrise to sunset.

Canoe tours are designed to get visitors on the water so that they can see the shoreline and learn about nature from a different perspective. The 20-passenger, 36-foot-long voyageur canoe cruises daily during the summer for a two-hour tour. The excellent water clarity allows passengers to see lots of St. Lawrence River fish during the trip.

Winter: Seven miles of cross-country ski trails are at the nature center. Ski equipment and snowshoes are rented and the nature center's fireplace is the perfect place to enjoy a hot drink.

Nearby state parks: Grass Point and Keewayden state parks aren't far away. The Canoe Picnic Point State Park is accessible by canoe only and has camping and cabins. DeWolf State Park, known as a fisherman's park, is on the Lake of the Isles in the St. Lawrence River and has 14 cabins and 14 camping sites. Waterson Point is a boat access-only state park that many fishing guides use for shoreline lunches. Mary Island State Park offers boat access only.

Insider tips: Pets must have a current rabies certificate to enter the park. Check out the Waterfront Theme Park, Graham Thomson Museum and Boldt Castle on Hart Island, Cornwall Building, Brown Mansion, Brownsville Railroad Museum, Tibbet's Point Lighthouse, Horns Ferry, Thousand Island Museum, Oxbow Historic Homes, whitewater rafting, Thompson Park Zoo and observation towers (especially the 400-foot-tall tower on Hill Island). Boldt Castle is a must see.

In-line skates are not permitted on park roads.

THOUSAND ISLAND REGION

PHONE	PARK
315 482-2593	THOUSAND ISLANDS REGION
315 654-2324	Burnham Point
315 654-2522	Canoe-Picnic Point
315 654-2522	Cedar Island
315 654-2522	Cedar Point
315 654-2522	Cedar Point
315 386-5636	Coles Creek
518 563-5240	Cumberland Bay
315 482-2012	DeWolf Point
315 393-1138	Dewolf Point
315 686-4472	Eel Weir
315 262-2880	Grass Point
315 375-6371	Higley Flow
315 482-3331	Jacques Cartier
315 482-2444	Keewaydin
315 649-5258	Kring Point
518 643-0225	Long Point
315 654-2522	Macomb Reservation
315 769-9933	Mary Island
315 654-2522	Robert Moses
518 563-0369	Point Au Roche
315 393-1977	St. Lawrence
315 846-5338	Southwick Beach
315 482-2722	Waterson Point
315 482-2722	Wellesley Island
315 482-2722	Waterson Point

Amenity columns:

- Tent/trailers sites (h = hookups, e = electricity)
- Trailer dump
- Showers
- Camper recreation
- Cabins
- Food
- Store
- Picnic tables
- Shelters (• reservations)
- Swimming beach (• bath house)
- Swimming pool (• bath house)
- Recreation programs (• performing arts)
- Hiking
- Biking
- Nature trails
- Fishing
- Playground
- Golf (•clubhouse)
- Tennis
- Pond or lake (• power boats ok)
- River or stream (• power boats ok)
- Launching site (• hand launch only)
- Boat rental
- Marina (• anchorage)
- Pump out
- Ice skating (•rentals)
- Cross-country skiing (• rentals)
- Snowmobiling
- Sled slopes

374

Other great books by
Glovebox Guidebooks of America

- ***State Parks on the Great Lakes,*** by
Dean Miller   ISBN 1-881139-17-4

- ***Pennsylvania State Parks Guidebook,***
by Bill Bailey   ISBN 1-881139-15-8

- ***Virginia State Parks Guidebook,*** by
Bill Bailey   ISBN 1-881139-14-X

- ***Ohio State Parks Guidebook,*** by
Weber & Bailey   ISBN 1-881139-16-6

- ***Kentucky State Parks Guidebook,*** by
Bill Bailey   ISBN 1-881139-13-1

- ***Indiana State Parks Guidebook,*** by
John Goll   ISBN 1-881139-12-3

- ***Illinois State Parks Guidebook,*** By
Bill Bailey   ISBN 1-881139-11-5

- ***Fish Ohio: 100 Lakes Atlas,*** by
Bill Bailey   ISBN 1-881139-19-0

To order visit your favorite bookstore or
call 1-800-289-GUIDE
(4843)

About the author

Bill Bailey has written 13 books, including six guide-books to state parks. He is one of America's foremost experts on outdoor recreation, public information and communication. Bill lives with his wife and two sons.